PARALLEL PATTERNS OF SHRINKING CITIES AND URBAN GROWTH

In memoriam Caroli, qui omnes res urbanas amavit

Parallel Patterns of Shrinking Cities and Urban Growth

Spatial Planning for Sustainable Development of City Regions and Rural Areas

Edited by

ROBIN GANSER
Nürtingen-Geislingen University, Germany

and

ROCKY PIRO
Puget Sound Regional Council, Seattle, Washington, USA

Routledge
Taylor & Francis Group

LONDON AND NEW YORK

First published 2012 by Ashgate Publishing

2 Park Square, Milton Park, Abingdon, Oxon OX14 4RN
711 Third Avenue, New York, NY 10017, USA

Routledge is an imprint of the Taylor & Francis Group, an informa business

First issued in paperback 2016

British Library Cataloguing in Publication Data
Parallel Patterns of Shrinking Cities and Urban Growth: Spatial Planning for Sustainable
   Development of City Regions and Rural areas. – (Urban Planning and Environment)
   1. Cities and towns – Growth. 2. Shrinking cities. 3. City planning. 4. Sustainable
   urban development.
   I. Series II. Ganser, Robin. III. Piro, Rocky.
   307.1'216–dc23

Library of Congress Cataloging-in-Publication Data
Ganser, Robin.
   Parallel Patterns of Shrinking Cities and Urban Growth: Spatial Planning for
   Sustainable Development of City Regions and Rural Areas /
   by Robin Ganser and Rocky Piro.
        p.   cm.
   Includes bibliographical references and index.
   1. City planning – Environmental aspects. 2. Rural development – Environmental
   aspects. 3. Sustainable development. I. Piro, Rocky. II. Title.
   HT166.G255 2012
   307.1'216–dc23   2012026364

ISBN 978-1-4094-2741-4 (hbk)
ISBN 978-1-138-26866-1 (pbk)

Contents

List of Figures

List of Tables

Acknowledgements

Our thanks go to all those involved in writing and producing this book. We are grateful to all the contributors for their chapters and for showing such enthusiasm for the project. We are indebted to Valerie Rose and the staff at Ashgate Publishing for their pertinent comments, production assistance and flexibility in working with us on this book. Our gratitude also goes to Kathleen Kreßmann for her tireless formatting but also sub-editorial work throughout the manuscript.

The preparation of this book would not have been possible without the support of the Dutch Ministry of Housing, Spatial Planning and the Environment (now: Ministerie van Infrastructuur en Milieu), and our gratitude goes especially to Hans Verspoor for his dedication and help.

Our appreciation goes to colleagues of the International Urban Planning and Environment Association (IUPEA), particularly to Prof. Donald Miller, and also to Prof. Gerhard Steinebach and colleagues at the Department of Town Planning, University of Kaiserslautern, who hosted the UPE8 Symposium which brought together many of the authors included in this book.

We wish to express our deepest gratitude to our families for their support during the preparation of this book. In particular we would like to give our warmest thanks to Katja Ganser and Bev Piro for all their support and patience during the intensive work involved in bringing this book to completion.

Notes on Contributors

Stephen V. Ward

Steve Ward, Professor of Planning History at Oxford Brookes University, is a former President of the International Planning History Society 1996–2002 and remains a member of its governing Council. He is also a former editor of the refereed journal Planning Perspectives and continues as a member of its Editorial Board. He is also an Editorial Board member of the American refereed Journal of Planning History. He has published widely on historical matters relating to planning with many books, book chapters, articles and other outputs to his name.

Peter Hall

Professor Hall has a special interest in the application of research to planning and regeneration policy, especially the relationship between transport development and urban and regional change. He writes regularly on this and other topics for the magazines Town and Country Planning and Planning. He is author or editor of nearly 40 books on urban and regional planning and related topics. He was Director of the Institute of Urban and Regional Development at the University of California at Berkeley (1980-92), where he is Professor Emeritus of City and Regional Planning.

Johann Jessen

Johann Jessen is Professor of Local and Regional Planning at the Institute of Urban Planning and Urban Design, University of Stuttgart. Before this (1983 to 1991) he was lecturer at the Department of Urban and Regional Planning, University of Oldenburg, where he earned his doctorate (1981) and his habilitation (1990). His research concentrates on the social aspects of urban development and the methodology of urban and regional planning. Recent books and articles focus on strategies for metropolitan regions as well as comparative research of housing and urban regeneration in Europe, and new methods in urban planning.

Hélène Roth

Dr Hélène Roth is Lecturer and Research Assistant at the University of Clermont, France, and a member of EA 997 CERAMAC, a Research Centre specialised in Geography. One of her key research interests is in shrinking cities.

Emmanuèle Cunningham-Sabot

Dr Emmanuèle Cunningham-Sabot is an Associate Professor of Urban Planning at the University of Rennes 2 and a member of UMR ESO 6590, a Research Centre specialised in Geography. She teaches Globalisation, Urban Economics and Urban Planning. Having been awarded several research grants, her expertise is in urban regeneration, specifically shrinking cities. She is also Chair of the Shrinking Cities International Network (SCiRN).

Lea Holst Laursen

Lea Holst Laursen (PhD, M. Sc.eng. in urban design) is an Associate Professor at the Department of Architecture, Design and Media Technology, Aalborg University. Her research is placed within the fields of differentiated urban development and spatial restructuring, with a view to explain the causes for different development pathways as well as exploring planning interventions in the context of spatial restructuring. In both fields focus is placed on best practice but also on the further development of strategies, including landscape strategies, participatory planning and urban design.

Christian Strauß

Christian Strauß studied Urban and Regional Planning. His research interests focus on environmental resources as management objects and space as a base for political control against the background of global change. He is currently working as a scientific assistant at Leibniz-Centre for Agricultural Landscape Research (ZALF), Institute of Socio-Economics, Müncheberg, Germany. He is member of the scientific coordination project 'Sustainable Land Management' funded by the German Federal Ministry of Education and Research.

Anja Kübler

Anja Kübler is based at TU Braunschweig, Germany. Before that, she was scientific assistant and project manager at Leipzig University. Her expertise was in regional planning, geographic information systems, land use management and quantitative statistical methods.

Barbara Warner

Dr. Barbara Warner holds a PhD from the University of Leipzig. Since 2002 she is a Research Fellow at the Department of Social Geography, Martin-Luther-University Halle-Wittenberg, Germany. Her research is focused on demographic change and the resulting demands on spatial planning in the eastern regions of Germany after the reunification.

Stefan Fina

Stefan holds a degree in geography from the University of Eichstätt, Germany. After graduation in 2001 he worked in the GIS industry. From 2003 onwards he was employed as a transport and land use planner in New Zealand, and in 2007 he joined the Institute of Regional Development Planning at the University of Stuttgart, Germany. His publications to date and his current research agenda focus on indicators of spatial development. He now spends most of his time teaching quantitative methods in spatial planning and works as a GIS consultant.

Simone Planinsek

Dr.-Ing. Simone Planinsek is a project manager in the housing industry. Her research interests and practice focus on socio-demographic change, energy efficiency and employment of renewable energies in housing. Until 2011 she worked as a research assistant at the Institute of Regional Development Planning at the University of Stuttgart (IREUS) and completed her PhD at the Institute of Urban, Regional and Land Use Planning at the University of Karlsruhe (KIT). In her dissertation she developed GIS and data models for the analysis of population and land use in residential areas.

Philipp Zakrzewski

Philipp received his diploma in architecture from the Coburg University of Applied Sciences and he also holds a master's degree in European urban studies from the Bauhaus-Universität Weimar. He worked as a research assistant at the Leibniz Institute of Ecological and Regional Development (IOER) in Dresden and in 2007 he joined the Institute of Regional Development Planning at the University of Stuttgart (IREUS). His research interests include the analysis of urban development, empirical urban and neighborhood research as well as planning policy and history.

Christian v. Malottki

Dr Christian v. Malottki is a project manager at the 'Institut Wohnen und Umwelt GmbH' (Institute for Housing and Environment) a publically funded research institute that advises public administrations at different levels in the fields of housing policy, integrated urban development and sustainable energy use. Christian's main research interests are energetic aspects in urban regeneration, house price analysis and the spatial effects of housing and energy subsidies in the German welfare system.

Joachim Kirchner

Dr Joachim Kirchner is also a project manager at IWU. His main research topics are housing market forecasts and housing policy with a recent focus on the coordination of housing subsidies and the other instruments of the welfare system.

Holger Cischinsky

Dr Holger Cischinsky is also a project manager at IWU. His research is focused on primary data collection and he carries out large surveys of housing markets e.g. the energetic state of the German building stock or the strategy of private landlords .

Kiyonobu Kaido

Kiyonobu Kaido is Professor of Engineering at the Faculty of Urban Science, Department of Urban Science, Meijo University, Japan. He worked at Japan Regional Development Corporation from 1975 to 1995 as a planner and engineer. He was made an associate professor at 1995. His research mainly focuses on sustainable urban form, especially the compact city, urban spatial change and policies in the context of urban shrinking processes. This also includes urban design review systems.

Tsuruta Yosiko

Professor Dr Tsuruta Yosiko works at the Gifu National College of Technology, Department of Architecture, Japan. Before this she worked as an engineer at the Architectural Bureau of Nagoya from 1989 to 1990. She was made a research associate in 1990, a lecturer in 1995, an associate professor in 1999. Her research mainly focuses on the process of urbanisation, the improvement of residential areas and urban design review systems.

Nicole Gurran

Dr Nicole Gurran is an associate professor in the Urban and Regional Planning Program at the University of Sydney, Australia. Her research focuses on comparative planning approaches to ecological sustainability, housing, and climate change. Prior to joining the University of Sydney, she practised as a planner in several government roles, focused on local environmental plan-making and housing policy.

Barbara Norman

Professor Dr Barbara Norman is the Foundation Chair and Head of Discipline in Urban and Regional Planning, University of Canberra. She is a member of the national Coasts and Climate Change Council and the Regional Development Australia Fund Advisory Panel. She has extensive experience in the public sector at all levels of government. Her research interests include coastal planning, sustainable cities, urban and regional planning, climate change adaptation and urban governance. She is Life Fellow and past national president of the Planning Institute of Australia.

Elisabeth Hamin

Dr Elisabeth M. Hamin is an associate professor of regional planning in the Landscape Architecture and Regional Planning department at the University of Massachusetts. She previously taught at Iowa State University, and holds a Ph.D. from the Department of City and Regional Planning at the University of Pennsylvania. Her teaching and research centers on land use and climate change. A particular focus is placed on the nexus between adaptation and mitigation as well as local planning.

Finbarr Brereton

Finbarr Brereton is a Research Fellow at the UCD School of Geography, Planning & Environmental Policy. His PhD focused on the topics of Quality of Life and the Economics of Happiness in Ireland and his research interests centre on the areas of environmental economics; environment and happiness; environmental valuation; survey design and GIS. He has published in international journals such as Ecological Economics, European Urban and Regional Studies and the Economic and Social Review examining the influence of the environment on subjective well-being.

Peter Clinch

Between June 2008 and January 2011, Peter served as Special Adviser to An Taoiseach (the Irish Prime Minister) advising on, inter alia, medium-term economic development policy, enterprise policy and environmental policy. Peter's research interests include economic growth; sustainability and quality of life; behavioural economics; policy analysis; market-based instruments; cost-benefit analysis and environmental valuation; economics of land use and land markets; energy economics and policy. He is author of over 100 publications including books, book chapters and international journal articles as well as over 60 reports and other documents.

Menelaos Gkartzios

Menelaos is a Lecturer in Rural Development at Newcastle University. He holds a PhD from University College Dublin, School of Geography, Planning and Environmental Policy, which focused on processes of counterurbanisation and spatial planning implications in Ireland. His wider research interests are on rural social change, sustainable development, planning and housing studies in rural contexts and international comparative research.

Mark Scott

Mark Scott is currently Head of Subject for Environmental Policy and Director of Research in the UCD School of Geography, Planning and Environmental Policy. He is a graduate of Queen's University Belfast with a PhD in Environmental Planning. In addition, to planning practice, he has worked in the University of Ulster and Queen's University Belfast. Mark's research interests revolve around three core themes: rural transformation and planning; exploring the role of spatial planning in building sustainable and resilient places; and environmental governance and active citizenship.

Sophie Schetke

Dr. Sophie Schetke is post-doctoral researcher at the Department of Urban Planning and Real Estate Management at the University of Bonn. Sophie´s research areas comprise sustainable settlement development, Multi criteria assessment, Decision Support Systems as well as the assessment of Ecosystem Services and Quality of Life in urban areas. She teaches courses in urban planning and urban renewal. Sophie is a graduate of the University of Leipzig and holds a diploma in Geography. She received her Phd in urban planning from the University of Bonn in 2010.

Theo Kötter

Prof. Dr.-Ing Theo Kötter studied Geodetic Sciences and Spatial Planning at the University of Bonn. He was assistant at the Institute of Urban Planning and afterwards chair of the urban planning branch of urban development companies in Munich and Bonn. Since 2003 he is Chair of the Department for Urban Planning and Real Estate Management at the University of Bonn. His professional and research interests comprise all aspects of sustainable town and country development, land management, land valuation and GIS based decision support tools in spatial planning.

Dagmar Haase

Dagmar Haase holds a PhD from the University of Leipzig, Department of Geography, and focused her research on modelling and monitoring water and matter fluxes in disturbed and landscape systems. 1999 she finished her PhD thesis on modelling matter fluxes of disturbed urban floodplain forests. Since 2009 she is professor in Landscape Ecology at the Department of Geography, Humboldt University, Berlin. She also works as a guest scientist at the UFZ, Leipzig, continuing her work on urban land use change modelling, urban ecosystem services and flood risk assessment.

Fabiano Lemes de Oliveira

Fabiano Lemes is a Senior Lecturer at the Portsmouth School of Architecture, in England. He holds a PhD in History and Theory of Urbanism awarded by the Technical University of Catalonia (UPC), in Barcelona; an Mphil and a Degree in Architecture and Urbanism, both awarded by the University of São Paulo. He is the coordinator of the MA in Urban Design, teaches design studio and history, theory of architecture and urban design. Fabiano is a frequent contributor to conferences and seminars with publications on sustainable urbanism, green infrastructures and planning history.

Lorraine Farrelly RIBA

Lorraine Farrelly is Professor of Architecture and Design and Deputy Head of the Department of Architecture at the University of Portsmouth and teaches architecture, interior and urban design. Lorraine's specialist lecture areas are representation and freehand drawing. Research interests are in the area of urban regeneration with conference presentations and papers published internationally. Lorraine has a postgraduate urban design studio, which has made mixed use and housing proposals for European sites in Dublin, Paris, Amsterdam, Vienna, Venice, Rotterdam and London.

Robin Ganser

Dr Robin Ganser is Professor of Urban Planning at Nürtingen–Geislingen University, Germany, and also works as consultant in planning practice. Before this he was Professor at the University of Applied Sciences, Lübeck, and he held a position at Oxford Brookes University as Senior Lecturer in Spatial Planning. He joined the Board of Directors of the International Urban Planning and Environment Association in 2004. His teaching and research specialisms include: rural issues; management of planning procedures; regeneration and brownfield development.

Rocky Piro

Dr Rocky Piro serves as growth management program manager at the Puget Sound Regional Council in Seattle. He oversaw the policy work for VISION 2040 and manages the Council's Plan Review. He is on the Board of Directors for the International Urban Planning and Environment Association and is first vice-chair of the Regional and Intergovernmental Planning Division of the American Planning Association. He is the past chair of the City of Shoreline (Washington) planning commission. In 2008, he received the Myer Wolfe Planning Award for Professional Achievement in Washington state.

Introduction

Spatial development pressures and decline are unevenly distributed at the macro and micro level within city regions, as well as around the globe. Growth tends to be concentrated in global cities and major agglomerations, including in designated growth areas, but how does this impact the towns and villages that surround these successful urban areas? And what happens to declining cities and regions which are not connected to growth and where the viability of infrastructure, regeneration, and brownfield redevelopment pose great challenges? Even in growing city regions, pockets of decline and physical dereliction occur regularly, such as industrial brownfield sites or surplus military sites. The parallel growth and shrinking of cities and urban regions is a global phenomenon – with numerous examples in western and central Europe, North America, Japan, China and elsewhere.

Planning and the environment

Both spatial development processes – rapid growth and decline – challenge planning and the achievement of sustainable urban and rural development. In this context a range of environmental impacts are specifically related to growth. These include, for example, the loss of soil, flora and fauna or fragmentation of habitats due to development, a lack of sites for ecological compensation measures and as a result degradation of the local environment, conflicts with neighbouring land uses in already densely built up settlement structures, as well as additional traffic and related emissions.

In a spatial context of shrinkage one might impulsively assume that no, or at least far less, environmental impacts are to be expected. However, the opposite may be the case as the following problems may occur in a shrinkage scenario: loosening of environmental regulations as increased weight is given to economic considerations in planning decisions, loss of cultural landscapes as mobile parts of the population leave an area in search of career opportunities, and compromised opportunities for more soft-end reuse of brownfields due to of a lack of funding for remediation.

The academic discourse to date

This book addresses the parallel occurrences of urban growth and decline, with a focus on shrinking cities and wider urban regions. For several decades academicians and practitioners in North America and Europe have focused on growth management and on physical, as well as social regeneration of urban areas. Recently the phenomenon of 'shrinking cities' has been (re)discovered. The term – shrinking cities – refers to municipalities or urban regions that have experienced a dramatic loss in population, often due to the loss of industries or commerce and out migration.

The existing literature covers analyses of the underlying causes of shrinkage and tries to come up with explanations for and descriptions of the phenomena of demographic as well as economic decline (see, for example, Ebers 2007). There are also a host of interesting discussions of case studies available – many of them focus on Detroit, Leipzig, Manchester and Liverpool – which appear to have achieved the status of 'the usual suspects' among shrinking cities (see for example Ebers 2007; Oswalt 2004). Another set of research efforts, mainly based on case studies, focus not so much on the explanation of reasons behind shrinkage and growth, but also seek to analyse and define best practice in dealing with the outcomes and spatial consequences of shrinkage (see for example Oswalt 2005; Rugare, Schwarz 2008).

Of particular interest is the recent shift in focus away from declining industrial urban areas grappling with economic restructuring, to the problems in so-called boom cities, such as 'Sun Belt' cities in the southern and western United States (e.g., Phoenix, Las Vegas, and Orlando) (see Hollander and Popper, 2011).

While most recent literature focuses on municipalities, especially inner city areas, it is valuable to widen the spatial context and also shed light on areas within and adjacent to urban regions – thereby covering the entire city region, urban fringe, and rural areas. In doing so, this book also extends the academic discussion by combining theoretical or typological, conceptual and planning practice related approaches. The existing theoretical and typological framework in particular, is still not well developed for areas experiencing physical decline and/or demographic shrinkage. At the heart of the discussion is an analysis of spatial consequences, along with related planning concepts from theory and practice. This analysis aims to further the sustainable development of city regions, the urban fringe, and rural areas – whether they are experiencing decline or some combination of both growth and decline.

In this context, international comparisons provide more practical conclusions and suggestions for the further development of planning concepts and tools, than would be possible by focusing on a single country or on existing planning strategies. This international comparative perspective considers the situation in Europe and North America, but also includes examples from Asia and Australia, where on-going demographic and economic structural changes also result in parallel patterns of growth and shrinkage. Germany, in particular, makes an interesting case due to the rapid structural changes which followed its reunification. In this context the phenomena of growth and shrinkage has occurred – and is still occurring–at a fast pace along with spatial consequences.

Perspectives on and facets of growth and shrinkage

This book makes an important contribution by examining the phenomenon of urban growth and shrinkage from a number of perspectives. History, theory (with a focus on typology), housing, redevelopment, and strategic planning are all discussed within a common framework of sustainability. In this context, sustainable planning approaches for *either* growth *or* decline are pursued with a view to strengthen social, economic, and environmental resiliency, while bolstering the capacity to address adverse challenges – including resource depletion, adequate infrastructure, urban decay, and climate change.

From a historical context, growth and shrinkage are not new phenomena. Indeed, looking at different 'eras' of spatial planning, one can identify responses that range from major and strategic interventions to those that embrace acceptance of general spatial development trends. Typically, spatial planning philosophy is linked to economic and political development. If this holds true, then global economic and environmental challenges experienced at any given moment will define changes and transportation in how spatial planning is conducted.

In Chapter 1, Ward provides a valuable historical context of spatial planning, tracing how planning practice has had to evolve from focusing on growth and urbanisation to needing to develop various approaches for addressing physical urban decline and demographic shrinkage.

Hall (Chapter 2) presents insights into strategic planning challenges – including regional growth and shrinkage – being faced in the twenty-first century. He draws from recent reports on the state of cities in Europe in general, as well as in the United Kingdom more specifically.

Theory and practice are closely related in the discipline of spatial planning. Various models and evaluation methods have been developed to describe urban form and existing conditions, as well as to provide alternative scenarios for what the future may hold. Nevertheless, a systematic typology of shrinking cities has not yet been developed. Jessen (Chapter 3) takes on this subject with a view to provide a better theoretical or typological understanding of shrinking cities, concentrating on the 'de-population' of cities in eastern Germany and the subsequent 'de-urbanisation'.

Roth and Cunningham-Sabot (Chapter 4) have collaborated to look at two 'shrinking cities' – one in France and the other in the United Kingdom – to consider whether there are possibly standard strategies for restructuring and redeveloping cities which have experienced population decline.

Strategic planning and its policy implications are of particular importance in areas which face either rapid growth or substantial shrinkage. Strauß (Chapter 6) examines the 'shrinking city' experience from the viewpoint of public policy and planning process. The urban redevelopment programme for eastern Germany provides some intriguing approaches to managing population loss from a spatial planning approach designed to advance sustainability principles.

Kuebler, Strauß, and Warner (Chapter 7) look at urban shrinkage from a regional land use perspective. Spotlighting the Halle-Leipzig urban region in eastern Germany, the authors take into account economic development, residential needs, and stabilisation of land use.

The housing market and spatial planning are closely linked. Whether the housing situation is one of high demand for a limited supply of residential units in a growing region, or an oversupply of housing in a shrinking region, there are infrastructural, social, economic, and ecological consequences. Fina, Planinsek and Zakrzewski (Chapter 8) consider the ageing housing stock in Germany and what the future housing needs are for the country as it faces changing demographics over the coming decade and beyond. New housing choices are discussed, especially as they relate to strategies for revitalisation, conversion, and demolition.

Malottki, Kirchner and Cischinsky (Chapter 9) examine housing demand in both growing and shrinking urban regions. Special attention is given to the German state of Hessen – which includes both areas of population growth and decline. Policy implications of housing programmes are discussed, focusing on the critical need for coordinated urban planning.

Kaido and Yosiko (Chapter 10) share lessons learned from the Nagoya metropolitan region in Japan – a country facing a dramatic decline in population in coming decades. They consider changes which have been taking place in suburban residential districts and the implications they have on evolving into more sustainable urban forms. Their study considers demographics, access to jobs and services, environmental conditions, and housing types.

Gurran, Norman and Hamin (Chapter 11) provide a perspective on growth and change in non-metropolitan areas of coastal Australia. They assess demographic and economic trends for more than five dozen areas along the country's coast.

Brereton, Clinch, Gkartzios and Scott (Chapter 12) investigate perceived benefits and limitations of both rural and urban living in the Republic of Ireland within the context of sustainable development. Environmental and quality of life issues are the primary factors considered, including health and well-being, exposure to pollution, transport and traffic, stress, crime, access to jobs and services, and housing.

Adaptive reuse of sites and infill development are particularly significant strategies for ensuring the vibrancy and sustainability of shrinking cities. Spatial planning plays a critical role in ensuring the successful regeneration of previously developed land.

A unique form of regeneration involves the closure of military bases, which not only results in an abandoned site, but also the loss of personnel and civil sector jobs. Ganser (Chapter 14) considers the challenges of converting military sites to new uses, in situations where the spatial context is one of slow growth or urban shrinkage and, conversely, at locations which are characterised by development pressures. Sustainable brownfield development is examined from a policy perspective.

Farrelly and Lemes (Chapter 15) look at the British naval city of Portsmouth and its efforts to regenerate itself following the closure of military sites and dockyards. This is also a good example of how pockets of decline (structural changes in some areas of Portsmouth) in an overall setting of growth (South East of England) can occur and which challenges for spatial planning arise in this context.

Questions arising from the different facets of growth and shrinkage

The above elements of growth and shrinkage and related consequences for spatial development and planning interventions cover a set of interesting questions which will be explored throughout this book:

1. Is there a need for a new planning paradigm and how do spatial planning systems change as well as respond to the challenges ahead?
2. Further to this point: Do we need more or less strategic planning processes and instruments?
3. As housing and the living environment appear to be key issues in the context of growth and of shrinkage, what are the specific challenges for spatial planning in order to further sustainable residential development and linked quality of life?
4. An overarching objective of spatial and urban planning is to make the best possible use of land in order to achieve sustainable development. It is therefore pertinent to ask: Which reuse options and approaches for previously used land are available in order to achieve an effective and efficient use of land?

Of relevance to all questions posed above are challenges and opportunities with regards to the environmental sustainability principle which are associated with trends of growth and decline. These questions are addressed in the individual chapters that follow and are picked up again in the form of an integrative synopsis in the concluding chapter.

References

Ebers, M. 2007. *Shrinking cities, the hidden challenge.* München: GRIN Verlag GmbH.

Hollander, J.B. and Popper, F.J. 2011. *Sunburnt cities: The great recession, depopulation, and urban planning in the American sunbelt.* 1st Edition. London: Routledge.

Oswalt, P. (ed.). 2004. *Schrumpfende Städte: Band 1: Internationale Untersuchung.* Ostfildern-Ruit: H. Cantz.

Oswalt, P. (ed.). 2005. *Schrumpfende Städte: Band 2: Handlungskonzepte.* Ostfildern-Ruit: H. Cantz.

Rugare, S. and Schwarz, T. (eds.). 2008. *Cities growing smaller.* Cleveland, OH: Cleveland Urban Design Collaborative, College of Architecture and Environmental Design, Kent State University.

Chapter 1

Spatial Planning Approaches to Growth and Shrinkage: A Historical Perspective

Stephen V. Ward

Introduction

Initially in western nations, but increasingly throughout the world, the functioning of increasingly complex economies has required the growing concentration of population in towns and cities. Modern spatial planning appeared as a series of ideas and actions to manage the various economic and social contradictions which followed from that urban growth. It soon began to include localised attempts to slow, relocate and even, to some extent, reverse or prevent the effects of urban growth. This chapter reviews how and why these concerns appeared. It also considers the kinds of practical remedies that were proposed and applied. Finally, it reflects on the main factors which generated changes in thought, policy and practice.

The main elements and examples used in this story are from western Europe and North America since this was where modern urban and regional planning largely emerged during the later nineteenth century. Just as would later prove the case elsewhere, the appearance of this new approach to organising human settlements was spurred by urban growth. The first modern planners were not, initially at least, faced with any need to manage urban decline. In most countries, the relative shift to mass urban living began against a background of marked absolute population growth. This ensured that urbanisation was initially accompanied by a decline that was only relative even within the rural regions from where most of the new urbanites came.

Increasingly, however, as urbanisation continued and overall population growth slowed, rural regions experienced real population shrinkage, albeit earlier and more acutely in some countries than others. Later cyclical and structural shifts within industrialised economies introduced further areas of decline as older urbanised industrial regions dwindled and new economic activities arose elsewhere. Within planning various ways of addressing decline were developed, from seeking its outright reversal through a less ambitious acceptance and management or even acceleration of decline.

Urban growth, spontaneous and otherwise

These later planning responses did not appear immediately. Few of the first generation of European and American planning theorists and practitioners did other than accept the inevitability of a relatively spontaneous process of urban growth. In 1899 the American statistician, Adna Ferrin Weber, showed just how dramatic and widespread had been the phenomenon of urban growth during the century that was just ending (Weber 1963 [originally 1899]). Its scale went far beyond that which could have been achieved by the conscious actions of local or even national governments. Already, through trade and colonial exploitation, urbanisation was spreading across the globe, exceeding all previous experiences of urban civilisation.

In the core regions of Europe and equivalent parts of the United States, cities themselves needed to do little to make growth happen. This was not so in more marginal regions, however. Here, where capital, technical knowledge and labour skills were scarce, civic and business leaders had to compete hard to attract these factors of production. The result was that, during the nineteenth and early twentieth centuries, many ambitious cities in these regions adopted boosterish and promotional policies.

Particularly notable were the subsidies that towns and cities in the southern and western states of the United States and in Canada gave to attract railroads and manufacturing industries from around 1850 (Ward 1998: 9–25, 145–50). Such place competition was particularly intense in North America because, unlike Europe, there was simultaneous competition to populate and build up both cities and rural territories as the settlement frontier moved westward. Cities subsequently as important as Los Angeles, Atlanta and Winnipeg gave incentives to foster growth in their early history. However, the major givers of subsidies to private businesses during this period were typically less prominent manufacturing cities such as Kitchener (originally Berlin) and Oshawa in Canada (Bloomfield 1983).

There was nothing comparable at the time in Europe but some cities (and higher governments) offered incentives to offset the effects of foreign competition. The city of Łódź, shielded by tariff walls set up by the (Russian) Kingdom of Poland, deliberately attracted large numbers of German textile workers to settle in the early nineteenth century (Koter, et. al.1993: 12–18). Their own German markets had been lost to more advanced mechanised production from the cotton mills of Lancashire in Britain. Łódź became a haven where they could adjust to the new technologies and market realities, allowing the city to make itself into 'Poland's Manchester'.

Fascinating though they are, such early local policy innovations to kick-start urban growth on the margins were far from typical. Even cities which indulged in such practices for a time were quick to wean themselves off the most draining subsidies. And they had little impact on the ideas and practices associated with urban planning emerging later in the century. The new movement's dominant concerns were to give urban growth a physical form that was, in varying degrees, efficient, healthy and beautiful. Due attention was given to the enhancement of urban infrastructures that would assist the future prosperity of business but this was scarcely dominant. Planning was also a movement to civilise the ugliness and squalor of the dynamic cities that industrialism was creating. Interestingly, boosterish cities were often amongst the first to make this policy transition. They were usually eager to show how far they had moved beyond the crude upstart places of just a few years earlier (Scott 1969: 1–46).

The garden city as a model of balanced spatial development

The earliest theorists of planning did not question the process of urban growth itself. There had been utopian thinkers and communitarian activists who had imagined or attempted to build small model settlements that rejected the big concentrated city. The pastoral impulse which romanticised the pre-industrial, rural life was also strong, especially so in Britain where the extent of nineteenth century urbanisation was then unprecedented. The recent acceleration of similar trends in Germany and the United States was also encouraging similar sentiments.

It was not until 1898 that such concerns were convincingly drawn into the emergent discourse of planning. In that year, a hitherto obscure Englishman, Ebenezer Howard, published his important book, *To-Morrow: A Peaceful Path to Real Reform* (Howard 2003). Famous for introducing the key planning idea of the garden city, Howard was also notable in the present context for his theorising and questioning approach to urban growth and uneven development. In the well-known 'Three Magnets' diagram from his book, he highlighted the contrast between the two extremes of late nineteenth century urban development – the big, concentrated city and the declining countryside. The former could offer high wages, social opportunity and places of entertainment but at the price of congestion, poor environment and high living costs. The latter had all the beauties and healthful qualities of nature but also low wages, poor opportunities and living conditions.

He characterised the prevailing pattern of urban development as a product of the capitalist land development process. The key to change lay in the surplus value that arose when land was converted from rural to urban use. If this increase could be harnessed for communal purposes rather than, as it usually was, retained for individual profit, Howard argued that a more balanced pattern of spatial development could be achieved. His vision was of a network of small, low density garden cities, closely integrated with a well-populated intervening countryside. He called this new pattern the 'social city' and wanted it to replace the dense urban concentrations of populations that were such a feature of the age. First the new garden cities would be set up, each one limited to a modest size of 32,000. Then the old concentrated cities would gradually wither away and be rebuilt as new social cities. In this new pattern, everyone could enjoy economic and social opportunities but combined with a healthy, beautiful environment and affordable, pleasant housing conditions.

Howard was not a lone voice but was giving the most coherent and widely acceptable expression to ideas that were 'in the air'. In Germany, the right-wing political activist and polemicist, Theodor Fritsch, had advocated his own vision in his book *Die Stadt der Zukunft* (The City of the Future) in 1896 (Schubert 2004). This had many features in common with Howard and Fritsch also saw land reform as the key to change. Underlining the similarities, the second edition of Fritsch's book carried the subtitle 'garden city'. Yet there were important differences. Fritsch's purpose was fundamentally agrarian, to forestall urbanisation, which was less advanced in Germany than in Britain. In addition, Fritsch's anti-metropolitan vision was grounded in rabid anti-Semitism and proto-Nazi thinking. This severely limited his political reach although his ideas enjoyed some vogue in extreme right wing circles, especially during the Nazi era.

Others spawned their own variants of the garden city. The French architect, Tony Garnier exhibited his vision of the Cité Industrielle, in 1904 (though published it in extended form only in 1917) (Pawlowski, Vechambre J.-M 1993). Like Howard, Garnier favoured a settlement ideal that combined industrialism with a rejection of the giant city. Yet Garnier's was essentially an architectural vision, premised on an ideal socialistic and regionalised society but with no clear sense about how it might be achieved. It had great appeal for the first generation of self-consciously modernist architects and planners in the 1920s. But it too lacked the wider appeal of Howard's garden city.

Together, however, these anti-metropolitan visions showed that emergent opinion was by the early twentieth century seeking more balanced forms of urbanisation. Henceforth planning would be characterised by efforts to modify urban growth to mitigate rural decline and the alienation of city from countryside.

Concepts to balance metropolitan growth

In practice, Howard's social city gradually metamorphosed during the 1920s and 1930s from a complete replacement of the concentrated city into several distinct ways for managing its growth. The first signs came in 1912 when the garden city planner, Raymond Unwin, imagined a pattern of growth that replaced continuous peripheral suburban development with planned satellite suburbs (Miller 1992: 134–38). This was an idea that was taken further between the wars especially by the German planner Ernst May, first at Breslau (now Wrocław in Poland) in 1921 and, more famously, at Frankfurt-am-Main during the later 1920s (Bullock 1978). Compared to the usual pattern of suburbanisation, planned satellite towns (as they were called) offered clear physical separation from surrounding urbanisation with the possibility of greater community identity linked to local service provision, usually grouped around transport hubs.

These early German examples were widely admired and emulated. The term 'satellite town' became part of the evolving terminology of the garden city movement between the wars. Though often applied rather loosely, the label was used in British planning proposals by the late 1920s. A pioneer was May's mentor, Raymond Unwin who, during 1929–31, produced advisory plans for the Greater London Region (Miller 1992: 189–209). Though never implemented, they were important as rehearsals for post-war proposals. The interwar plans reacted to the massive growth of relatively low density suburbs around London and other big cities. This growth enlarged the built up area of Britain by an estimated 40 per cent in just twenty years. It reflected a combination of both subsidised, largely municipal, housing construction and, especially in the 1930s, a huge boom in private housebuilding.

Already by the late 1920s, there were growing calls to find some alternative. Conceptually, Unwin's plans can be seen as marking the completion of the shift from Howard's social city model. There was no longer any suggestion that London would ultimately wither away. Instead various elements of the repertoire of garden city planning were deployed to encourage the growth of industrial garden cities, at some distance from the city and with their own strong local employment bases. Nearer to the suburban fringe there would be satellite towns, more connected to the core metropolitan economy. The physical separateness of both would be maintained by an encircling belt of open country. The latter drew on Howard's proposal for an agricultural belt limiting the spread of his garden city. But it was also influenced by German precedents, especially Fritz Schumacher's 1923 plan for Cologne. Unwin even labelled the London country belt as a 'green girdle', directly drawn from the German term 'Grüngürtel' (Greater London Regional Planning Committee (GLRPC) 1929: 44–49).

This last was the only part of these proposals that began to be implemented before 1939 (though using the more enduring term 'green belt'). However, other British cities began to adopt parts of this ambitious new decentralist agenda for metropolitan expansion (Ward 2004: 47–55). Although the most typical growth pattern remained peripheral expansion accomplished through a combination of private and municipal construction, ideas to protect some parts of the urban fringe from suburbanisation had begun to take hold. Cities such as Birmingham and Sheffield had begun to sterilise large rural areas by 1939. Other cities also adopted the notion of satellite towns. A notable example with some tangible results by 1939 was Wythenshawe in Manchester, which ultimately housed about 100,000 people (Deakin 1989). It was planned in 1931 by one of the leading garden city planners, Barry Parker. Another satellite town, planned a few years later was the smaller example of Speke in Liverpool (Post-War Redevelopment Advisory (Special) Committee (PWRASC) 1947: 32–37). What was notable about both these examples is that they had local employment, if never enough for all the resident local workers (an aspect which will be considered further in the next section.)

Another, more convoluted, strand in the thinking about planning urban growth grew from an amalgamation of Howard's ideas with those of the Spanish engineer Soria y Mata (1996). Soria had in 1882 proposed the idea of a linear city, a low density ribbon of development along a transportation artery such as a tramway or rail line. Relatively little notice was taken of this, despite Soria's launch of a small demonstration project in Madrid in 1894. He also proposed vast linear cities that would span continents. In the ferment of planning ideas in the first decade of the twentieth century, however, elements of his thinking were taken up elsewhere. In Britain, James William Petavel, a prolific writer on social and Indian matters at this time, advocated closer linkage of transport investments and improved housing development in British cities (Petavel 1909).

Petavel's ideas partly followed Howard's reasoning and this link was pressed with more energy when it was taken up by the French reformer and garden city enthusiast, Charles Benoît-Levy (Buder 1990: 138–40). This was an unorthodox direction compared to the mainstream of the garden city movement but it bore some conceptual fruit after 1919. There was notable interest amongst some city planners within the new Soviet Union where different variants of the linear concept briefly flowered (Miljutin 1974). Some of this knowledge spread back to Western Europe during the 1930s. It could be detected as a minor theme in planning in many countries. One of its clearest expressions came in the proposals made by the British Modern Architectural Research (MARS) Group for the linear expansion of London (Gold 1997: 145–63). These appeared in a mature form in 1942. At this time, however, these fascinating ideas had no real practical effect.

Planning in a context of decline

The interwar decades were also notable because they marked a period of real crisis in global economic and urban growth. This had important implications for those towns, cities and regions which depended on declining economic sectors. The most acute contractions occurred in areas dependent on primary production for export markets but many export-dependent sectors of manufacturing were also very badly affected. Where impacts were especially severe and prolonged, they were likely to bring population loss and simultaneous contraction of tax revenues and increase in need for public services. In Britain, for example, local tax bases had to bear the costs of relieving poverty which became a crippling charge (amounting to 50 per cent or more of total local expenditure) in the most depressed areas (Ward 1988: 155–206). This was despite the fact that central government increasingly funded most payments to relieve short and medium term unemployment. The consequences were that local governments in such areas found it very difficult to fund capital projects that might have created new employment and improved the area's attractiveness for new industries.

There was also great central reluctance to sanction public capital spending, in the belief that doing so would encourage people to stay in areas without long term prospects (Ward 1986). This ensured that these areas quickly had noticeably worse standards of welfare and infrastructure than elsewhere. Explicit policies to encourage labour out-migration were also introduced from the mid-1920s. These accelerated an existing process whereby the most able-bodied and skilled workers departed, leaving behind a progressively more dependent population. Meanwhile, the main business ministry rather disingenuously encouraged (but gave no financial support for) local and regional boosterish initiatives.

Many of the areas most acutely affected were relatively small mining settlements. However some were significant towns such as Merthyr Tydfil (in South Wales) and Jarrow on Tyneside. The financial impacts of the depression on the former (which had had over 70,000 inhabitants at the end of World War I) were so acute that a Royal Commission on the town was established. In 1936 this recommended downgrading the town's municipal status to transfer poverty relief to the county's geographically wider tax base (Royal Commission on Merthyr Tydfil (RCMT) 1936). The recommendations were not followed but Merthyr's problems remained serious. The influential and progressive 'think-tank' Political and Economic Planning could seriously recommend in 1939 that the existing town should be entirely abandoned and a new one established in a more favourable location closer to the English border (Morgan 1981: 341). The complete abandonment of smaller depressed settlements and more conscious policies to concentrate development in parts of regions with better prospects were also more widely canvassed (Bulmer 1978: 176–78).

These ideas directly shaped some aspects of post-war policy for the economically weaker regions. Yet in the 1930s the boldest attempts to tackle these types of spatial development problems lay elsewhere. Under Fascist dictatorships, Germany and Italy adopted vast schemes of public works to combat the effects of the depression. Especially notable were the national programmes to create national high speed road systems. New towns were also created in association with new industrial initiatives or other development schemes. Hitler launched what became the Volkswagen car in 1937, creating a new town (now Wolfsburg) where it was built. A new steel works occasioned another new town (now Salzgitter) (Hass-Klau 1990: 127–37). Mussolini's government created several planned new towns, most famously those associated with his project to drain and settle the Pontine Marshes (Ghirardo 1989).

The projects associated with President Roosevelt's New Deal in the United States became far more potent examples of democratic planning from 1933. Most important for urban and regional planners were the green belt new settlement programme and above all the Tennessee Valley project (Lilienthal 1944; Ghirardo 1989). This tackled a large rural area which had suffered acute economic and social decline and environmental degradation as a result of unwise farming practices. The special purpose Valley Authority re-established forests, dammed and controlled the river's flow, and harnessed its energy for power generation. It also instituted scientific farming practices, initiated tourism development and generally created a long term basis for more sustainable economic and social development.

There was nothing comparable to these initiatives in Britain or most other democratic countries. In Britain, the Conservative-dominated National Government which led the country for most of the 1930s put its faith in low interest rates rather than any spatially focused intervention. The 1934 Special Areas Act marked a very tentative beginning of centrally funded regional assistance (Ward 1988: 211–25).

But it was not until 1936 that this programme began (initially very modestly) to fund regional development (notably in creating new industrial estates) to attract new industries. The following year, the national government also began to give much greater local grant assistance to depressed areas. Yet these shifts were more important as a dress-rehearsal for post-war regional policies than a source of any real change at the time. It was rearmament which by the early 1940s had reinvigorated the depressed regions.

Less noticed were various efforts by local governments in several countries to boost economic development in areas of decline. Much the most important were in the southern United States (Cobb 1993). The economic recovery saw several notable efforts to attract industries. In 1936, the state of Mississippi launched its pioneering Balance Agriculture with Industry (BAWI) programme. The intention was to reduce dependence on cotton growing which had been devastated by successive blows from boll weevil infestation in the 1920s and depression in the following decade. It worked essentially by encouraging municipalities to issue bonds, the proceeds of which could be used to subsidise new industrial development. These were certainly not the first local incentives which, though unconstitutional, were already widely used across the South. What was notable about the new policy was that the actions were fully sanctioned by the state of Mississippi itself. The state also created an Industrial Commission which promoted the state for industry and acted as an intermediary and advisor in dealings with incoming companies.

As the economy improved and especially during the boom period of World War II, the Balance Agriculture with Industry policies proved their worth. Though the municipal bond funds typically attracted only low wage employers, even this was preferred to the grinding poverty and deprivation associated with cotton growing. Mississippi's lead was widely followed across the South, especially after 1945. Eventually this mechanism of local bond funding was adopted (though not necessarily used to the extent they had been in the South) by most US states.

In Britain municipal subsidies were traditionally strongly discouraged by national government, to avoid local tax payers underwriting wasteful inter-authority competition (Ward 1990). Yet several towns and cities achieved notable successes in attracting industries during the later 1930s. Lancashire, which received little benefit from central government's limited regional assistance policies, was the main scene of these initiatives. Most notable were Manchester and, more ambitiously, Liverpool where the city councils used local legislation to provide factory sites (and buildings in Liverpool's case) and offer loans for incoming industrialists. Other towns similarly used local powers, often in legally dubious ways, to tackle decline. A particular interest of the Manchester and Liverpool schemes was, however, their integration into metropolitan decentralist planning thinking (Royal Commission on the Distribution of the Industrial Population (RCDIP) 1940: 282–83) . Both created new industrial estates as part of wider plans for new satellite towns at Wythenshawe and Speke respectively. As evident in the more ambitious schemes of Germany, Italy and the United States, planning concepts to tackle both growth and decline had begun to converge.

Planning in Britain during the long post-war boom

In most parts of the world, the experiences of global conflict, following economic crisis, strengthened the growing interest in spatial planning. In Europe especially, democratic governments approached reconstruction with stronger planning powers. Over the first three post-war decades they applied these powers to promote more spatially balanced forms of development than had ever before been attempted. The intention was to reduce disparities between urban and rural, between different towns and cities and between different regions. Many of the concepts which had been tentatively rehearsed in the interwar years were now applied with more enthusiasm.

Britain was one of the most complete expressions of this new strengthened approach. The 'British way' was epitomised by the 1944 Greater London Plan prepared by a team led by Patrick Abercrombie (Abercrombie 1945). In many respects it developed and streamlined ideas rehearsed by Unwin in the 1929–31 advisory regional plans. Overall growth pressures in the London region were to be dampened by regional policies to push new industrial development into less favoured regions. Future spread of Greater London's continuously built up area would be prevented by a containing green belt, now much larger than Unwin's green girdle, around existing suburbanisation.

New freestanding towns and expanded small country towns beyond the green belt would henceforth be the main settings for new growth and, more importantly, be reception areas for net population and employment shifts from inner districts. The plan envisaged shrinkage of population and jobs in inner London, as the older, more decrepit parts were redeveloped not as low density garden cities, as Howard had envisaged, but as medium density areas of terraced housing and apartments.

Greater London developed much as the plan intended. Eight new towns, each planned originally for 50–60,000 population, were developed at locations including Stevenage, Crawley and Harlow (Cullingworth 1979). They were intended to be self-contained in service provision and broadly match local jobs to resident workers. These objectives were largely achieved. In the 1960s, a period when much higher population growth was expected, the principles behind Abercrombie's thinking were applied to the whole greater South East region (Ministry of Housing and Local Government (MHLG) 1964). Three larger new towns (Milton Keynes, Peterborough and Northampton) were designated at locations further from London. Existing new towns were also expanded and greater use made of planned expansions of existing towns such as Basingstoke. These locations were successful in attracting new industrial and service growth that otherwise would probably have located in suburban Greater London.

Alongside all this, inner London experienced population and employment decline. By the early 1970s, however, this was on a much greater scale than the planned growth of new and expanded towns (Ward 2004: 275–78). Much outward movement reflected accelerating loss of inner city jobs as major employers declined or relocated. Bigger proportions of a more affluent population were also looking to buy private housing in the outer metropolitan area, in villages and small towns within or beyond the green belt.

Similar principles informed planning in other British metropolitan regions. The difference was that traditionally less buoyant regions now received some new employment which regional policies was steering away from London and the South East. Building on the tentative pre-1939 precedents, significant financial and other incentives were given to industries to locate in the least favoured regions. Within those, there would be major policies to renew the pattern of urban development. New towns such as Cwmbran in South Wales, East Kilbride and Glenrothes in Scotland and Peterlee and Newton Aycliffe in County Durham were used as bridgeheads for new inward investment and points to consolidate settlement (e.g., Bowden 1978; Patton 1978).

As in London and the South East, the policies were taken further in the 1960s with many more new towns being used in this way, partly influenced by French theories about growth points (Aldridge 1979; Cullingworth 1979). They included Skelmersdale, Runcorn and Warrington in the North West, Washington in Durham and Livingston and Irvine in Scotland. Meanwhile, the inner areas of cities in less favoured regions, such as Liverpool, Glasgow and Newcastle, declined markedly (Hausner 1986). As in London, this decline initially reflected planning intentions for housing and employment. But it was intensified by very sharp declines in traditional employment and the inner city housing market, more acute than those which affected London.

This shrinkage was only partly planned. However, quite deliberate and very draconian steps were taken in one region from the late 1940s to eradicate what were seen as the least viable settlements outside the main cities. The 1951 County Durham development plan placed all villages into one of four categories according to their deemed future suitability for new investment (Pattison 2004). Category 'A' comprised those seen as likely to grow in population where capital investment was desirable. At the other extreme, Category 'D' villages were those where population was likely to decline (typically because of colliery closure) where there was a presumption against any future capital investment. The so-called 'D' village policy soon became infamous and was not overtly replicated elsewhere. A popular protest movement gathered strength as actual villages began to be completely eradicated by slum clearance measures and the policy was finally dropped in 1977. By that stage, greater mobility and the growing attractions of home ownership had drastically changed thinking about what made a settlement viable.

In contrast to this, the wider countryside generally fared much better (Gilg 1996). A strong policy of government support for agriculture and planning policies in different ways gave increasing protection to village life and rural landscapes, especially so in the new National Parks designated during the 1950s. In most areas these policies were sufficient to slow or even stem rural depopulation.

Experiences in other countries

Among western nations, the United States presented the most striking contrast with British experience. In many older cities of the eastern seaboard and upper mid-west, aggressive policies of urban renewal brought declines in inner populations (Fox 1985; Jackson 1985). There was also huge and largely unplanned growth of privately developed suburbs, all the more dramatic because there was no equivalent to British green belt policies. Most large American cities outside the South and West consequently experienced real population declines after 1950. This became acute as factories, shops and offices followed an increasingly suburbanised population out of the metropolitan core cities. There was already strong opposition to extending city boundaries and this intensified. The polarisation between growing suburbs and shrinking cities thus became a feature of the American urban pattern much earlier than elsewhere.

In contrast, most other western European countries had a portfolio of interventionist planning policies for growth and decline broadly equivalent to those of Britain, though with some differences in detailed approaches. This was particularly so in countries where the proportion of the population living in urban areas was lower than Britain's. In France and Sweden for example, only about half the population was urbanised in 1945 compared to over 80 per cent in Britain. In such countries, planning was able to play a more direct role in shaping metropolitan growth rather than reacting quite so much to already established patterns.

By comparison with the 'British model' of an encircling green belt and freestanding new towns or expanded settlements beyond it, a more common European model involved rail transit corridors of growth with planned satellite towns developed at station nodes (Bosma, Hellinga 1997). This was thought more appropriate than the more static British model for countries where bigger increases in urban populations were expected. It was a pattern typical of Scandinavia, especially the famous 1947 'finger plan' for Copenhagen and the equivalent 1952 plan for Stockholm (Hall 1991; Vlassenrood 1997). Green wedges of countryside between the transit routes were the equivalent of British green belts. Like the British model it also enjoyed some international resonance and was deployed (abortively) in the 1961 plan for the Washington DC region and (more productively) in several later Australian metropolitan plans (Scott 1969: 573–80, Morison 2000).

It also had a big impact on planning for the French capital, though after considerable policy evolution. The growth of Paris had traditionally been at the expense of the rest of France. Over the 1940s, there emerged a strong political determination to strengthen provincial and rural France. Geographer Jean-François Gravier's influential 1947 book Paris et le désert Français played an important role in focusing this historic concern (Marchand, Cavin 2007). Policies of agricultural support (increasingly from the nascent European community after 1957) were used to slow rural France's decline. The 1950s also saw the emergence of policies to promote regional balance by encouraging the growth of regional cities, the so-called métropoles d'équilibre, as counterbalances to the Paris region (Hansen 1968).

French planning for historically lagging regions was strengthened by important theoretical thinking associated with François Perroux and Jacques Boudeville about the promotion of growth points (Boudeville 1966). Their theory was originally concerned with the clustering of 'propulsive industries' within 'economic space'. However, it soon took on a more straightforwardly geographical dimension (in which form it later had some influence in Britain, as already noted).

In the event, the spatial unevenness of French growth never reappeared in its previous extreme form. After 1945 there was a sustained increase in the total French population which made it easier to achieve greater spatial balance. By 1965 the provincial cities had experienced sufficient growth that it was even possible to produce an overtly expansionist structure plan for the Paris region (van Hoogstraten 1997). This famous plan was effectively a scaled up version of earlier Scandinavian plans. Major transport investments opened up corridors of development which were given shape by creating major new towns. Unlike British examples, the transport links of these villes nouvelles allowed them to be closely integrated into the wider metropolitan economy (Merlin 1971; Rubenstein 1978).

Provincial métropoles and their regions received comparable investments and growth. The Marseilles region received major industrial investment and a new town, centred on the Étang de Berre. In Toulouse there was major investment in aerospace, university provision and a satellite town at Le Mirail. Lille gained a new town at Villeneuve d'Ascq, along with important investments in transport and university infrastructure. As this suggests, French spatial planning was closely integrated with national economic planning and public investment programmes, more so than in most other Western European countries. This meant that spatial decisions about growth locations did not rely, British-style, largely on regional incentives to, or restraints upon, private investment. They were backed by major planned and co-ordinated commitments to investments in physical and social infrastructure etc.

Planning and the neo-liberal era

Since the 1970s, these established planning strategies in relation to the management of spatial growth and decline have everywhere diminished. As economic activity became increasingly globalised, traditional policies promoting spatial balance became less viable. At varying rates, national governments recognised that the nature of spatial imbalances had completely changed (Dicken 2007). The bewildering new hypermobility of both capital and information, combined with business's capacity to organise production and service delivery across national and continental frontiers have rendered traditional policies much less effective. New low cost locations for routine processes of production and service delivery have emerged in the former developing world. Meanwhile Western cities have suffered unprecedented economic disinvestment. This has produced serious declines in employment and population and especially within the specific areas of cities affected by change.

The policy effects have varied. Former government efforts to encourage economic development in particular parts of national territories are now organised more at supra-national level, especially so within Europe. More striking, however, has been the trend to greater localisation and 'bottom-up' regionalisation of spatial economic policy (Ward, Jonas 2004). In the United States, this policy turn was not entirely unfamiliar. The new policies to promote local economic development had strong echoes of old-style boosterism, if now on a much larger stage. Some Southern cities had never stopped their drive to attract new industries but the targets were now global rather than domestic corporations.

What is different is that the new approach is less focused on attracting mobile manufacturing and more on promoting the 'knowledge industries' and boosting all forms of consumption. As manufacturing declined, culture, heritage and tourism became important elements in city promotional policies. Cities, sometimes supported by higher governments, concentrated on using regeneration to re-image themselves. New consumption spaces such as museums, aquaria and conference centres were created from obsolete waterfronts or industrial sites to attract tourists. The American cities of Baltimore and Boston were leaders in the reuse of waterfront areas and during the 1980s they were widely imitated nationally and across the world (Ward 2006). Another pioneer was New York, where the state in 1977 launched its famous 'I♥NY' campaign (Ward 1998). In New York City the campaign was credited with having hauled the city back from the fringe of bankruptcy.

These approaches soon spread to western Europe, especially Britain. The New York campaign was emulated by the Scottish city of Glasgow which in 1983 launched its well-known 'Glasgow's Miles Better' campaign (Struthers 1986). Intended initially to boost Glaswegians' perceptions of their long shrinking city, it was soon widened to interest potential investors and tourists. There were initial, fruitless hopes that the campaign might promote industrial revival to offset the decline in shipbuilding and heavy engineering. Instead the city pioneered a regeneration strategy based on cultural development to boost tourism and promote Glasgow's attractiveness for creative and other knowledge industries. In 1990 it became European City of Culture, ensuring that its approach was widely noticed and emulated (Booth, Boyle 1993).

Many port cities, faced with the dramatic effects associated with containerisation and other changes, followed Baltimore and Boston's lead in reusing their redundant older docks for cultural and tourist development (Ward 2006). Again British cities such as London and Liverpool were amongst the first to take notice. They further elaborated the approach beyond the tourism and cultural orientation to pioneer housing and major financial development within such settings. Over the 1980s other cities in Europe and farther afield began to follow these early leads, adding their own innovations and individuality. Notable examples were Rotterdam and Barcelona, both inspired by Baltimore but with features that made them in turn models for other cities (Ward 2011). Nor was this confined to Europe, with cities such as Sydney, Melbourne, Osaka, Cape Town, Buenos Aires and many others making it a truly international model.

One of the principal reasons for this rapid globalisation of planning and development approaches was the importance of the private development sector. The planning models in the 1945–75 period had relied on governments being the major driving force. Regeneration in the neo-liberal era was much more a function of the private sector. Governments now shared the 'driving seat' with private developers and 'partnership' was the watchword of the new approach. Yet in some cases, especially the London Docklands during the 1980s, initiative was virtually ceded to private developers. This could produce dramatic transformations, evident especially in the major new financial district which sprang up at Canary Wharf during the late 1980s and early 1990s (Brownill 1990). However it also marked a return to planning approaches that were less balanced in their consideration of wider infrastructural and social issues. Some reaction to more extreme forms of this developer-led approach occurred in the 1990s.

These regeneration strategies also began to shape all aspects of planning. They worked best in cities that had growth potential but were noticeably less successful in less buoyant cities, where it was difficult to attract sufficient private in relation to public investment to match the boosterish rhetoric. There were few places with the potential for a Canary Wharf and even dynamic cities were vulnerable to property market slumps. These were now far more significant for spatial planning than under the more managed national economies of the post-war boom.

More widely, it is even less possible in the neo-liberal era than it was during the post-war boom for spatial planners simply to push growth back into shrinking parts of cities and regions. Where major new investments in infrastructure are occurring, it is more feasible. In Britain, for example, the Thames Gateway strategy attempts to use investments in high speed rail and those promised in regional rail to extend the dynamism of the London Docklands to the traditionally less favoured eastern side of London (Cohen, Rustin 2008). But many major generators of growth such as airports lie well away from the areas of shrinkage. The result is that the goal of balanced development remains more elusive than ever.

Conclusions

Standing back from the detail of the history of western planning thinking and policies in relation to growth and decline, certain broad tendencies become apparent. The story starts as a pragmatic and unquestioning acceptance of the prevailing broad patterns of market-led development. Any policy responses to vary this were essentially local. There was then a more questioning phase with first rather utopian ideas appearing which were then modified into more realistic but still ambitious policies to lessen unevenness and instability in development patterns. In turn this phase has given way to something that is again much closer to acceptance of prevailing patterns of development. The most that is now attempted is to change these patterns at the margins, mainly in a localised way, using the overall dynamism of city regions to drive regeneration of the less dynamic parts of these same areas. But cities which really are on the margins are now left very much to their own devices, assisted only a little by the policies and actions of higher governments.

A key question is why there was a retreat from the post-1945 policies aimed at promoting more balanced urban and regional development. More balanced development is surely a quality highly regarded in contemporary desires for sustainable development. Yet, although great show is made of pursuing such goals, especially within Europe, the tangible action taken to achieve it remains less than in former decades.

In turn this question goes back to one of the principal aims of this chapter, about what it is that actually shapes the kinds of responses that are pursued. The dangers of massive overgeneralisation are clear but there do seem to have been similarities of policy responses between different eras when the world economy was being dramatically reformulated. During such periods, spatial (and other) policies appear to have been premised largely on the notion of competition. Conversely it was during an era of political formulation of the world order, tentatively and inconclusively after 1918 and rather more decisively after 1945 that competitive forces could be stabilised, paving the way for more ambitious policies to manage spatial order.

If this interpretation is correct then we will need to wait for some major political reformulation of the world order to manage the forces of international competition which are now largely unfettered before really fundamental changes in the nature of spatial policies can be expected. We may hope, though, that this reformulation will occur more peaceably than during the twentieth century, driven perhaps by a common response to global environmental crisis and without need for international conflict. What is clear though is that the role of the West in any such reformulation is likely to be rather less than it was in 1945, something which will inevitably impinge on the new spatial order which will result.

References

Abercrombie, P. 1945. *Greater London plan 1944: A report prepared on behalf of the Standing Conference on London Regional Planning.* London: His Majesty's Stationery Office (HMSO).

Aldridge, M. 1979. *The British new towns: A programme without a policy.* London: Routledge & Kegan Paul.

Bloomfield, E. 1983. Boards of Trade and Canadian Urban Development. *Urban History Review*, 12(1), 77–99. Available at: http://urbanhistoryreview.ca/june1983english.html.

Booth, P. and Boyle, R. 1993. See Glasgow, See Culture. in *Cultural policy and urban regeneration: The West European experience*, edited by F. Bianchini. Manchester: Manchester University Press, 21–47.

Bosma, K. and Hellinga, H. (eds.). 1997. *Mastering the city: North-European city planning, 1900–2000*. Rotterdam, The Hague: NAI Publishers; EFL Publications.

Boudeville, J.R. 1966. *Problems of regional economic planning*. Edinburgh: University Press.

Bowden, P. 1978. The origins of Newton Aycliffe. in *Mining and social change: Durham County in the twentieth century*, edited by M. Bulmer. London: Croom Helm, 202–17.

Brownill, S. 1990. *Developing London's Docklands: Another great planning disaster?* London: Paul Chapman.

Buder, S. *Visionaries and planners: The garden city movement and the modern community.* [Online] Available at: http://site.ebrary.com/lib/academiccompletetitles/home.action.

Bullock, N. 1978. Housing in Frankfurt, 1925 to 1931 and the new Wohnkultur. *Architectural Review*, 113, 335–42.

Bulmer, M. 1978. Change, policy and planning since 1918. in *Mining and social change: Durham County in the twentieth century*, edited by M. Bulmer. London: Croom Helm, 167–201.

Cobb, J.C. 1993. *The selling of the South: The Southern crusade for industrial development 1936–1990*. 2nd Edition. Urbana: University of Illinois Press.

Cohen, P. and Rustin, M.J. 2008. *London's turning: Thames Gateway: prospects and legacy*. Hampshire: Ashgate.

Cullingworth, J.B. 1979. *Environmental planning, 1939–1969. Volume 3. New towns policy.* London: Her Majesty's Stationery Office (HMSO).

Deakin, D. 1989. *Wythenshawe, the story of a garden city*. Chichester: Phillimore.

Dicken, P. 2007. *Global shift: Mapping the changing contours of the world economy*. 5th Edition. New York, NY: Guilford Press.

Fox, K. 1985. *Metropolitan America: Urban life and urban policy in the United States, 1940-1980*. Houndmills: Macmillan.

Ghirardo, D. 1989. *Building new communities: New Deal America and Fascist Italy*. Princeton, NJ: University Press.

Gilg, A.W. 1996. *Countryside planning: The first half century*. 2nd Edition. London: Routledge.

Gold, J.R. 1997. *The experience of modernism: Modern architects and the future city, 1928–53*. 1st Edition. London, New York: Spon.

Greater London Regional Planning Committee (GLRPC). 1929. *First report*. Westminster: Knapp, Drewett & Sons.

Hall, T. (ed.). 1991. *Planning and urban growth in the Nordic countries.* 1st Edition. London: Spon.

Hansen, N.M. 1968. *French regional planning.* Bloomington: Indiana Univ. Press.

Hass-Klau, C. 1990. *The pedestrian and city traffic.* London: Belhaven Press.

Hausner, V.A. (ed.). 1986. *Critical issues in urban economic development.* Oxford: Clarendon Press.

Howard, E. 2003. *To-Morrow: A peaceful path to real reform.* London: Routledge.

Jackson, K.T. 1985. *Crabgrass frontier: The suburbanisation of the United States.* New York, NY: Oxford University Press.

Koter, M., Liszewski, S., Marszał, T. and Pączka, S. 1993. Man, environment and planning in the development of Łódź urban region. in *Planning and environment in the Łódź region,* edited by T. Marszał and W. Michalski. Łódź: Zarząd miasta Łodzi, 9–33.

Lilienthal, D.E. 1944. *TVA (Tennessee Valley Authority): Democracy on the march.* 7th Edition. New York: Harper.

Marchand, B. and Cavin, J.S. 2007. Anti-urban ideologies and planning in France and Switzerland: Jean-François Gravier and Armin Meili. *Planning Perspectives,* 22(1), 29–53. Available at: http://www.unil.ch/webdav/site/ipteh/shared/Publications/Joelle/RPPE_A_205100_O_Joelle_antiurbain.pdf [accessed: 14 July 2011].

Merlin, P. 1971. *New Towns: Regional planning and development.* London: Methuen.

Miljutin, N.A. 1974. *Sotsgorod: The problem of building socialist cities.* Cambridge, Mass: MIT Press.

Miller, M. 1992. *Raymond Unwin: Garden cities and town planning.* Leicester: Leicester University Press.

Ministry of Housing and Local Government (MHLG). 1964. *The South East Study 1961–1981.* London: Her Majesty's Stationery Office (HMSO).

Morgan, A. 1981. The inter-war years. in *Merthyr Tydfil: A valley community,* edited by Merthyr Teachers Centre Group, W.D. John and G.J. Coombes. Cowbridge: Brown.

Morison, I. 2000. The Corridor City: Planning for Growth in the 1960s. in *The Australian metropolis: A planning history,* edited by S. Hamnett and R. Freestone. London: Spon, 113–30.

Pattison, G. 2004. Planning for Decline: The 'D' Village policy of County Durham. *Planning Perspectives,* 19(3), 311–32.

Patton, K. 1978. The foundations of Peterlee New Town. in *Mining and social change: Durham County in the twentieth century,* edited by M. Bulmer. London: Croom Helm, 218–33.

Pawlowski, K.K. and Vechambre J.-M. 1993. *Tony Garnier: pionnier de l'urbanisme du XXe siècle.* Lyon: Les Creations du Pélican.

Petavel, J.W. 1909. The town planning of the future. *The Westminster Review,* 172, 398–405.

Post-War Redevelopment Advisory (Special) Committee (PWRASC). 1947. *City of Liverpool: Illustrated brochure issued in connection with the introductory Town Planning Exhibition to be held at Radiant House, Bold Street, Liverpool (by Courtesy of the Liverpool Gas Co.), Monday 30th June to Saturday, 26th July, 1947.* Liverpool: The Committee.

Royal Commission on Merthyr Tydfil (RCMT). 1936. *Report: (Cmd 5039).* London: His Majesty's Stationery Office (HMSO).

Royal Commission on the Distribution of the Industrial Population (RCDIP). 1940. *Report: (Cmd 6153).* London: His Majesty's Stationery Office (HMSO).

Rubenstein, J.M. 1978. *The French new towns.* Baltimore, MD: Johns Hopkins University Press.

Schubert, D. 2004. Theodor Fritsch and the German (völkisch) version of the Garden City: the Garden City invented two years before Ebenezer Howard. *Planning Perspectives,* 19(1), 3–35.

Scott, M. 1969. *American city planning since 1890: A history commemorating the fiftieth anniversary of the American Institute of Planners.* Berkeley, CA: University of California Press.

Soria y Mata, A. 1996. The Linear City, (translated by M. D. Gonzalez) Stanford. Stanford University Program on Urban Studies, reprinted 1998. in *Selected essays,* edited by R.T. LeGates and F. Stout. London: Routledge/Thoemmes Press.

Struthers, J. 1986. *Glasgow's Miles Better: 'They said it' About Glasgow.* Glasgow: Struthers.

van Hoogstraten, D. 1997. Paris 1965: Schéma Directeur d'Aménagement et d'Urbanisme de la Région de Paris. in *Mastering the city: North-European city planning, 1900–2000,* edited by K. Bosma and H. Hellinga. Rotterdam, The Hague: NAI Publishers; EFL Publications, 324–29.

Vlassenrood, L. 1997. Stockholm 1952: Generalplan för Stockholm. in *Mastering the city: North-European city planning, 1900–2000,* edited by K. Bosma and H. Hellinga. Rotterdam, The Hague: NAI Publishers; EFL Publications, 290–97.

Ward, K. and Jonas, A.E.G. 2004. Competitive city-regionalism as a politics of space: a critical reinterpretation of the new regionalism. *Environment and Planning A,* 36(12), 2119–39. Available at: http://ideas.repec.org/a/pio/envira/v36y2004i12p2119-2139.html.

Ward, S.V. 1986. Planmaking versus Implementation: The Example of List Q and the Depressed Areas 1922–1939. *Planning Perspectives,* 1(1), 3–26.

Ward, S.V. 1988. *The geography of interwar Britain: The state and uneven development.* London: Routledge.

Ward, S.V. 1990. Local industrial promotion and development policies 1899–1940. *Local Economy,* 5(2), 100–18. Available at: 10.1080/02690949008726035.

Ward, S.V. 1998. *Selling places: The marketing and promotion of towns and cities, 1850–2000.* London: Spon.

Ward, S.V. 2004. *Planning and Urban Change.* 2nd Edition. London: Sage Publications.

Ward, S.V. 2006. 'Cities are Fun!': Inventing and spreading the Baltimore model of cultural urbanism'. in *Culture, urbanism and planning*, edited by J. Monclús. Aldershot: Ashgate, 271–85.

Ward, S.V. 2011. Port Cities and the Global Exchange of Planning Ideas: The Transformation of Former Dock Areas. in *Port cities: Dynamic landscapes and global networks*, edited by C. Hein. London: Routledge.

Weber, A.F. 1963 [originally 1899]. *The Growth of cities in the nineteenth century: A study in statistics.* Ithaca, NY: Cornell University Press.

Chapter 2
Balancing European Territory.
The Challenge of the Post-Neoliberal Era

Peter Hall

Introduction

At the start of the twenty-first century, Europe – indeed the entire developed world – faces multiple challenges of economic and spatial reorganisation. The basic phenomena are well-known and well-rehearsed. The most basic is the shift to a service-based economy in which manufacturing forms a negligible part of employment and even the gross domestic product (GDP); services dominate and the distinction between producer and consumer services becomes critical; advanced producer services – not just financial and business services, but also the media and the design professions – become the main economic driver, and even the distinction between manufacturing and services erodes through the critical role played by logistics.

This fundamental shift has major spatial impacts on cities and regions. Differences emerge both between regions and within them. National governments and the European Union Commission seek to reduce core-periphery differences by such measures as improved transport and communications, and the improvement of human capital through education and training programmes. Measuring city performance, both nationally and internationally, becomes an important key to policy.

Two major comparative reviews

Here, two comprehensive reports give exceptionally valuable overviews: the State of the English Cities from the United Kingdom government (Department for Communities and Local Government 2006), and the European Union's *State of European Cities* (European Commission 2007). The United Kingdom report builds on a preceding study (ARUP 2005), which clearly established a series of key geographical divides: an old-established North-South divide, evident since the 1930s, between a prosperous London and South East Region and the old industrial regions of Northern England, South Wales and Central Scotland; a distinction between the major provincial 'Core Cities' and the rest of Northern and Midland England, observable since the 1990s; and a more subtle distinction within these core cities, between their central business districts and their residual middle and outer rings, which seems to have developed since 2000. The North-South divide, analysed in the *Regional Futures* report from the consultants (Arup and Partners, 2005) is measured by regional gross value added (GVA) per capita: the North has failed to develop a broad structure of private services, and remains over-dependent on public services; in addition, both private and public services have been attracted to the core cities at the expense of the remainder of these regions. The *State of the Cities* report reinforces this conclusion in much richer geographical detail, showing that northern cities suffer from lower per capita gross value added and higher poverty, but that the core cities perform distinctively better than the remainders of their regions, while old industrial cities around them – together with some seaside resorts, which in their way are a special variety of old one-industry towns – do worse. And this gap appeared to be increasing in the early years of the twenty-first century. In contrast, the so-called South East Mega-City Region, stretching up to 160 kilometres from London, constituted a vast growth zone in which small and medium-sized cities, physically separate but intensively networked, constituted the dynamic core of the United Kingdom economy. A dramatic illustration of this comes from research from the Globalisation and World Cities team at the University of Loughborough, who show that London is indisputably one of only four top global cities in terms of global business organisation, but that only two other British cities, Birmingham and Manchester, manage to scrape into the lowest category showing 'Some Evidence of World City Formation' – though, recently, they have made significant advances in the global hierarchy. The *Index of Multiple Deprivation*, issued every three years by the United Kingdom government, suggests that the core cities remained deprived but that some were improving their condition, while non-core cities were often becoming more deprived. That was a point underlined by the 2006 *State of the English Cities* report, which concluded that:

'The economic performance of English cities has been diverging for many decades. The overt policies adopted so far and the unintended spatial consequences of others have either failed to close this gap or actually made it worse. Among the results of this is that 31 out of the 56 city regions studied here lagged the English average growth rate in GVA per capita during the late 1990s and early 2000s. This is a major, persistent and long term problem for the English economy as a whole. The scale of change required can only be affected by central government with the active collaboration of local authorities and in conjunction with the private sector'(Department for Communities and Local Government 2006: 15).

The 2006 report attempted a comparison between major cities across Europe. Particularly striking here were the major differences in per capita gross value added: the major cities generally 'punched above their national weight', but United Kingdom cities conspicuously failed to do so (Figure 2.1 – Figure 2.4). Cities generally were strong in knowledge jobs, were highly innovative, but with

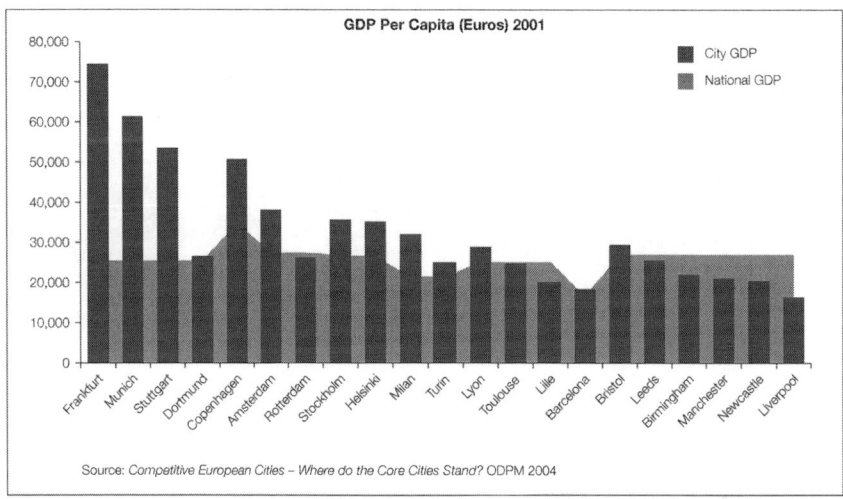

Figure 2.1   National and urban economic competitiveness: a comparison

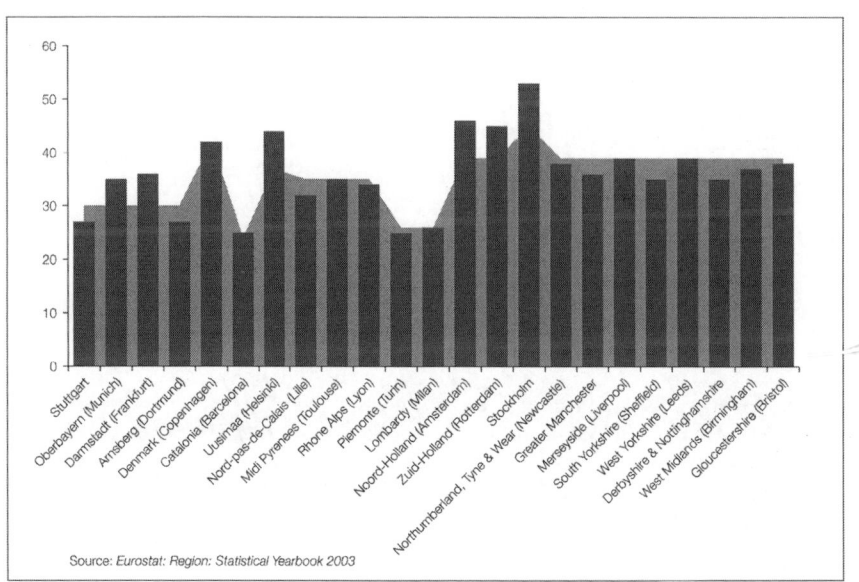

Figure 2.2   Employees working in knowledge intensive sectors

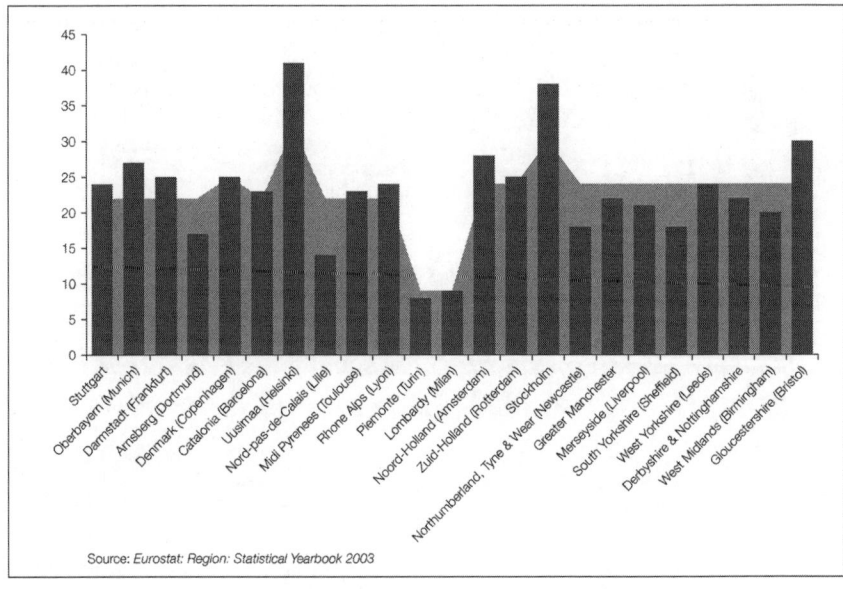

**Figure 2.3   Percentage of population (25–34 years) with 3rd level
               education – 2000**

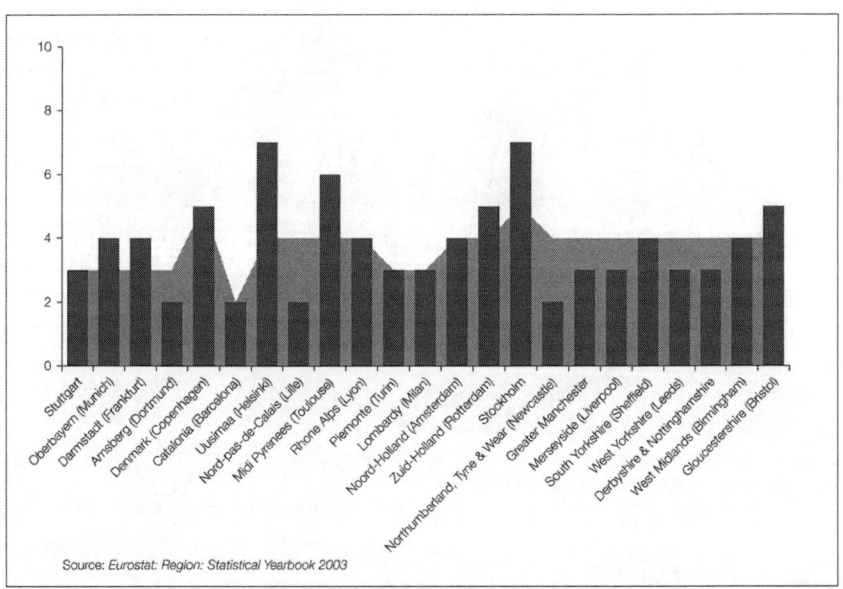

Figure 2.4   Employees working in high tech service sectors (percent)

big differences, were attractive to higher education students, and were strong both in high-tech manufacturing and in high tech services – but again, United Kingdom cities lagged behind the national average, and comparable mainland cities.

In 2007 there followed a major international comparison of European city performance, commissioned by the European Union's DG-Regio. The *State of the European Cities Report*, produced by ECOTEC Research and Consulting, shows that in the early 2000s there were still big differences in GDP (Gross Domestic Product per head) between western and eastern Europe; per capita GDP was highest in northwest European and Alpine region cities, while eastern European cities showed values only 50 per cent as high as those in the 'old' EU-15 (European Commission 2007). The good news was that cities were converging: gross domestic product per head was rising fastest in the cities of Scandinavia, Southern Europe and Poland, while also in individual member states – for instance in the United Kingdom, where the major cities of northern England were catching up on London. However, across many parts of Europe there remained an urban paradox: many cities were underperforming their national averages, with lower numbers employed and higher levels of unemployment, with disappointing levels in southern and eastern European cities, occasioned by low birth rates and high-out migration. There were also major differences within individual cities, and most disturbingly these reached a maximum where overall unemployment was highest, suggesting that such cities had a particular problem in absorbing their least-qualified citizens into the workforce (Figure 2.5 – Figure 2.6).

The *State of the European Cities* report sought to provide a composite index of performance, by asking how well cities scored on the so-called Lisbon benchmark – a measure based on the 'Lisbon Agenda', combining per capita gross domestic product, labour productivity, percentage in employment, percentage of older workers in employment, percentage in long-term unemployment among older workers, youth education levels and youth unemployment (Figure 2.7) (European Commission 2007). This produced a complex picture: the best-performing cities were those in Scandinavia, the Netherlands and western Germany, together with Paris, Madrid and Lisbon; otherwise, cities in southern and eastern Europe generally performed poorly, and there was no obvious relationship to size.

The most important contribution of the ECOTEC Research and Consulting report was its attempt to produce a taxonomy of European city types based on their principal economic functions. In all they distinguished three major groups, subdivided into thirteen types (Figure 2.8) (European Commission 2007).

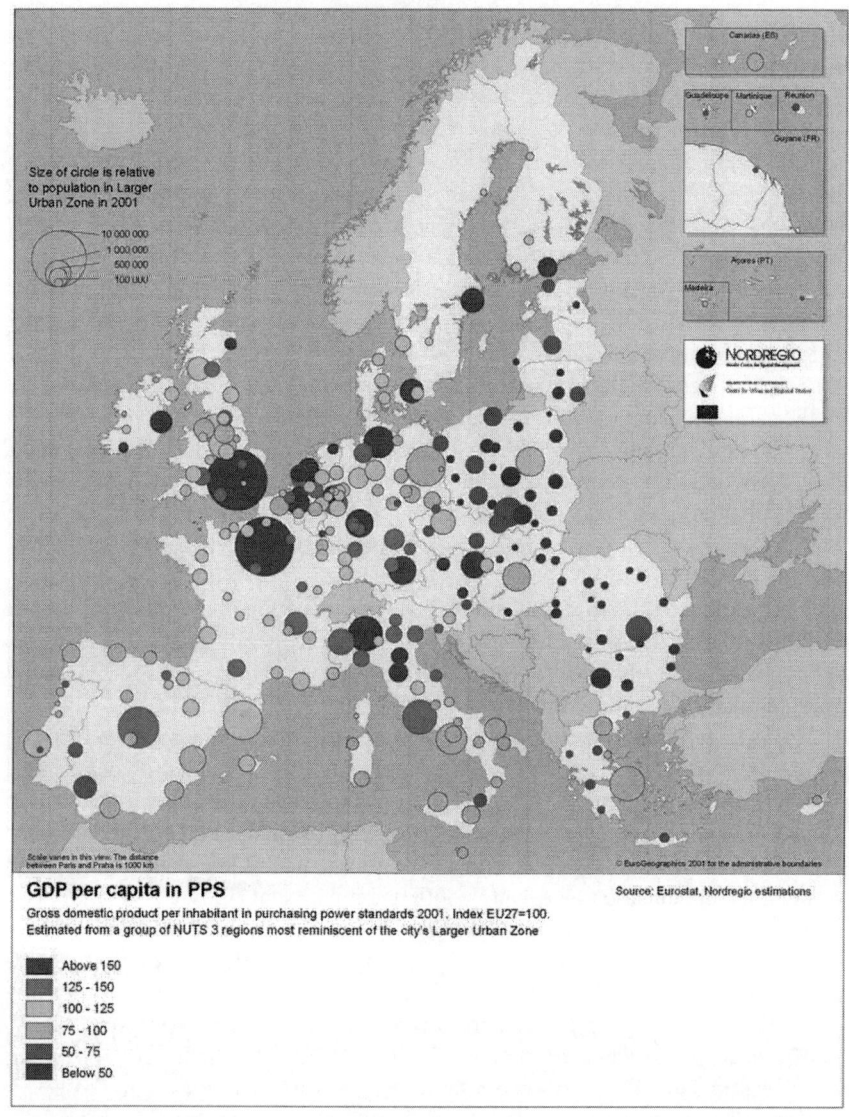

Figure 2.5   GDP per capita in PPS

Note: Gross domestic product per inhabitant in purchasing power standards 2001, Index EU27=100. Estimated from a group of NUTS 3 regions of the city's Larger Urban Zone.

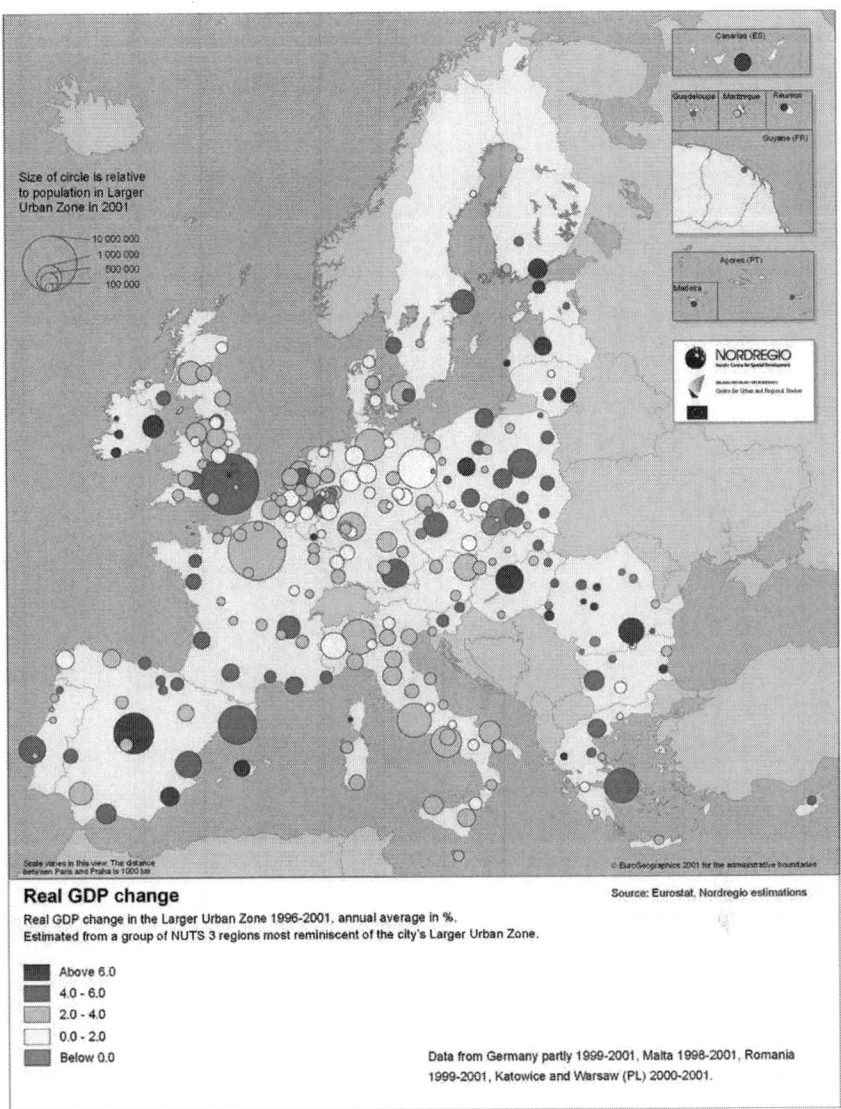

Real GDP change

Real GDP change in the Larger Urban Zone 1996-2001, annual average in %.
Estimated from a group of NUTS 3 regions most reminiscent of the city's Larger Urban Zone.

Source: Eurostat, Nordregio estimations

- ■ Above 6.0
- ■ 4.0 - 6.0
- ▨ 2.0 - 4.0
- ☐ 0.0 - 2.0
- ■ Below 0.0

Data from Germany partly 1999-2001, Malta 1998-2001, Romania 1999-2001, Katowice and Warsaw (PL) 2000-2001.

Figure 2.6   Real GDP change

Note: Real gross domestic product change in the Larger Urban Zone 1996-2001, annual average in percent. Estimated from a group of Nomenclature of Territorial Units for Statistics (NUTS)regions (specifically the NUTS 3 regions) of the city's Larger Urban Zone

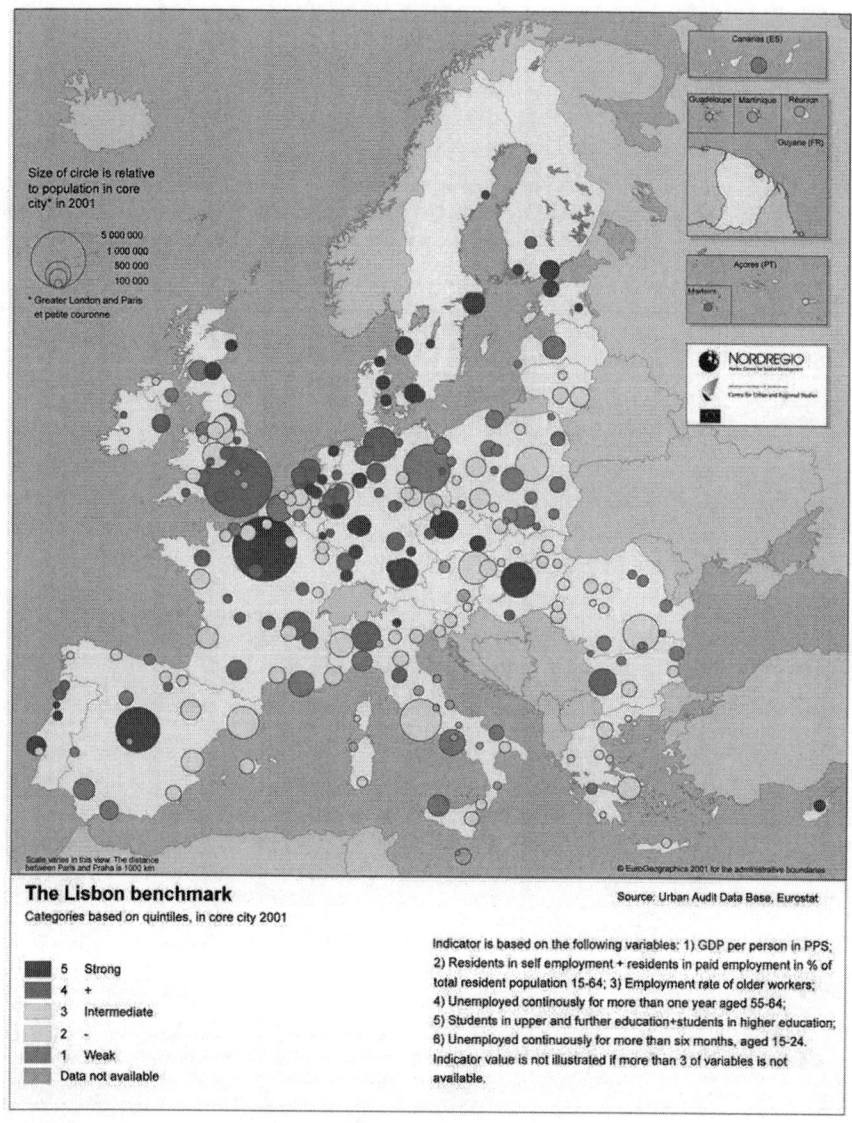

The Lisbon benchmark

Categories based on quintiles, in core city 2001

Source: Urban Audit Data Base, Eurostat

Figure 2.7   The Lisbon benchmark

Note: Categories based on quintiles, in core city 2001

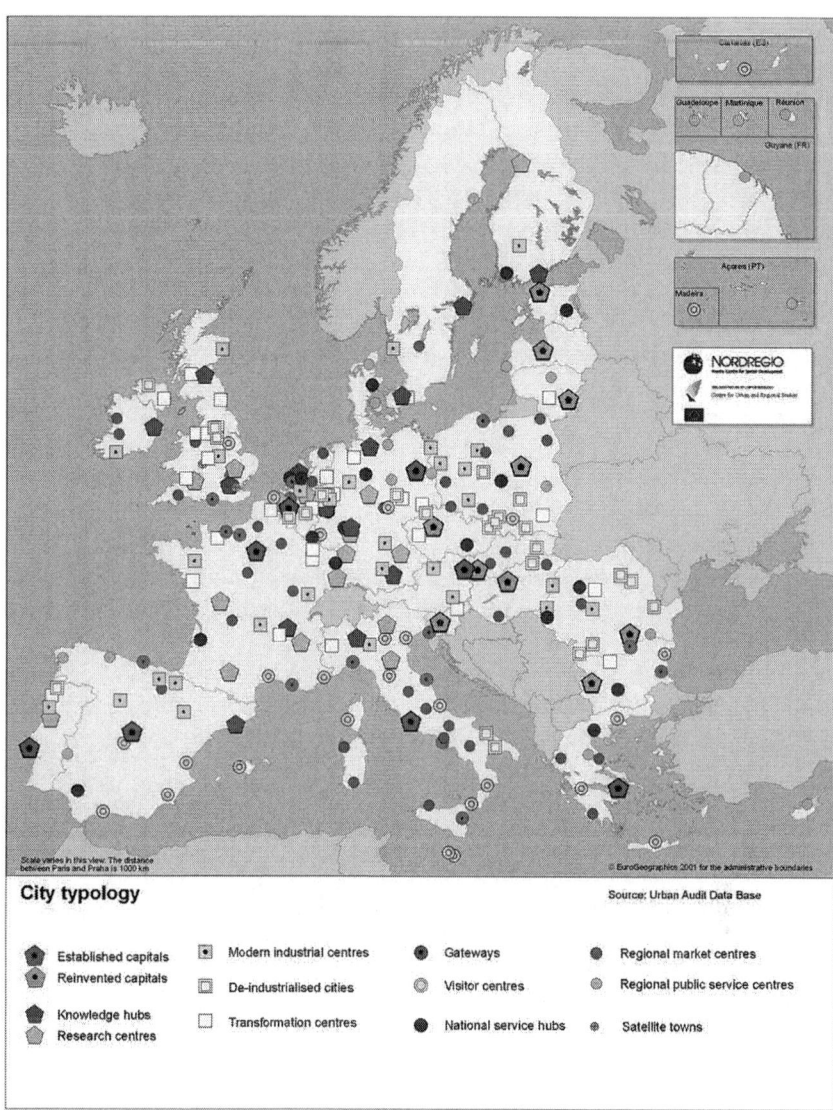

City typology

Source: Urban Audit Data Base

Established capitals	Modern industrial centres	Gateways	Regional market centres
Reinvented capitals	De-industrialised cities	Visitor centres	Regional public service centres
Knowledge hubs	Transformation centres	National service hubs	Satellite towns
Research centres			

Figure 2.8   City typology

International hubs

- Knowledge hubs: these top the league both in size and international importance, and in their recent economic performance. They include London, Frankfurt, Copenhagen and Barcelona;
- Established capitals: these shared many of the same characteristics, topping their national hierarchies but performing less spectacularly in the global economy. Examples include Paris, Madrid, Berlin and Rome;
- Re-invented capitals: these are the capital cities of the EU's new accession countries, paradoxically showing shrinkage of the population but an expanding economy. Examples include Prague, Warsaw and Budapest.

Specialised poles

- National service hubs: these play a strong administrative role for prosperous, dynamic regions, and demonstrate good growth records. Examples include Hannover, Utrecht and Seville;
- Transformation poles: these are old industrial cities, more or less successfully making the critical transition to the 'new knowledge economy'. Examples are Lille, Glasgow and Turin.
- Gateways: these are port cities heavily dependent on a transport-based economy, suffering from high unemployment and a poorly-qualified labour force. They include such places as Rotterdam, Marseille and Genoa.
- Modern industrial centres: in stark contrast, these are Europe's high-tech powerhouses. Examples include Augsburg, Tilburg and Göteborg.
- Research centres: these are strong higher education and research and development centres with associated high-tech corporate activities, generally quite small but well-connected to the wider world. Examples are Karlsruhe, Grenoble, Eindhoven and Cambridge.
- Visitor centres: these are tourist centres serving big flows of international visitors, reasonably successful economically. Examples are Trier, Málaga and Kraków.

Regional poles

- De-industrialised cities: these are old industrial cities suffering from major problems of adaptation to the new knowledge economy, both in western and eastern Europe. Examples include Charleroi, Halle, Katowice and Sheffield.
- Regional market centres: these serve a crucial role in providing personal, business and financial services, including business services, for their local sub-regions. They are performing modestly well. Examples include Erfurt, Reims and Palermo.
- Regional public service centres: these also are important in providing

administrative, health and educational services to their local regions, but suffer from remote locations and weak markets. Examples include Schwerin, Odense and Umeå.

- Satellite towns: these are a rather special case, constituting quite dynamic specialised subcentres within wider urban regions, depending on a combination of commuters from larger core cities and local service economies. Examples include Stevenage, Worcester and Setubal.

Figure 2.9, from the ECOTEC Research and Consulting report, plot the economic performance of these 13 different types on three different criteria: employment rate, qualified residents, and multimodal accessibility. The results are startlingly clear: there is a clear array across the categories, from success to relative failure. And the central explanation is the basis of the taxonomy: economic structure. Certain kinds of places, in certain locations, are successfully making the transition from the older to the newer economy; others are not. The question is what, if anything, public policy can do about this.

The European Union, in their 1999 *European Spatial Development Perspective* (European Commission 1999), had one clear answer: to encourage greater polycentricism at the European scale, out of the central Pentagon region and towards the peripheries of Europe. Not stated at that point, but explicit in the reallocation of the European Union budget after 2007, was the diversion of structural funds from older less-successful industrial regions of western Europe into mainly rural regions in the accession countries. However, over the period 2000–2010, it is clear that the main effect – even anticipating the actual diversion of funds – has been to aid rapid development of the capital city regions in these countries: Budapest, Prague, Warsaw and smaller capital cities became the new European boomtowns, just as Madrid, Lisbon and Dublin had begun to be in the previous enlargement (European Commission 1999). In other words, paradoxically, it appears that encouraging European-scale polycentricism may promote monocentricism at the national scale. At the same time, cities like London, Paris, Milan, Munich and Hamburg, all significantly sited right on the edge of Pentagon, appear to be expanding outwards into larger city regions, this expanding the scale and influence of the Pentagon itself. The law of unintended consequences thus seems to be operating massively within the European urban system.

There is no simple answer that will unlock the problem of regional and urban imbalance, either within Europe or within its member states. The United Kingdom has been grappling with this problem since the 1930s, and other European countries almost as long, with very modest success. But there are two possible policies that are worth examining; improving access to under-performing cities and regions, and upgrading their human capital.

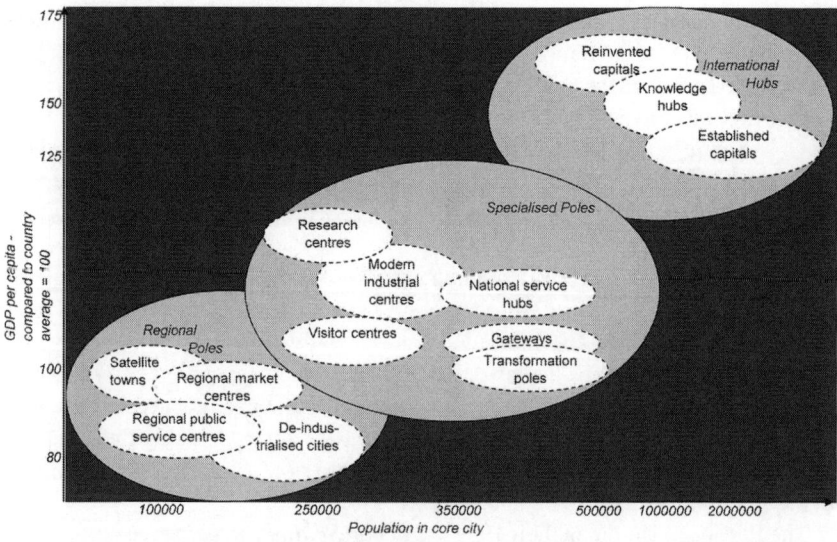

A. Employment levels

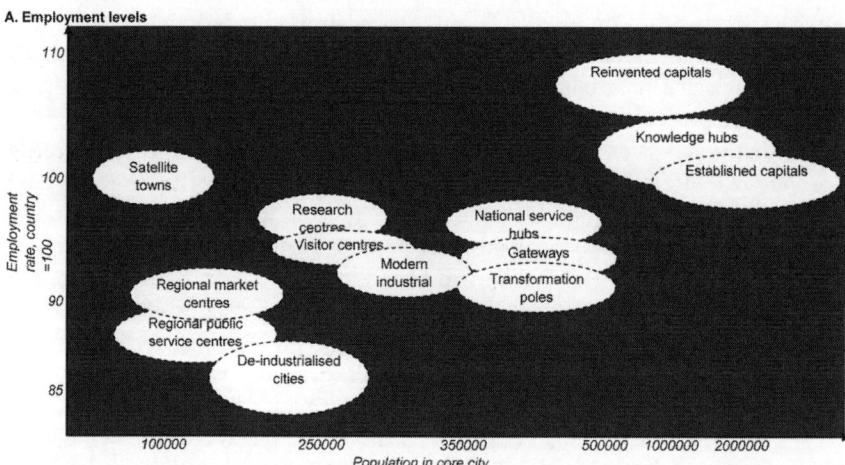

Figure 2.9   City types positioned – by some driving factors of competitiveness

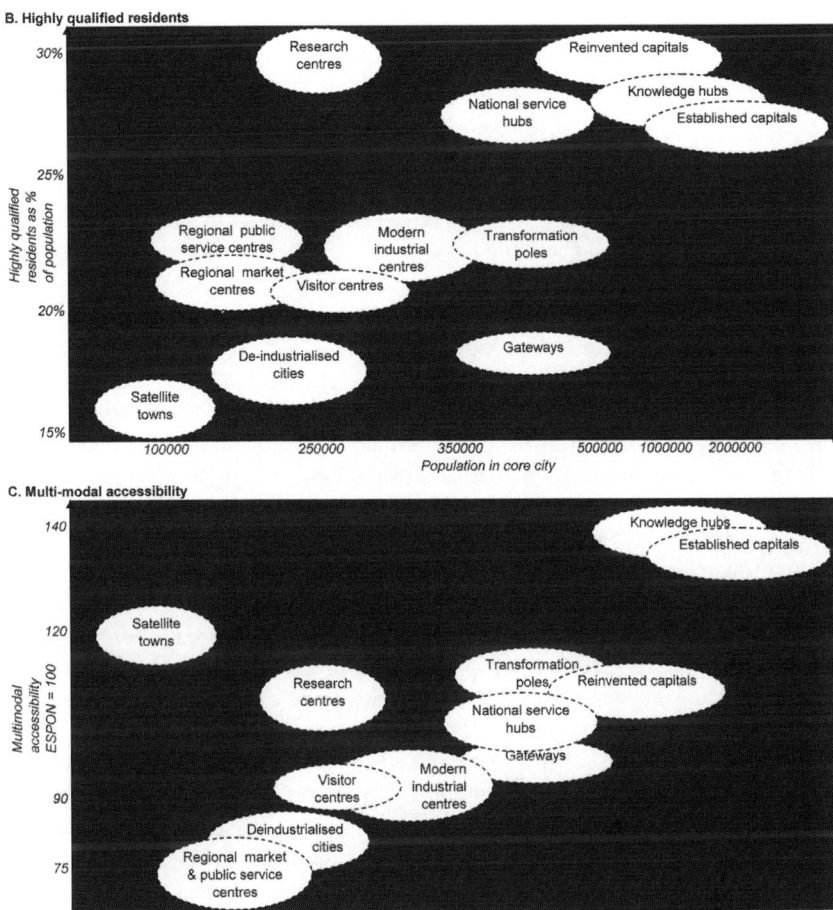

Figure 2.9   Concluded

Improving accessibility

This, it could be argued, is a necessary but not a sufficient condition. Since 1980, but recently at an accelerating pace, high-speed train travel has shrunk effective distances in Europe, making remoter regions accessible (Figure 2.10). But the effects have often been quite highly differentiated: times between major core cities (London to Manchester, Paris to Lille) have been dramatically reduced, but to the smaller places in their surrounding regions accessibility has not been improved as radically, or may have even declined because the new networks have not extended there. The contrast between Manchester and Burnley in the North West region of England is a particularly telling example (Lucci, Hildreth 2008). A key choice here is whether to extend high-speed train service directly to these other places (as has been done in the Nord-Pas de Calais region of France) or to create seamless web easy transfers to local metro or tram systems (as now in most French cities), or both. Recent evidence from France and the United Kingdom suggests that a direct TGV (*Train à Grande Vitesse*, meaning *high-speed train*)service may aid direct connection between old industrial cities and their capital cities, but that internal linkages to the regional core city (Lille, Manchester) may show little or no improvement (Chen, Hall 2011a, Chen, Hall 2011b).

A particular question concerns a relatively new technology, the tram train, first developed in the German city of Karlsruhe in the early 1990s and now being widely emulated elsewhere in Europe, whereby trams extend from city streets on to regional rail systems (Figure 2.11). There, as later in Kassel and then in a host of European cities that are following their examples, tram trains offer all kinds of new connection possibilities, linking in city centres to high-speed and inter-city rail and effectively extending rail networks into new areas that earlier were poorly served. In the United Kingdom, where a national trial is under way, they have a special role in extending tram service, via hybrid electric-diesel vehicles, to extend tram service on to the many hundreds of kilometres of non-electrified lines – although the United Kingdom trial has been considerably complicated by new European Union emissions regulations for diesel motors. In any case, the main motivation of the United Kingdom Department for Transport is clearly to find ways of operating branch lines at lower costs, by taking them out of the national rail network altogether and reconfiguring them as light rail lines. This will take several more years of experimentation. The European Union Interreg-financed Sustainable Integrated Tram-Based Transport Options for Peripheral European Regions (SINTROPHER) project is playing an active role by assisting the development of tram train systems, linked to multimodal transport hubs, in five subregions of North West Europe: Kassel (Germany), Nijmegen (the Netherlands), Westvlaanderen (Belgium), Valenciennes (France) and Fylde Coast (United Kingdom).

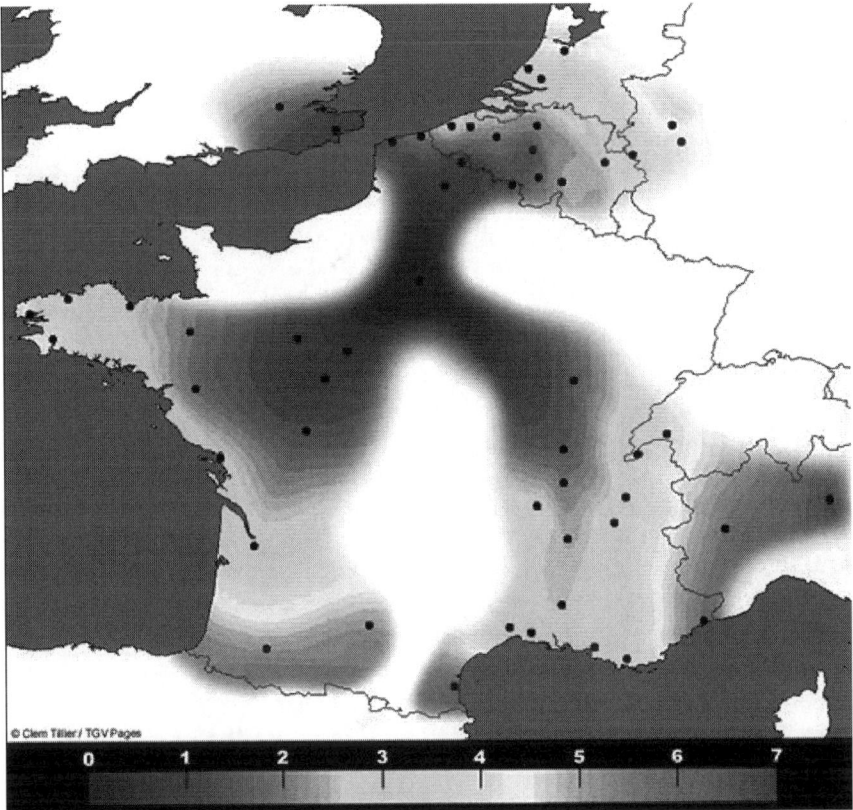

Figure 2.10   Travel time from Paris

Note: Black dots represent selected cities with TGV /Thalys / Eurostar service

Upgrading human capital

It can and will be argued that better accessibility is not enough. Regions will not successfully adapt from the manufacturing to the knowledge economy unless they succeed in re-educating and retaining their workforces. This appears to be particularly a problem in old industrial regions formerly based on mining and heavy industrial work, where a predominantly male workforce has found it difficult to adjust to the demands of the 'new economy', not only in specific professional and technical skills but in the 'soft skills' of human relations. In the United Kingdom, for instance, the workforce is underskilled and this is even more evident in the older industrial regions (HM Treasury 2006). Here, a combination of policies appears to be needed. In the core cities of such declining regions the need is to strengthen the knowledge economy through investment in higher

Figure 2.11   The Tram train

education and the research base; around them, transport policies are crucial, developing and improving linkages into the core city, in the way already evident around a successful world city like London, so developing new-style networked MEGAs (Mega City-Regions). And in more remote older industrial towns in such regions, the priority is to supplement private investment in new 'Unique Selling Propositions', so effectively developing a new economic base like the 'Weavers' Triangle' in the northwest England cotton weaving town of Burnley, which lost its basic industry decades ago. Even more distantly, in the remote rural regions: the need will be to exploit natural qualities and resources as a basis for developing local economies, with 'niche' activities (rural production, tourism) as model exemplars of sustainable economic development. There is no single model here; the challenge will be to develop uniquely innovative solutions that answer to the particular qualities of the local location and the local environment. But developing these solutions may involve breaking negative path dependencies that spring from the regional economic past, in the form of inherited social and cultural attitudes that may inhibit the path of adaptation to the economic future – whatever, in the particular context, that solution may be.

Conclusion

There is no easy answer to the problem of cities and regions that are caught up in processes of structural economic change, threatening their traditional economic base and forcing them and their citizens to find new ways of earning their living. These processes have operated through centuries of economic history, constituting the 'creative destruction' which the economist Joseph Schumpeter regarded as central to the capitalist economy (Schumpeter 1942). But a critical new element in the new global economic geography is the development of mega-city regions, linking individual cities and towns into networked systems of specialised production. This new form of spatial organisation, distinctive to the early twenty-first century, simultaneously offers both a challenge and an opportunity: within it, each place can develop its own specialised economic niche. Improving the physical conditions for interchange – of people, of goods and of information – is one key. But developing the potential of a place's human capital is equally important, indeed critical. In the new knowledge economy, human intelligence is all.

References

Arup and Partners. 2005. *Regional Futures: England's Regions in 2030 (Final Report)*. London.

Chen, C.-L. and Hall, P. 2011a. The Impacts of High-Speed Trains on British Economic Geography: a Study of the UK's InterCity 125/225 and its Effects. *Journal of Transport Geography*, 19(4), 689–704. Available at: 10.1016/j.jtrangeo.2010.08.010.

Chen, C.-L. and Hall, P. 2011b. The Wider Spatial-Economic Impacts of High-Speed Trains. A Comparative Case Study of Manchester and Lille Sub-Regions. *Journal of Transport Geography*, 19 (forthcoming).

Department for Communities and Local Government. 2006. *The Competitive Economic Performance of English Cities*. London: Department for Communities and Local Government.

European Commission. 1999. *ESDP: European spatial development perspective: Towards Balanced and Sustainable Development of the Territory of the European Union; agreed at the informal Council of Ministers responsible for Spatial Planning in Potsdam May 1999*. Luxembourg.

European Commission. 2007. *State of European Cities Report: Adding Value to the European Urban Audit*. [Brussels]: European Union Regional Policy, DG Region.

HM Treasury. 2006. *Prosperity for all on the global economy: World class skills (The Leitch Report)*. London: His Majesty's Stationary Office (HMSO).

Lucci, P. and Hildreth, P. 2008. *City Links: Integration and Isolation*. London.

Schumpeter, J.A. 1942. *Capitalism, Socialism and Democracy*. New York: Harper & Brothers.

Chapter 3

Conceptualizing Shrinking C·
A Challenge for Planning Theu.

Johann Jessen

Introduction

While much is known about the spatial patterns and underlying mechanisms that make up growing cities, less is known about what those mechanisms are in shrinking cities. In this chapter the case is made for the need to conceptualize the change of urban patterns in shrinking cities, specifically, how does demographic change (loss and ageing of population) and economic decline affect the functional, spatial and morphologic structure of cities? In the first part, the question is addressed of why it is relevant to think about shrinking cities in a new way. The second part touches upon the relationship between urban growth and urban theory. Thirdly some early observations on structural changes of urban patterns in shrinking cities are made. The conclusion offers research questions that should be put on the agenda for further consideration.

Shrinking Cities – an important issue in Germany

Why is the subject of shrinking cities so important, at least in Germany? Almost every city in eastern Germany is shrinking. With the breakdown of communism and the fall of the 'iron curtain', eastern Germany faced an abrupt and tremendous loss of jobs and population. Hannemann described this as interrelated processes of 'de-economization, de-population, and de-urbanisation' (Hannemann 2004: 200). Within ten years, most of eastern Germany's cities lost up to 20 per cent of their former inhabitants through labour-oriented migration to western Germany, through dramatic decline in the already very low birth rate, and a kind of 'catch-up suburbanisation'. The continuous loss of population and jobs had tremendous impacts: an unemployment rate at a persistently high level (17–20 per cent on average), a constantly high rate of people depending on social welfare, a rapidly ageing population, decreasing housing rents, decreasing land prices, reduced purchasing power and reduced local tax revenues. The effects became more and more visible. The cities were marked by huge abandoned industrial brownfields, streets with many vacant shops and offices, dilapidated factory and residential buildings and by underutilized or abandoned social and technical infrastructure.

Both speed and scale of urban decline in eastern Germany have been unique. However, all forecasts show that the phenomenon of shrinking cities is not restricted to eastern Germany, but will extend to the country as a whole: Due to demographic change there will be more and more shrinking cities, concentrated in old industrial regions and in more rural areas.

Currently, shrinking cities and regions are predominantly characterized by the means of images, episodes and statistics. Spacious brownfields, abandoned factories, vacant housing, derelict railway stations and boarded-up schools still make for bizarre motifs with an ambiguous aesthetic appeal. Inhabitants of non-declining cities are still shocked by these pictures, as they fundamentally contrast with people's everyday perceptions. In this sense, these images are self-explanatory. In numerous portrayals of the individual destiny of cities and their inhabitants, this traumatic experience becomes tangible (Kil 2004). Long-term statistics tellingly explain why these cities or parts of them are no longer needed: decline of industrial branches, reduction in jobs, decrease and ageing of population due to mortality surplus and migration, dwindling spending power and fiscal revenue, shutdown of public infrastructure because of a shortfall in demand (Gatzweiler, Meyer, Milbert 2003).

But how does the functional, spatial and morphologic structure of cities change, when it is subject to demographic change (loss and ageing of population) and economic structural decline? Is the process of decline ruled by an inherent logic analogous to the development of growing cities, and what determines it? It may seem overhasty to adopt such an unemotional perspective on the future of these cities, one which is not influenced by images of the desired or envisioned urban regeneration. But sooner or later, such a perspective will become necessary. All projections agree that the number of shrinking cities in Germany will increase. Therefore, this mode of urban development will represent the normal case and lose the dramatic touch that hitherto characterized the processes in eastern Germany. For this reason, it seems unlikely that the high level of public interventions that were performed within the National Funding Programme Stadtumbau Ost ('Urban Restructuring East Germany') will be maintained. This programme provided substantial amounts of public funding in an exceptionally rapid manner – this approach to funding will not be sustained. Options to steer and moderate this process will narrow and market developments will more noticeably impact on urban structure. Furthermore, experts widely agree that urban planning, when deprived of public funding, will lose its ability to influence spatial development in shrinking regions, not least because stakeholders have a wide range of options when choosing future business or residential locations. These in turn are not necessarily in line with planning objectives.

Until now, the scientific community, for understandable reasons, predominantly focused on the urban structure of cities in eastern Germany. Questions of future development were mainly addressed from a perspective that was dominated by urban regeneration efforts. There have been some typologies of shrinking cities submitted by urbanists, derived from the special case of eastern Germany. In one typology a distinction is made between (1) the perforated and fragmented city, and (2) the transformed and the dissolving city, applying the potential for successful urban regeneration strategies as the central distinctive feature (Göschel 2003: 607). Another empirical study on shrinking small towns in east Germany follows the same line (Hannemann 2004: 213f.). Four types of shrinking cities are defined which differ in their chance to cope with the crisis related to shrinkage: (1) the consolidated city, (2) the stabilized city, (3) the stagnating city, and (4) the eroding city. The analysis shows that present and anticipated structures are flexible enough to adapt to future needs or desired urban models. However, how they develop, and according to which underlying principles they will probably develop are not always addressed.

Obviously there is a research gap. This chapter cannot close it, but strives to contribute some observations. An urban vision after which the future of shrinking cities will solely be guided by market forces – similar to the Burgess (1925) growth model of the capitalist city that totally ignored planning and political interventions – is not realistic. Of course, planning and regeneration interventions will continue to influence the development of shrinking cities – but, due to dwindling resources, in a less effective way and sometimes with unintended effects.

The existing gap in knowledge may go back to the fact that other city types were the well-known protagonists for urban transformation: the American city of the 1970s and 1980s on one hand, and the German socialist city on the other. The declining American city of the 1970s and 1980s, that German urban planners became aware of because of reports on cities such as Detroit, is not a suitable reference for the understanding of shrinking processes in western Germany (van Buren Jones 1995, Plunz 1995). The specific conditions of urban development in the United States of that time became apparent in former industrial cities such as Detroit, Pittsburgh, Cleveland or Philadelphia, but they apply to other growing American metropolises as well. They led to spatial patterns that are often described as 'doughnut development': a hole in the middle that is surrounded by a blown-up ring:

- deteriorating centres that lose their functions and face dereliction whereas agglomerations in suburbia (edge cities) prosper and where growth is accelerated by the expansion of the motorway network.
- processes of growth that, in US cities, always go along with a quick abandonment of existing buildings: this inherent decay and the evolvement of 'derelict landscapes' within vital regions have been described as 'collective wasting' that is immanent in the process of American urban development (Jakle, Wilson 1992)
- a course of development that is ruled by an outwards movement: first, inner city centres decay because they have been abandoned in favor of better developed new centres in the peripheries. This 'decay within growth' has now advanced to the point that the first suburban rings of development are affected. There, the existing housing stock from the 1950s, 60s and 70s no longer fits the market demand (Lucy, Phillips 2000).

The example of Detroit illustrates that the American model does not serve as a comparable frame of reference for German cities in deep structural crisis. Although alarming pictures show an advanced state of de-urbanisation of Detroit, contrary to popular opinion this formerly vital American city is actually the empty core of a region that is nevertheless still thriving (Callagher 2004). There is analysis which shows that wastelands and urban decline have always been an inherent part of dynamic urban development in American cities. In different phases of postwar America this phenomenon has been connoted, interpreted and strategically used to support arguments by different groups in many different ways (Beauregard 1993).

Furthermore, it turns out that this growth is the prerequisite for amazing processes of re-urbanisation that we can witness – albeit not in Detroit, but in deserted and functionless urban cores and inner-city neighbourhoods of other American metropolitan areas, including Los Angeles, Baltimore, Chicago, Portland, Washington D.C., and others (Birch 2005, Fishman 2005). In these cases, urban policy that is geared towards inner city revitalisation can resort to a flexible, 'disposable quantity' of activities that can be used to fill the hole in the middle and revive the empty core (Giseke, Spiegel 2007, for Portland/ Oregon: Jessen, Mayer 2010). However, this does not mean that there are not other comparable shrinking cities in the United States at all connected with regional structural industrial decline (Pallagst, Wiechmann 2005).

The general discussion on shrinking cities in Germany is determined by the debates on the federal programme Stadtumbau Ost ('Urban Restructuring East Germany') and the latest development of cities in the 'Neue Länder' (federal states established from the former East Germany), although it is well known that the latter have been shaped by certain particularities:

- by 40 years of socialist urban development which generated other urban structures than in capitalist Western Germany: no suburbanisation, dominance of public and cooperative standardized housing, no private housing development, only marginal individual homeownership, neglect of the older housing stock that already featured high vacancy rates before the political turn-around in East Germany, facilities for childcare and other services organized by state enterprises, not by the local communities;
- by a dramatically fast process of economic decline and de-population after the German reunification and large-scale retail development at out-of-context locations;
- by a wide-ranging national funding programme probably unparalleled in history with conflicting effects: rapid modernization of the historic housing stock and retrofitting of technical infrastructure, new construction of rental housing in the peripheries of large cities that was triggered by tax incentives within the first years and that is partially responsible for the widespread vacancies nowadays.

In the first place, these particularities account for the exceptional vehemence of decline processes in eastern Germany. They must be interpreted as a singularity in history that is even unparalleled by the developments in post-socialist central and eastern Europe. On one hand, the cities in eastern Germany represent the most up-to-date and comprehensive illustrative material available on shrinking urban structures in modern societies. On the other hand, wide generalization of the processes witnessed there does not appear appropriate. Shrinking cities in western Germany considerably differ from cities in eastern Germany as far as their initial urban structure and the recent history is concerned. Here, urban structure usually changes in a more continuous manner and at a slower pace.

Urban growth and planning theory

The nineteenth and twentieth century in Europe and the United States can be considered as the age of continuous urban growth, characterized by various stages or phases (van Berg et al. 1982): urbanisation, suburbanisation, counter- and/or de-urbanisation and now re-urbanisation (the latter being subject to debate). Since the age of industrialisation from the early nineteenth century all towns experienced a growth of population and jobs; new towns like the 'coketowns' occurred, towns turned into cities, cities turned into big cities and into metropolitan regions. They keep on expanding their boundaries, there is a continuous change of spatial, functional and social as well as physical patterns following different paths in different parts of the world.

Urban and regional planning emerged as modern professional disciplines. They can be considered as true offspring of the rapid urban growth in the second half of the nineteenth century. From the very beginning, urban planning was meant to mitigate or to avoid the negative consequences of urban growth. Planning was and still is predominantly about optimizing the spatial allocation of uses in order to compensate for market failure of growing cities.

It has been stated earlier that all our spatial models – from the Garden City to the Compact City of today – are about 'taming' and modifying urban growth and fighting its unwanted consequences. Shifts of planning paradigms, e.g. the change from the notion of comprehensive planning to that of disjointed incrementalism, took place within the context of urban growth. This applies to all their derivatives as well: all planning legislation, planning systems and our curricula in planning education are oriented towards planning of, and for, growing cities – rather than for shrinking and declining ones.

Of course this does not mean that no shrinking cities existed in the last two centuries. Old industrial regions (homes to the textile, steel, and mining industries) were the first modern urban landscapes that faced structural changes with substantial decline of jobs and inhabitants (Benke 2005). However, declining regions were an exception and only represented a small, negligible minority of cities. This changed dramatically, at least in Germany, due to the combined effects of the political repercussions of Germany's reunification, its economic restructuring and demographic change.

Characteristic structural features of shrinking cities

Urban development has always been a combination of city extension, urban regeneration and structural transformation – whereas shares varied during different eras. At least this is true for growing cities. But to what extent does it also apply to shrinking cities? How do these functional and spatial characteristics of urban development change in declining cities that suffer from permanent loss of population and jobs? What conclusions can we draw from the experiences within the last decades (former coalfields in western Europe such as northern England, northern France, the Ruhr Basin and Saarland in Germany) and from the exceptional case of eastern German cities in which decline was accelerated by political change? What are the patterns of functional and socio-spatial differentiation particular to shrinking that have emerged in these cities?

The functional and socio-spatial differentiations and the morphology of growing cities have been widely described by urban sociologists and urban geographers, in order to ascertain the dimensions that may be relevant for analyzing the structural change of shrinking cities. In their theoretical models and empirical studies they identified different cultural paths of urban growth all over the world. While the focus in this chapter is on European cities, most of the subsequent observations may apply to cities in other parts of the world. Growing urban cities in Europe are characterized by at least five features:

- *Continuous land consumption:* The increase of population and/or jobs leads to continuous expansion of settlement area. With growing wealth, land consumption becomes super-proportional to growth of jobs and population as the demand of space per household and workplace is growing as well. These processes of growth undulate – there are phases of accelerated growth and phases of stagnation or little growth in small steps. This is also expressed in the respective scale of growth: the more dynamic the growth, the larger are the units of city extension or transformation.
- *Separation of land uses:* In the course of development, the functional structure of cities changes. Uses start to segregate. The spatial distance between place of living and place of work increasingly grows. The separation of uses is accelerated by augmenting car ownership and expansion of the public transport network. Large areas of housing, industry and offices emerge. The number of commuters rises, more and more time is spent on travel.
- *Densification of built-up area:* In growing cities, the settlement area expands. But at the same time, the uses within built-up areas are intensified by conversion, upgrading or replacement of buildings, predominantly in

favourable locations (highly accessible or/and attractive sites (landscape amenities as hillside and waterside situations). While building density increases, the occupancy rates decrease as the demand of space per workplace and household keeps constantly growing in the cities of most Western countries.

- *Social differentiation:* In the course of city growth, an opportunity opens up for all city dwellers to gradually improve their housing situation – albeit not at the same rate and not to the same level. On the lines of the existing income distribution, residential areas differentiate into 'preferred addresses', 'less upscale' and 'ordinary' neighbourhoods; the more distant to the centre the neighbourhoods, the higher the income and the better the housing quality. According to this model in the course of a lifecycle city dwellers move in regard to the site in an outwards direction and in regard to housing quality in an upward direction. For industrial areas, commercial and retail areas, a similar value gap emerges, that is expressed in differing price levels for rent and land.
- *Formation of centres:* In the course of urban growth, the city core, that often goes back to pre-industrial roots, contains the most important commercial and cultural uses, expands. Like the city as a whole the city centre expands while simultaneously facing growing density caused by ever larger single investments. In larger conurbations sub-centres emerge, either by incorporating neighbouring suburbanised town centres of previously independent municipalities or by agglomerating functions along important arterial roads or close to railway stations. The concentration of commercial facilities at locations in the urban periphery that are easy to reach by car, is a historically rather new phenomenon that did not started until the middle of the twentieth century.

Driven by the land market, all these processes of concentration, de-concentration and intensification take place continuously and simultaneously, but they do not affect every part of the city in the same way. For example, suburban neighbourhoods with single-family homes are considered stable structures as the social mix and the buildings usually only change gradually. In contrast, neighbourhoods which are close to the city centre transform more rapidly due to the development pressure of the core. Therefore, the structural change of growing cities can be characterized as 'coexistence of asynchrony'. Thus, comparably stable and gradually changing structures can be found next to structures that are subject to rapid change and repeated transformation. This has included the existence of areas of urban decline and urban blight within growing city regions which preferably then became subject to regeneration strategies.

Also, most of us are likely to agree on the role and impact of urban policy and planning when accounting for modern urban patterns in Europe. Local spatial planning has always sought to shape these processes of urban growth in order to modify and mitigate their negative consequences (such as land consumption, conflicts in use, and gentrification):

- by allocation of social and technical infrastructure
- by danger and damage prevention
- by providing affordable housing
- by regulating the type and degree of land use
- by protection of endangered goods and species (nature conservation, monument protection)
- by stimulating the development of land and the use of resources in situations where market processes fail to do so (urban regeneration).

Therefore planning is about optimizing the spatial allocation of uses in order to compensate for market failure and to protect goods that are endangered to fall victim to market processes.

The urban growth paradigm is based on settlement area expansion, separation of uses, densification, social differentiation and centre formation as well as on urban planning interventions that strive to steer and organise growth. This applies to the way European cities grow, to the morphology of growing cities, and to the role that planning plays in that process.

But, if all this characterises urban growth, what are the equivalent processes in the context of shrinking cities? There is some interesting current research on shrinking cities. Many surveys study the changing social and demographic structure, the change in living conditions and so forth. Some studies explain why these cities or parts of them are no longer needed and finally, above all, there has been lot of policy-oriented research about shrinking cities. The policy related research in Germany is reflecting the tremendous planning efforts and financial state support of urban regeneration, in the old industrial regions and especially in eastern Germany. However, it is amazing and not easy to explain, that up to now there has been almost no empirical research or theoretical efforts addressing the following questions: Which new land uses replace existing urban functions when a city becomes subject to decline? What new uses emerge in which place and in which physical form? Can we identify a particular temporal order of follow-up uses? What shifts occur in the patterns of socio-spatial distribution?

What is missing, is what may be called an 'inverse urban morphology' of shrinking cities. As Iris Reuther points out: 'It is hard to predict how the land use setting in declining cities will warp and what physical forms and spatial patterns will evolve from a decreasing, stagnating or only relatively increasing demand on an oversupplied real estate market. In this sense, development is hardly planable' (Reuther 2003: 584).

Of course, we must not perceive the process of urban decline as a film playing in reverse – even if the currently dominating pictures of spectacular demolition may suggest that. Processes of shrinkage are the result of balancing powers, where processes of decline and decay outweigh the processes of growth and regeneration that continue to take place. In comparison to the processes in growing cities, structural change in declining cities may currently be described as follows. The description takes into account some observations from eastern German cities from the last decade.

- *Reduced land consumption:* The spatial expansion of settlement area (turning farmland to building land) slows down its pace but still proceeds in most cases. Suburbanisation is still ongoing: residential suburbanisation as construction of single-family homes in the countryside or urban fringe, commercial suburbanisation by new shopping malls while other suburban commercial sites might decline (de-malling) and at times industrial suburbanisation – for instance new locations for industrial and commercial development that are too big to be placed on inner city brownfields.

- *Transformation of land use – industrial uses:* At the same time, former industrial and commercial areas turn into wasteland. The mechanisms that determine when and where dereliction occurs, but also why some locations persist, is not clear. It may be different for each type of land use. Future industrial brownfields will probably occur more within the areas that were developed on the outskirts during the 1960s and 1970s. The chronological order of abandonment and the spatial order, i.e. the distribution of industrial brownfields are the outcome of 'random' business developments and decisions, even though there might still be some undiscovered regular patterns. These brownfields have been mostly converted to retail or cultural uses, which are often temporary and only partial conversions of sites. In this regard, older locations with historic industrial buildings seem obviously more attractive for reuse than postwar sites (Hauser 2004). But if reuse fails, inner city brownfields interfere much more with the urban structure than industrial wasteland in the periphery which is often not noticed at all. The abandonment of railway land and military bases goes back to political decisions that are not taken at the municipal level either. Here, the rule also applies that resuming uses, if any, usually differ in type from their predecessor. They can only be attracted when the space on offer fits their needs in a long-term perspective.

- *Transformation of land uses – housing:* Unlike the situation for industrial use, a decreasing housing demand (due to a decreasing population) does not instantly lead to vacancies. It seems that the remaining households extend their floor space within the existing housing stock as soon as prices start to decline or stagnate. When and where housing vacancies occur depends on the market position of the individual unit. 'Poor' housing is abandoned first: the 'poorest' apartments of a building, the 'poorest' buildings of a neighbourhood, the 'poorest' neighbourhoods of a city. In this case, restructuring efforts are guided by falling rent and real estate prices. These are merely plausible speculations that should be thoroughly analysed. A special case is obviously the extensive housing stock of housing associations and cooperatives which includes partly rent-controlled 'social housing'. Here, the chronology of withdrawal (respectively preservation) is mainly determined by the business strategy of the owners and therefore can be barely influenced by planners or politicians. There seem to be divergent trends at the same time. In some of the more attractive cities in eastern Germany there are signs of a lively process of reurbanisation. After years of losing residents, there is an absolute increase of population of the inner city, while at the same time the population in the outskirts is decreasing (for Dresden see: Siedentop, Wiechmann 2007, for Leipzig see: Haase 2010). It is not known whether this is a stable process. The growing demand for inner city living that cannot be fully met in growing cities may be met and satisfied in shrinking cities.

- *'decompression' instead of densification:* Another characteristic feature of declining cities is the extensification of use, respectively the 'de-compacting' of housing and business areas that are marked by decreasing density (even low-income households can afford more floor space) and fragmentation. Gaps between buildings are no longer filled in and instead of compact housing, single-family homes are built at inner city locations. The market-driven mechanism, through which economically weak land uses are displaced by more efficient uses has partially been repealed.

- *Separation of land uses:* The basic principle of separated land uses is hardly affected by processes of decline. The functional enrichment of segregated and less dense structures does not seem likely, except for the fact that more options for inner city housing, cultural activities and small businesses arise. This situation may lead to the revitalisation of abandoned sites and create a new functional mix. In contrast, it can be expected that the separation of uses will increase within traditionally mixed zones, as neighbourhood-oriented enterprises will even suffer more from a diminishing customer base and increasing vacancies.

- *Socio-spatial polarization:* There is evidence that socio-spatial polarization will be amplified in shrinking cities. The functional and spatial processes of decline probably lead to increased social disintegration. 'Altogether, not only do functional and spatial processes of decline lead to a less dense settlement structure, but also to increased social disintegration: the 'thinning out' of cities reinforces segregation and tendencies of fragmentation' (Doehler-Behzadi et al. 2005: 72). Private households benefit from housing market relief because they gain more freedom of choice. Whether this will lead to more barriers between neighbourhoods and to the prevalence of 'gated communities' is not foreseeable today. Therefore, one of the main criteria for successful urban regeneration in shrinking cities, as it is discussed today, might be whether the social and cultural cohesion of the European City can be sustained during times of decline.

- *Differentiation of public open spaces:* Nature will return to the city in a transformed mode. The cityscape of shrinking cities is determined by an enormous diversification of open spaces in regard to location, size, design and use that emerge due to an increasing number of brownfields. Nature will recapture former railway lands that are spacious but difficult to access as well as small gaps where no infill development takes place. Ingo Kowarik (2003: 112) coined the term of 'nature in the fourth manner' as the specific description of post-industrial green spaces: 'Unplanned, untended by gardeners, resulting from perfect assimilation to the urban conditions of location and use. It comprises barren wall and sidewalk vegetation as well as spontaneous growth of 'forests' on empty lots, former railroad tracks or abandoned industrial sites.' Depending on what demands – from nature conservation to intensive temporary use – and degrees of intervention, design standards and maintenance costs are put forth, urban green spaces will diversify into different types, from 'urban jungle' to agricultural cultivation or parks with a new aesthetic appeal (Giseke 2007).

- *Impairment of centres:* The central business district, the district and neighbourhoods centres are all challenged by shrinkage. They may stagnate or they may be reduced in size, and some of the neighbourhood centres may even disappear completely. Tendencies of trading down are an inevitable long term result of dwindling purchasing power and declining household incomes. City dwellers are not only confronted with less supply options but also with trading down tendencies in retail that have become striking in neighbourhood centres in shrinking cities.

What is true for growing cities, also applies to shrinking cities: Urban development is a combination of city extension, urban regeneration and structural transformation, but with varying weights and partly differing trajectories. It has to be assumed that as with different 'profiles of decline,' respectively different types of shrinking cities can be identified. It has been observed that smaller and medium-sized towns and cities that owe growth to political locational decisions or an imbalanced economic structure (domination of a single branch of industry) often become much more exposed to massive transformation than larger cities with a differentiated economic base and important administrative or infrastructural functions for the region. Nevertheless, a systematic typology of shrinking German cities in this perspective has not yet been developed.

In English cities, two phases of decline which predate the ongoing German spatial restructuring process can be identified: In the first phase, dramatic loss of jobs and population take place which heavily affect the cityscape (extensive vacancies and demolition). The second phase is characterized by consolidation of a downsized level of activities (Brombach et al. 2005: 51). During this phase, extensive vacancies disappear, but scattered buildings persist that are empty, deteriorating or neglected – even in the city centre or adjacent to new neighbourhoods and buildings. Even shining examples of urban regeneration such as Manchester feature fragmented patterns of contrast between 'islands' of decline and emerging areas. Unfinished and provisional solutions seem to be the norm and the badge of the diminished city. In the context of demographic trends in both countries – the United Kingdom is currently third in the European population table and is expected to overtake Germany by 2043 – it remains to be seen if this pattern observed in the United Kingdom will be reproduced in German cities or if a different course of development will evolve from a much more sweeping demographic change.

During processes of decline, spatial planning loses ground. The remarkable efforts of new planning strategies and regeneration approaches in eastern German cities may be interpreted as a creative attempt to regain the lost room for manoeuvre (Jessen 2006). However, this 'wave of innovations' in planning for shrinking cities cannot change the fact that urban regeneration still heavily depends on external resources such as public subsidies and funding programmes from the states, the federal government and the European Union – not only in eastern Germany. These resources will become scarcer in the future as the loss of population progresses and shrinking cities no longer constitute exceptional cases. Options to steer and moderate this process will become narrower and market developments will have more impact on urban structures.

Nevertheless, one result becomes apparent: German post-war urban development was highly determined by the housing industry and its corporate structures. It seems ironic that the transformation of socialist housing ('Plattenbau') and the large public housing estates in the Western regions seem to follow the same path. Obviously, at present the rhythm of demolition is predominantly defined by the needs and the business strategy of the major housing companies with their powerful lobby. When it comes to implementing restructuring measures, important public interests such as the preservation or efficient adaptation of infrastructure, monument protection and last but not least strategic comprehensive urban planning, are forced onto the defensive – despite all of the remarkable concepts and planning instruments which are available. Needless to say, these observations are little more than conjectures, mixing empirical facts with plausible speculation and they need to be substantiated.

Of course, planning and regeneration interventions will continue to influence the development of shrinking cities. However, due to dwindling resources they may be less effective and sometimes may even cause unintended effects. As it is still too early to evaluate the outcome of urban restructuring measures and to investigate the unexpected side effects of urban regeneration, this research field will have to be addressed over the next decade or so.

Conclusion

As stated at the outset, much is known about the spatial patterns and underlying mechanisms of growing cities, but less is known about those mechanisms that govern shrinking cities. This knowledge is needed, because moving to the policy perspective of how to come to terms with shrinking will fail without such a deeper, conceptual understanding. While being aware of premature generalization, there is a need to look more closely at empirical cases in order to arrive at such a more informed conceptual understanding for our policies of urban regeneration. Missing are more theoretical foundations and empirical studies, including the following:

- functional, physical and social characteristics of the shrinking process
- urban morphology of shrinking cities
- profiles of decline: typology of shrinking cities

Considering that studies on shrinking cities have expanded considerably in the last years, it appears safe to assume that there will be further research along these lines in the future and that there will be enough bold propositions that will enrich our debates and, in doing so, will extend our knowledge of this still undiscovered area.

References

Beauregard, R.A. 1993. *Voices of decline: The post-war fate of US cities.* 1st Edition. Oxford: Blackwell.

Benke, C. 2005. Historische Schrumpfungsprozesse. Urbane Krisen und städtische Selbstbehauptung. in *Jahrbuch StadtRegion 2004/05: Schwerpunkt: Schrumpfende Städte*, edited by N. Gestring, H. Glasauer and C. Hannemann. Wiesbaden: VS Verl für Sozialwiss, 49–70.

Birch, E.L. 2005. *Who lives downtown?* Washington, D.C: Brookings Institution, Metropolitan Policy Program.

Callagher, J. 2004. Suburbanisierung Detroits. in *Schrumpfende Städte: Band 1: Internationale Untersuchung*, edited by P. Oswalt. Ostfildern-Ruit: H. Cantz, 242–48.

Doehler-Behzadi, M., Keller, D.A., Klemme, M., Koch, M., Lütke Daldrup, E., Reuther, I. and Selle, K. 2005. Planloses Schrumpfen? Steuerungskonzepte für widersprüchliche Stadtentwicklungen. Verständigungsversuche zum Wandel der Planung. *disP,* 41(161), 71–78. Available at: www.nsl.ethz.ch/index.php/de/content/download/1106/6813/file [accessed: 28 June 2011].

Fishman, R. 2005. Longer View: The Fifth Migration. *Journal of the American Planning Association,* 71(4), 357–66. Available at: 10.1080/01944360508976706.

Gatzweiler, H.-P., Meyer, K. and Milbert, A. 2003. Schrumpfende Städte in Deutschland? Fakten und Trends. *Informationen zur Raumentwicklung,* (10/11), 557–74. Available at: www.bbsr.bund.de/nn.../DE/.../10_11GatzweilerMeyerMilbert.pdf [accessed: 28 June 2011].

Giseke, U. 2007. Und auf einmal ist Platz. Freiräume und beiläufige Landschaften in der gelichteten Stadt. in *Stadtlichtungen: Irritationen, Perspektiven, Strategien*, edited by U. Giseke and E. Spiegel. Basel/Gütersloh: Birkhäuser, 187–217.

Giseke, U. and Spiegel, E. (eds.). 2007. *Stadtlichtungen: Irritationen, Perspektiven, Strategien.* 1st Edition. Basel/Gütersloh: Birkhäuser.

Göschel, A. 2003. Stadtumbau – Zur Zukunft schrumpfender Städte vor allem in den neuen Bundesländern. *Informationen zur Raumentwicklung,* (10/11), 605–16. Available at: www.bbsr.bund.de/nn_74508/BBSR/DE/.../10_11Goeschel.pdf [accessed: 28 June 2011].

Haase, A.H.G.K.S.S.A. 2010. Reurbanisierung in ostdeutschen Städten. *disP,* 180(1), 24–35. Available at: www.nsl.ethz.ch/index.php/de/content/view/full/2029.

Hannemann, C. 2004. *Marginalisierte Städte: Probleme Differenzierungen und Chancen ostdeutscher Kleinstädte im Schrumpfungsprozess.* Berlin: BWV Berliner Wiss.-Verlag.

Hauser, S. 2004. Industrieareale als urbane Räume. in *Die europäische Stadt,* edited by W. Siebel. Frankfurt am Main: Suhrkamp, 146–57.

Jakle, J.A. and Wilson, D. 1992. *Derelict landscapes: The wasting of America's built environment.* Savage, Md: Rowman & Littlefield.

Jessen, J. 2006. Stadtumbau – Blick zurück nach vorn. Die Bedeutung von Leitbildern bei Neuerungen in der Stadtplanung. *Deutsche Zeitschrift für Kommunalwissenschaften,* 45(1), 23–43.

Jessen, J. and Mayer, H. 2010. Flächenrecycling und Reurbanisierung – Stuttgart und Portland. *Informationen zur Raumentwicklung,* (1), 27–42.

Kil, W. 2004. *Luxus der Leere: Vom schwierigen Rückzug aus der Wachstumswelt : [eine Streitschrift].* Wuppertal: Müller + Busmann.

Lucy, W.H. and Phillips, D.L. 2000. *Confronting suburban decline: Strategic planning for metropolitan renewal.* Washington, D.C. ; Covelo, CA: Island Press.

Pallagst, K. and Wiechmann, T. 2005. Shrinking smart? Städtische Schrumpfungsprozesse in den USA. in *Jahrbuch StadtRegion 2004/05: Schwerpunkt: Schrumpfende Städte,* edited by N. Gestring, H. Glasauer and C. Hannemann. Wiesbaden: VS Verl für Sozialwiss, 105–27.

Plunz, R. 1995. Detroit is Everywhere. *Stadtbauwelt – Themenheft der Bauwelt,* 127(36), 2012–13.

Reuther, I. 2003. Learning from the East? Über die Suche nach neuen Leitbildern zum Stadtumbau. *Informationen zur Raumentwicklung,* (10/11), 575–88.

Siedentop, S. and Wiechmann, T. 2007. Zwischen Schrumpfung und Reurbanisierung. Stadtentwicklung in Dresden seit 1990. *RaumPlanung,* 131, 57–62.

van Berg, L.d., Drewett, R., Klaasen, L., Rossi, A. and Vijverberg, C.H. 1982. *Urban Europe: A Study of Growth and Decline.* Oxford: Pergamon.

van Buren Jones, D. 1995. Stadtgeschichte Detroit. *Stadtbauwelt – Themenheft der Bauwelt,* 127, 2004–11.

Chapter 4

Shrinking Cities in the Growth Paradigm: Towards Standardised Regrowing Strategies?

Hélène Roth, Emmanuèle Cunningham-Sabot

Introduction

In the current context of economic and urban development in Europe, cities have to cope with intense economic restructuring (Bontje 2004). Contemporary globalisation processes (Amin, Thrift 1994), with an economy that is 'spatially dispersed, yet globally integrated' (Sassen 2001), have been accompanied by generalised de-industrialisation, which has in turn set in motion changes in formerly industrial cities. Every city and its local government has to face the issue of increasing global mobility of capital and jobs (Kantor, Savitch, Haddock 1997), which sets up de facto a fierce competition among cities. This results in growing inequalities between the cities that have integrated into the global networks and those that are not succeeding in finding a place in these networks (Scott, Storper 2007, Castells 2000b).

Knowledge, innovation, networking and learning appear as key factors of economic performance and spatial differentiation (Arthur 1996, Castells 2000a). Some places attract investments and the most qualified workers, while others lose their economic base, their jobs and thereby their population. Cities that focused on only one branch or one cluster of economic activities were particularly harmed by this process (Friedrichs 1993, Lang 2005). Former industrial cities tend to be sidestepped by globalisation; they play for high stakes and usually struggle to re-enter or find a new place in the current worldwide economic competition (Martinez-Fernandez, Audirac, Fol and Cunningham-Sabot, 2012).

Saint-Etienne and Glasgow are emblematic of this fate. In recent decades, they have endured among the most severe shrinkage, economic as well as demographic, of all cities in their respective countries. They both have fought and tried to gain competitive advantages to reverse the shrinkage pattern they suffer, and the future of both is being constantly questioned. The policies and strategies implemented in both cities reveal the strength of the urban growth paradigm. The post-industrial and culture-led strategies they chose are very similar and seem to have produced the same socio-economic effects.

Glasgow and Saint-Etienne: among the most intensive urban shrinkages in Great Britain and France

Urban shrinkage in France and Great Britain

In France, as well as in Great Britain, the transformation of local productive systems resulted in a polarisation of regional spaces and a growing imbalance among urban territories. City shrinkage is a common phenomenon for a number of countries in Western Europe, yet it takes various forms, as the examples of France and Great Britain clearly show (Cunningham-Sabot, Fol 2007, Cunningham-Sabot 2009). In Great Britain the areas affected by shrinkage are mainly large metropolitan areas and industrial areas clustered around the middle and north of the country. Scotland has been significantly affected by shrinkage, especially Greater Glasgow and the Western Isles.

In France urban decline affects mainly small cities with fewer than 50,000 inhabitants (Julien 2000) located in the middle of the country, as well as a few larger urban areas which used to specialise in mining, heavy industries or port activities. Saint-Etienne belongs to the second type (i.e., large urban area). It is, like Glasgow for Great Britain, the largest French shrinking city affected by the most dramatic population loss in the last decade. Both cities present a doughnut pattern, with industries leaving the central city along with the middle- and upper-class residents, leaving behind those who cannot afford to leave. Thus, Saint-Etienne and Glasgow offer a laboratory for analysing urban regeneration policies in the context of shrinkage.

A long trend of shrinkage, made of de-industrialisation and suburbanisation

Saint-Etienne and Glasgow have experienced continuous decline in population for several decades. The city of Saint-Etienne has lost about 20 per cent of its inhabitants in the last 40 years. This demographic decline is due solely to migration effects, and contrasts with the growth of population in the region as a whole, especially in the neighbouring metropolitan area of Lyon. The city of Glasgow, in terms of demographic decline, is among the worst in advanced economy cities: in 1961 it had a population of 1,14 million, whereas today it has a population of 579,000. The loss is therefore more dramatic than in Saint-Etienne: during the last four decades, the city lost half of its population. The economic development of Saint-Etienne and Glasgow was based on textile and iron in the seventeenth and eighteenth centuries, then on mining and heavy industry in the nineteenth century. In both cities, shrinkage occurred with de-industrialisation. The economic decline in Saint-Etienne began after World War II, with the closure of its mining enterprises followed by the gradual closure of the major industrial firms in the 1970s and 1980s. As a consequence, Saint-Etienne lost thousands of jobs; and this trend continued in the 1990s. Glasgow's effective shrinkage began after World

War I, with the decline of shipbuilding and other heavy industries. Employment and population decreased within Glasgow. This trend continued after World War II, as the British government imposed the creation of new satellite towns around Glasgow. These new towns successfully attracted the most skilled and qualified workers. Middle- and upper-class income households moved out and to larger suburban homes. As the old economic base left the city, abandoned homes and a landscape of decay in the city fuelled further suburbanisation. At this time, shrinkage was not considered a problem; in fact, it was encouraged and planned as a solution to the city's former growth and overcrowding problems, leaving the city severely depressed and brain-drained.

The suburbanisation process in Saint-Etienne started much later – at the beginning of the 1970s. Half the negative migratory balance is due to migration from the city to the surrounding areas. As in Glasgow, surrounding areas attracted young families and skilled workers in search of their own property in a green environment, while low-skilled workers and unemployed people stayed in the inner city. Within the city of Saint-Etienne, the poverty concentration is found not only in the peripheral, social-housing neighbourhoods (built in the 1960s and 1970s), but also in older, very central ones. Saint-Etienne's and Glasgow's socio-spatial evolution displays patterns common with American cities.

Towards post-industrial cities

After a period of spectacular economic development for one century, Glasgow bore the full brunt of post-Fordist change to become a 'post-industrial' city. This meant that between 1950 and 1996, overall employment fell from 559,000 to 326,000 with at the same time a massive contraction in manufacturing (-90 per cent). Since then a significant turnaround has taken place, with total employment reaching 393,400 in 2004; services are on the rise. However, the new jobs and relevant qualifications do not correspond to the jobs lost and to the low skills of many inhabitants.

In Saint-Etienne, the economic landscape is now characterised by a number of subcontracting industrial Small and Medium Enterprises (SMEs), among which the mechanical, metallurgical and textile sectors still dominate. Unlike in Glasgow, the service sector has developed, but more slowly than in other French cities (Paulus 2004), and the geographical proximity of Lyon tends to hinder the development of metropolitan functions (National Institute for Statistics and Economic Studies (INSEE) 2006: 4). Saint-Etienne's SMEs generally suffer from a lack of innovation (Chalaye, Massard, Largeron 2006), although many public teaching and research institutions exist there. In fact, the university and several high schools attract thousands of students to Saint-Etienne, who – after completing their education – have to leave the city to find appropriate jobs.

Similar ambitious regeneration strategies

In Europe, two ways of dealing with urban shrinkage can be distinguished: (1) fighting the decline by implementing growth oriented policies or (2) accepting and managing this decline (Baron et al. 2010). Glasgow and Saint-Etienne belong to the first type. They both have implemented ambitious regeneration strategies, with a same 'categorical imperative': making the city more attractive to bring back taxable households. Culture and image have played and still play a central role in the regeneration policies, so that – following Boland 2007 – a standardisation of urban policies in the context of shrinkage is to be questioned: cities adopt the *same* regeneration toolkit, although culture and image are supposed to support an innovative approach against shrinkage.

Glasgow, a pioneer

Regarding urban regeneration, Glasgow was a pioneer in launching a marketing campaign and also in culture-led regeneration policies. These efforts started with the Mayfest Festival in 1981, followed by many campaigns and festivals. The city continued a rather successful culture-led regeneration policy in tourism and leisure and its role as a major shopping centre. Leaving behind its former image as a 'city of production', city policy was geared towards making it a 'consumer city' (Sabot, Vant, Thompson 1999). But the city's heritage has left it facing a major challenge similar to that of Saint-Etienne: a financial crisis. Moreover, the entire population of the metropolitan area of Glasgow benefits from the infrastructures of Glasgow city, which are financed solely by the city; at the same time, Glasgow's means are already reduced as it lodges a significant number of non-taxable households. This unfair tax situation was similar in Saint-Etienne until the establishment of a cooperative taxation agreement with the surrounding local authorities in 2000.

For this reason, planning decisions taken by the Glasgow city authorities in recent years have been aimed at attracting not only companies, but also average and high-income (i.e., taxable) households to live within the city boundaries, particularly on regenerated brownfield sites which had been left by the manufacturing industries. Glasgow's main challenge still is to become more competitive, vis-à-vis its surrounding city-region, in attracting families with children and retaining households with two working adults. The policies aimed at recovery for the core city, have had a definite impact on growth patterns within the larger urbanregion. In the city centre, and particularly on the banks of the River Clyde, Glasgow has undertaken a series of upscale and prestigiousdevelopments. Govan, at the heart of this zone, once the 'shipbuildingest burgh in the world,' (Macdonald 1951) has been rehabilitated and now includes a series of high-rise luxury flats and numerous commercial complexes lining the river. In the short term these have not improved the overall financial situation, but it is hoped they will mean increased private investment and public-private partnerships. This situation is mobilising the inhabitants of Govan, who are proposing alternatives for a greater mix of housing, with building heights more in harmony with the rest of the quarter, and opposing the creation of two worlds side-by-side, the haves and have-nots, each in their own community.

Saint-Etienne, a late follower

In Saint-Etienne, re-imaging the city has been a concern for several decades (Vant 1981) but became a central issue in urban policies since the end of the 1990s (Sabot, Vant, Thompson 1999). Indeed, there was a two-stage recognition of the shrinkage of the city, which led to a switch from an initial defensive strategy to a more proactive one.

Over the span of two decades (the 1980s and 1990s), the imaging strategy consisted of the construction of cultural infrastructure, such as a golf course and a museum for contemporary arts, and marketing campaigns. This strategy has proven to be quite inefficient (Sabot, Vant, Thompson 1999). At the same time, local authorities adopted a defensive attitude towards the industrial crisis and focused public actions and funding on the stabilisation of employment and the maintenance of commercial enterprises by providing cheap real estate in the city. This led to a financial crisis, leaving Saint-Etienne one of the most debt ridden cities in France. These actions were completed in the early 1990s with the development of several industrial clusters whose impacts on economic vitality have been limited (Sabot, Vant, Thompson 1999, Tirmarche 1999, Le Gales 2006).

Saint-Etienne's 1999 census, which indicates a population decrease of 10 per cent over a nine year period, was the catalyst for an ambitious strategy aimed at breaking the patterns of decline. It served as a wake-up call in Saint-Etienne (Charvolin 2006) and supported the previous mayor's conviction of the necessity to break with the former short-term actions and to bring a broader, long-term vision to bear on Saint-Etienne's future.

The new strategy to revitalize Saint-Etienne is exactly like Glasgow's: making the city an attractive *place to live*, with ambitious action on public spaces, on housing estates' regeneration, and on cultural and design projects. The idea is to slow the demographic and social shrinkage by stopping the influx of poor people (attracted by very cheap rents until the 1990s) and, as in Glasgow, by attracting middle and upper classes from the surrounding area or from the urban agglomeration of Lyon. The efforts are concentrated on the development of attractive residential areas, thanks to an important state-funded housing renewal program, which contains both outlying social-housing quarters and quarters in the city centre. The re-imaging of Saint-Etienne is also based on the creation of a pleasant urban environment, the renovation of public spaces involving international architects (including Finn Geipel and Norman Forster), construction of a second tramway line, and development of culture-led regeneration projects like the creation of a 'Design village' (i.e. a creative industry cluster which is specialised in industrial design). This represents a break from former policies of short-term defensive action against the economic erosion, focused on employment and real estate provision for all sorts of enterprises.

The discourses of the mayor and other city leaders illustrate an ambition to make Saint-Etienne a 'creative city,' with many references to Glasgow and other European cities (Bilbao, Barcelona, and Turin). In Saint-Etienne's urban regeneration process, the development of cultural projects plays an important role. The aim is to change the image of the city and to improve its competitive advantage. Beside the construction of a concert hall and a contemporary music center, there has been a focus on developing a design cluster and on organising cultural festivals (Biennales, Transurbaines). This demonstrates an appreciation for place-making issues, and on making Saint-Etienne a 'Design city'. Moreover, Saint-Etienne's design- and culture-led projects contribute to an acceptance of other regeneration policies. Boland 2007 has underlined how the growing influences of competitiveness and place-marketing discourses shape local economic development policies, which consequently become similar from one city to another:

> 'Despite the aspirations to create local uniqueness, place marketing frequently results in sameness in both policy and practice. This is reflected in 'copycat' urban design strategies and 'karaoke architecture' where cities look for best practice but end up imitating each other' (Boland 2007).

Differences in governance

While the strategies in Glasgow and Saint-Etienne have been similar, the institutional contexts are different. The implementation of Saint Etienne's new strategy is based on the reorganisation of public players in this urban area and on new alliances with the municipality, the new intercommunal body Saint-Etienne-Métropole, the region and the state. The lack of cooperation between the city of Saint-Etienne and its surrounding communes – and thus the lack of urban planning strategies at this level- has long been a deterrent to Saint-Etienne's development (Cretin 1995; Vant, Gay 1997). It indirectly encouraged urban sprawl and created, as in Glasgow, a financial crisis. In Saint-Etienne's region, the first intermunicipal cooperative body was created in 1996 ('communauté de communes') and consolidated in 2000 ('communauté d'agglomération'). This was a step and condition for the implementation of regeneration projects, because it stopped the tax competition between the communes and allowed them to share the financial costs of parts of Saint-Etienne's infrastructure and regeneration projects.

This rise of cooperation between local authorities in France, encouraged by the state, is 'a dream that never came true' for Glasgow, despite the numerous local authorities' reorganizations (1990, 1996) and the devolution of the Scottish Parliament (1999). The successive boundary changes have redrawn the Scottish institutional landscape, restricted large cities' boundaries, and intensified the competition among the councils, putting into practice a convenient 'divide and rule' strategy led by the new Scottish Executive (Cunningham-Sabot 2007). The Glasgow municipality in conjunction with its economic development agency made the brownfield sites of Govan more attractive as a whole, cleaned up the place and built infrastructures for business and recreation that were both impressive and costly (e.g. the Scottish Exhibition and Conference Centre, the Science Centre, and the Millennium Tower). Private enterprise participated only after the investment risk was minimal, with profits guaranteed and at their maximum, thus providing them with a 'spatial fix' (Harvey 1989). The reoccupation of wastelands with clear urban development potential occurs when the differential profit ratio (the difference between real and potential rental income) is the greatest. This led Smith (1979) to define this particular process of gentrification as a return of capital, not necessarily of population.

The Glasgow local development agencies promoting urban economic growth are an integral part of what Molotch (1976) called 'growth machines,' assembling coalitions of public and/or private operators wielding decision powers over urban economic development. Their modes of operation demonstrate the shift of governance 'from managerialism to entrepreneurialism' (Harvey 1989), which could be characterised by the passage from a 'welfare-local authority' (after the Welfare State) to local authorities that have turned to 'capital-conscious welfare' (Sabot, 1999), somewhat neglecting their own communities. These local economic agencies, with their semi-public/semi-private status, no electorate to reign them in, and not accountable to the local community, do however need to balance their accounts. The quest for regular, sustainable capital by means of the creation and accumulation of industrial and commercial properties fits into their 'entrepreneurial' mode of thinking and planning.

In the French context, where national authorities still play an important role in urban and regional policies, the state is more intensively involved in Saint-Etienne's revitalisation. They have financed half of the major urban projects through housing renewal programs (Grand Projet de Ville and Agence Nationale Rénovation Urbaine) on the one hand, and on the other hand through the creation of a public planning agency (Etablissement public d'aménagement de Saint-Etienne – EPASE). The creation of such an agency is something exceptional, reserved for spaces with big challenges. This demonstrates the importance the state has given to Saint-Etienne's evolution. In fact, the national planning agency (DATAR) justified this national involvement with a regional argument: the decline of Saint-Etienne would impact the development of Lyon's metropolitan area, which is one of the priorities in spatial planning at the national level.

Impacts and limits of these urban policies

The regeneration strategies against shrinkage are more advanced in Glasgow than they are in Saint-Etienne. In Glasgow's core there is a huge amount of construction (houses and offices, leisure activities, shopping centres, hotels), and its economy, before the financial crises, was experiencing some growth, especially the service sector. Between 1996 and 2004 Glasgow's rate of employee job growth (20.5 per cent) was largely superior to Scotland's (11.3 per cent) and even to the national average in Great Britain (12.5 per cent). In 2004 the per capita gross domestic product (GDP) within the City of Glasgow reached 24,000 USD, which was 73 per cent of the average Glasgow Metropolitan level. This was a huge improvement since 1980, when the GDP was 64 per cent. In a top-10 list of the world's 'must-see' places for 2006 compiled by the travel publisher Frommer's, Glasgow was the only European city listed. Such elite status, superbly illustrated with the campaign 'Glasgow: Scotland with style,' was quite an achievement, and is the direct result of years of culture-led regeneration policies.

Glasgow's situation has indeed improved,

> 'but only for some – those able to cash in on the rebirth of the city centre as a post-industrial service centre' (Boyle et al. 2008).

All the signs now point to an 'inverted doughnut' with the former hole filling up (especially along the River Clyde and the part of Govan close to the city centre, Audirac, Cunningham-Sabot, Fol, Moraes, 2012), but leaving pockets on the edges of the doughnut as multi-deprived areas. While very high concentrations of well-educated people can now be found in the centre of Glasgow (European Commission 2007), still 19.5 per cent of the population has been in the bottom 5 per cent in SIMD for 2009[1]. Urban planning and economic regeneration as they have been conducted thus far have not solved the problems of unemployment, income disparity, and demography at some micro-local levels of the city. For instance, Govan is experiencing a distressing decline in its population with, above all, equally inexorable territorial imbalances that are setting in and being reinforced by these economic policies. We observe in Govan the departure of the middle and working classes, leaving only the most underprivileged, with a marginal influx of well-off populations in their luxury high-rise flats and marinas by the River Clyde.

Glasgow has managed to secure a position on the global map. But how long will this status last? Its enhanced reputation rests on continued consumption of services and culture, at a time when people suffer from so called 'credit-crunch' due to the financial crisis and the following global economic downturn. Moreover, while the city of Glasgow met with some success in reshaping its image and improving its former industrial areas, parts of the city have been sacrificed on the altar of this renaissance. The success of the anti-shrinkage policy implemented must be qualified, and may not necessarily be long-term.

---

1   The Scottish Index of Multiple Deprivation (SIMD) identifies small area concentrations of multiple deprivation across all of Scotland. It combines 38 indicators across 7 domains: income, employment, health, education, skills and training, housing, geographic access and crime.

Unlike for Glasgow, there is no serious data in Saint-Etienne to evaluate the demographic and social effects of its strategy[2]. Saint-Etienne's urban physical landscape has changed a lot in the last decade. This, coupled with rising property values until 2008, are early indicators of change in this shrinking city. The shock caused by the census results of 1999 made political actors at both the local and national levels aware of the seriousness of urban shrinkage and the necessity to implement a broad revitalisation strategy; but there was little indication of either a paradigm shift or significant commitment to innovation. Rather, the evidence points to a continuation of standard regeneration policies – even if they might be less ambitious after the global financial crisis of 2008–10. Indeed, the whole strategy implemented in the last decade is based on the idea that the creation of an attractive urban environment for middle and/or creative classes would be sufficient to halt the process of decline and induce urban growth. Inspired by other European examples of urban regeneration, and reinforced by Florida 2002, this idea – based on a causal logic – has since been largely contested, both in terms of its social implications (Paddison 1993) and its efficiency.

Despite discourses by municipal officials invoking creative, image-changing strategies, members of the local urban planning agency *Epures* express serious doubts about their relevance and the chance of Saint-Etienne to significantly attract any creative classes in the short or medium term. Some (more realistic?) local actors are aiming to attract a middle class rather than an upper or creative class. However, in the context of shrinkage, both the population loss and the national injunction of 'social mix' justify the implementation of a 'soft gentrification' strategy. New housing programs are being developed, with the construction of several hundred high-quality dwellings with private investment. Again, it is too early to confirm any gentrifying impact[3]. But this construction has contributed to the rise of property and rent prices[4], which is a growing cause for concern for some residents. There is concern even if the public actors (Agence Nationale pour la Rénovation Urbaine, ANRU) actually do a lot to re-house all the households affected by demolitions and try not to reduce the social housing availability. Although the progress made in local governance is recognised in a quite consensual way (Masboungi, de Gravelaine 2006), some respondents of the local agency *Epures* expressed their disappointment. Critics say that the new developments have been implemented to attract new residents, but few efforts have been made to maintain the current population.

---

2   The intermediary census 2005 showed evidence of the continuation of population loss, but without giving details on possible social restructuring.

3   The estimates by local actors about the occupants of the new high-quality dwellings are too different from each other to be taken seriously. Some of them refer to the arrival of elderly suburban people; others mention families and young couples, others the worrying turn-over of their residents, etc.

4   Prices of all types of old dwellings doubled from 2000 to 2006 (Chambre des notaires de la Loire, 2007).

In the case of Saint-Etienne, the culture-led regeneration policy is too young to measure its efficiency in terms of urban growth. Scott underlines, however, that 'any viable development programme focused on building a creative city must deal at a minimum, with setting up a local production system, training a relevant labour force, appropriate programming of urban space and ensuring that all the different elements involved work more or less in harmony with one another' (Scott 2006: 11). And yet in Saint-Etienne, the implemented revitalisation programme is not comprehensive and suffers from a lack of cohesive economic development strategy. That is why some doubts can be expressed about the sustainability of Saint-Etienne's latest urban changes. Indeed, economic development has become secondary, and no medium- or long-term vision exists for Saint-Etienne's economic future. The weakness of economic policies in Saint-Etienne is based on several factors, in which local governance problems play an important role, both inside the public sphere and in the existing public-private relationships (Béal, Dormois, Pinson 2006, de Banville, Venin 2000, Tirmarche 1999). Another possible cause of this weakness may be the somewhat neo-liberal conviction of the former mayor and his staff that the main role of the public sector is to support and encourage private enterprises by providing infrastructures and amenities. While the rise in property values (until 2008) and the involvement of major homebuilders (such as Nexity) might seem to confirm the aptness and efficiency of this approach in the housing field, this is not the case in the industrial and service sectors.

Conclusion

Population change within cities is a measure of their popularity as places to work and live. For both Glasgow and Saint-Etienne, the strategies implemented tend to confirm a standardisation of regeneration policies in old-industrial cities, leading us to question the long-term impacts and efficiency of these strategies, while it has been demonstrated that there is no evidence of a causal link between culture-led regeneration and urban growth (Evans 2005; Markusen 2006). Similar cities choose the same strategies for the same problems, although they are considered and referred to as 'unique.' This results in intensification of the (national and international) competition between cities. Local choices thus reinforce the globalisation process.

The fight against shrinkage that leads a city to becoming 'post-industrial' can also lead to a more divided city where the rich and the poor draw further apart from each other, both socially and spatially. The claim of being a post-industrial city or a 'recreated' city is a cover of a more trivial reality a 'dual' city.

The quest for growth has become like a quest for the Holy Grail, and in both our cities has led to questioning of this growth paradigm. It seems imperative to review the growth paradigm through the lens of the established views of urban development (Herfert 2004, Pallagst 2005, Audirac 2007), as shrinkage becomes more prevalent. Urban territories are not all affected in the same way by globalisation. Indeed, local context and strategies interact with globalisation to shape the transformation of city regions in different ways (Amin, Thrift 1994).

References

Amin, A. and Thrift, N.J. 1994. *Globalisation, institutions, and regional development in Europe.* Oxford ;, New York: Oxford University Press.

Arthur, W.B. 1996. Increasing returns and the new world of business. *Harvard Business Review,* 74(4), 100–09.

Audirac, Cunningham-Sabot, Fol, Moraes (2012), Declining Suburbs in Europe and Latin America, *International Journal of Urban and Regional Research (IJURR)* Vol. 36, n°2, March, p. 226-244.

Audirac, I. 2007. *Some Thoughts about Urban Shrinkage in a Sea of Growth: Paper to the International Conference The Future of Shrinking Cities: Problems, Patterns and Strategies of Urban Transformation in a Global Context, February 8–9, 2007.* University of California at Berkeley.

Banville, E. de and Venin, B. 2000. Un ancien 'territoire industriel' peut-il devenir un 'territoire de PME' ? Le cas de Saint-Étienne. in *Les dynamiques de PME: Approches internationales,* edited by B. Courault and P. Trouvé. Paris: Presses universitaires de France.

Baron, M., Cunningham-Sabot, E., Grasland, C., Riviere, D. and van Hamme, G. 2010. *Villes et régions européennes en décroissance: Maintenir la cohésion territoriale?* Paris: Hermès Lavoisier.

Béal, V., Dormois, R. and Pinson, G. 2006. Redeveloping Saint-Étienne. The weight of the inherited structure of social and political relationships in a French industrial city. in *Städtische Entwicklungspfade in der Schrumpfung: Hans-Joachim Bürkner,* edited by H.-J. Bürkner. Münster: LIT.

Boland, P. 2007. Unpacking the Theory-Policy Interface of Local Economic Development: An Analysis of Cardiff and Liverpool. *Urban Studies,* 44(5), 1019–39. Available at: 10.1080/00420980701320736.

Bontje, M. 2004. Facing the challenge of shrinking cities in East Germany: The case of Leipzig. *GeoJournal,* 61(1), 13–21. Available at: 10.1007/sGEJO-004-0843-7.

Castells, M. 2000a. *End of millennium.* 2nd Edition. Oxford: Blackwell.

Castells, M. 2000b. *The rise of the network society.* 2nd Edition. Oxford: Blackwell.

Chalaye, S., Massard, N. and Largeron, C. 2006. *Méthodologie pour l'observation des dynamiques localisées d'innovation: Une application à la région stéphanoise.* Saint-Etienne

Charvolin, F. 2006. Le milieu du renouvellement urbain à Saint-Étienne. Circulation des connaissances et territorialité. *Annales de la recherche urbaine,* (101), 139–45.

Cretin, C. 1995. *Saint-Etienne n'est plus dans Saint-Etienne: Plaidoyer pour un Pays urbain.* [Saint-Etienne]: Publications de l'Université Saint-Etienne.

Cunningham-Sabot, E. 2007. Polycentrisme et gouvernance dans la Central Belt, Écosse. *L'Espace géographique,* 36(4), 304–19. Available at: www.cairn.info/revue-espace-geographique-2007-4-page-304.htm [accessed: 18 July 2011].

Cunningham-Sabot, E. and Fol S. 2009. Shrinking Cities in France and Great Britain. A Silent Process? in *The Future of Shrinking Cities: Problems, Patterns and Strategies of Urban Transformation in a Global Context*, edited by K. Pallagst, J. Aber, I. Audirac, E. Cunningham-Sabot, S. Fol, C. Martinez-Fernandez, S. Moraes, H. Mulligan, J. Vargas-Hernandez and T. Wu. University of California at Berkeley, 24–35.

Cunningham-Sabot, E. and Fol, S. 2007. Schrumpfende Städte in Westeuropa. Fallstudien aus Frankreich und Großbritanien. *Berliner Debatte Initial,* 18(1), 22–35. Available at: http://www.berlinerdebatte.de/.

European Commission. 2007. *State of European cities report: Adding value to the European Urban Audit.* [Brussels]: European Union. Regional Policy.

Evans, G. 2005. Measure for measure: Evaluating the evidence of culture's contribution to regeneration. *Urban Studies,* 42(5), 959–83. Available at: 10.1080/00420980500107102.

Florida, R. 2002. *The rise of the Creative Class: And how It's Transforming Work, Leisure, Community and Everyday Life.* 1st Edition. New York (NY): Basic Books.

Friedrichs, J. 1993. A Theory of Urban Decline: Economy, Demography and Political Elites. *Urban Studies,* 30(6), 907–17.

Harvey, D. 1989. *The condition of postmodernity: An enquiry into the origins of cultural change.* 1st Edition. Oxford: Blackwell.

Herfert, G. 2004. Die ostdeutsche Schrumpfungslandschaft. Schrumpfende und stabile Regionen, Städte und Wohnquartiere. *Geographische Rundschau,* 56(2), 57–62. Available at: http://www.geographischerundschau.de/ [accessed: 18 July 2001].

Kantor, P., Savitch, H.V. and Haddock, S.V. 1997. The Political Economy of Urban Regimes: A Comparative Perspective. *Urban Affairs Review,* 32(3), 348–77. Available at: 10.1177/107808749703200303.

Lang, T. *Insights in the British Debate about Urban Decline and Urban Regeneration.* [Online] Available at: http://www.irs-net.de/download/wp_insights.pdf [accessed: 18 July 2011].

Le Gales, P. 2006. La restructuration des PMI à Saint-Étienne après la crise. Traces du passé et limites de l'intégration horizontale. *Sociologie du Travail,* 48(1), 17–36. Available at: 10.1016/j.soctra.2005.12.002 [accessed: 18 July 2011].

Macdonald, H. 1951. *Govan, Renfrew & Inchinnan.* Glasgow.

Markusen, A. 2006. Urban development and the politics of a creative class: evidence from a study of artists. *Environment and Planning A,* 38(10), 1921–40. Available at: 10.1068/a38179.

Masboungi, A. and Gravelaine, F. de. 2006. *Construire un projet de ville: Saint-Etienne 'in progress'.* Paris: Moniteur.

Martinez-Fernandez, Audirac, Fol and Cunningham-Sabot (2012), Symposia: Shrinking cities: urban challenges of globalisation, *International Journal of Urban and Regional Research (IJURR)* Vol. 36, n°2, March, p. 213-225.

Molotch, H. 1976. The City as a Growth Machine. Toward a Political Economy of Place. *American Journal of Sociology,* 82(2), 309–32. Available at: http://www.jstor.org/stable/2777096 [accessed: 18 July 2011].

National Institute for Statistics and Economic Studies (INSEE). *Rhône-Alpes, une région riche en emplois métropolitains supérieurs.* [Online] Available at: www.insee.fr/rhone-alpes [accessed: 18 July 2011].

Paddison, R. 1993. City Marketing, Image Reconstruction and Urban Regeneration. *Urban Studies,* 30(2), 339–49. Available at: 10.1080/00420989320080331.

Pallagst, K. 2005. *The End of the Growth-Machine. New Requirements for Regional Governance in an Era of Shrinking Cities: Paper presented at the Association of Collegiate Schools of Planning Congress.* Kansas City.

Paulus, F. 2004. *Coévolution dans les systèmes de villes: croissance et spécialisation des aires urbaines françaises de 1950 à 2000.* Paris.

Sabot, E., 1999. *Pour une étude comparée des politiques de développement économique localisé: Analyse franco-britannique de trois villes industrielles : Saint-Etienne, Glasgow, Motherwell.* Villeneuve d'Ascq: Presses universitaires du Septentrion.

Sassen, S. 2001. *The global city: New York, London, Tokyo.* 2nd Edition. Princeton: Princeton University Press.

Scott, A.J. 2006. Creative cities: conceptual issues and policy questions. *Journal of Urban Affairs,* 28(1), 1–17. Available at: 10.1111/j.0735-2166.2006.00256.x [accessed: 18 July 2011].

Scott, A.J. and Storper, M. 2007. Regions, Globalisation, Development. *Regional Studies,* 41(sup1), S191–S205. Available at: 10.1080/0034340032000108697.

Smith, N. 1979. Toward a Theory of Gentrification A Back to the City Movement by Capital, not People. *Journal of the American Planning Association,* 45(4), 538–48. Available at: 10.1080/01944367908977002.

Tirmarche, O. 1999. L'action publique de développement industriel à Saint-Étienne : le territoire réduit au plus petit dénominateur commun ? *Sociologie du Travail,* 41(4), 431–52. Available at: 10.1016/S0038-0296(99)00101-6.

Vant, A. 1981. *Imagerie et urbanisation: Recherches sur l'exemple stéphanois.* Saint-Etienne: Centre d'Etudes Foreziennes.

Vant, A. and Gay, G. 1997. Saint-Etienne Métropole ou le découpage du territoire minime. *Revue de géographie de Lyon,* 72(3), 177–90. Available at: 10.3406/geoca.1997.4691.

Chapter 5

Urban Transformations –The Dynamic Relation of Urban Growth and Decline

Lea Holst Laursen

Overview

Due to the economic and political changes marked by globalisation, neo-liberalism and post-industrialism, a changed spatial configuration has emerged in which an increased division is taking place. On the one hand, we are witnessing areas which are growing economically and demographically, and on the other hand, urban areas which are declining, and which are experiencing an erosion of the urban fabric and a de-concentration of people and capital (Laursen 2009).

In recent years the term 'shrinking cities' has emerged which describes the decline of urban areas. However, it is impossible to look solely at shrinkage without also looking at growth. In reality, there is a dynamic relationship between both growth and decline. Decline might, in some cases, be seen as an aspect of growth, while in other instances growth may be the result of decline taking place. With this approach the urban fabric can, therefore, best be described as a conglomerate of greater and smaller settlement concentrations 'living' in the same organism (Laursen 2009). Here the term *organism* describes the urban as a living object that changes and adapts to the different processes in society (Solà-Morales Rubió, Costa 1996). Further, the organism captures the entire built fabric and consists of both urban and rural areas which, thereby, enter into a dynamic relationship.

While the term shrinking cities might imply that shrinkage is something that happens on the city level, it could be argued that the relationship between growth and decline might be much more nuanced; that is, within a city region we should talk about both growing and shrinking districts.

Introduction

In the 1970s many mighty industrial cities and regions experienced difficult times and, due to structural changes in the economy, they began to stop growing and numerous inner cities began declining. This was not just a passing phase, but marked the beginning of a long term period of de-industrialisation. Manufacturing plants were getting more and more efficient, and the demand for heavy industries was no longer the same. On the contrary, new demands and technologies emerged that founded the basis for a new economy; creating a new era of capitalism – globalisation. Apart from this general shift from manufacturing industry to knowledge based businesses, historical changes – such as the 1970s oil crisis, the fall of the iron curtain, and the development of information and telecommunication technologies – have influenced the development of globalisation.

As a result of the increasing globalisation, neo-liberalisation has also emerged in recent decades, where the welfare state is under pressure and where the role of the nation state is weakened. The economy is less dependent on national regulation and the privatization of public services has increased. Furthermore, deregulation of the economic sector is the rule of the day, barriers to trade are broken down allowing a free flow of capital, and finally, labour unions and welfare states are under attack (Soja 2000). The degree to which the welfare state has been weakened, however, depends on individual states and their policies. Subsequently there are significant differences in the way in which the post-welfare state has manifested itself in Denmark (where the welfare state remains rather strong) and in the United States (where the welfare state has never been strong) (Laursen 2009). At the same time, some analysts suggest that globalisation may be reducing differences between American and European planning (Newman, Thornley 1996).

These development tendencies – with the shift from manufacturing to service society, the rising demands for well-qualified labour and the opening up of free trade and finance – have influenced urban structures. A constant movement of population, jobs, and capital is taking place, which does not only include the growth of territories, but also the decay and abandonment of buildings and locations (Beauregard 1993). Thus, contemporary city regions can be characterized as both growing and declining. On the one hand, a concentration within agglomerations into highly compact nodal points is emerging, and on the other hand a de-concentration of the urban fabric into less dense areas is taking place.

Shrinking cities

Shrinking cities is a recently invented term originating from Germany.[1] The research on shrinking cities draws attention to the challenges related to cities suffering from decline. Shrinking cities refer to cities with a declining demography and a declining economy, which may be due to a range of causes. As a consequence so-called shrinking cities experience a surplus of built structures, which can contribute to further fragmentation and decay.

The word 'loss' seems to be a good term for referring to shrinking cities. Architect, town planner and Head of the Department of Building, Housing and

---

1   One of the first contributions to the debate about shrinking cities can to be found in the book *Neue Urbanität* from 1987 by Hartmut Häußermann and Walter Siebel. In this book they elaborate on the declining cities discussing the relation between growing, stagnating and shrinking cities.

Architecture under the Federal Office for Building and Regional Planning Robert Kaltenbrunner, sees shrinkage as a downward spiral:

> 'structural economic weakness and a lack of jobs and job training opportunities; the departure of the young and the skilled; empty housing; rising poverty; a high percentage of old people; dwindling tax revenue to pay for the increasing costs of social security; a poor image and a reluctance to invest, all of which combine to reinforce the existing structural economic weakness – generates an overall downward spiral encompassing every aspect of urban life in the form of structural shrinkage'. (Kaltenbrunner 2006)

The shrinkage of cities is not new. In the decades since the end of World War II at least four factors have been identified as the main causes for urban shrinkage: (1) de-industrialisation, (2) change of urban structures (de-centralisation and suburbanisation), (3) demographic changes (such as declining birth rates) and (4) political changes (post-socialism) (Oswalt 2006).

The shrinkage of cities has occurred both in North America and in Western Europe. But since 1990 (with the fall of the Berlin Wall) there has also been a rise in the occurrence of shrinkage in the former communist countries in Eastern Europe. Cities in Russia, Ukraine and Kazakhstan are affected and countries like Japan and South Africa also have a number of cities which are suffering from shrinkage (www.shrinkingcities.com).

Shrinkage and growth in relation

Regional geographers John Allen, Doreen Massey and Allan Cochrane look at the relational aspect of growth and decline in their book *Rethinking the Region* (Allen, Massey, Cochrane 1998). The book looks at transformations in the southern part of England. This relational approach is about understanding space and place

> 'as constituted out of spatialized social relations' (Allen, Massey, Cochrane 1998: 2).

Thereby, the authors argue that 'regions' only exist in relation to particular criteria and that certain conditions constitute a given region (Allen, Massey, Cochrane 1998: 2).

> 'The identities of regions are constructed through their relationship to 'other' regions and naturally they come with a history in which they have already been 'placed' so to speak' (Allen, Massey, Cochrane 1998: 10).

This means that regions are part of a system in which they have a certain position, such as a core region, a peripheral region, a manufacturing region, high-tech region or another type of region (Allen, Massey, Cochrane 1998: 10). The point is that all regions cannot be a core region, but yet again, a core region can only establish its 'coreness' in relation to other non-core regions (Allen, Massey, Cochrane 1998: 53).

Patsy Healey, professor emeritus in the Global Urban Research Unit at Newcastle University, deals with the relational aspect of urbanism. She talks about contemporary urbanism as being in a world of multiplex and globalized relationships (Healey 2000: 517). This relational approach focuses on the dynamic and relational and on processes rather than on objects, where urban areas are

> '"driven" and "shaped" by different forces, interacting with each other in different ways, bypassing, conflicting, coordinating in complex trajectories'(Healey 2000: 526).

Also Robert Beauregard, professor at Columbia University, states that growth and decline are related.

> 'Growth and decline feed off each other as households, businesses, and capital switch incessantly from one place to another in search of the "good life" and political and economic reward' (Beauregard 1993: 21).

There is a tension and a connection between concentration and decentralization on all scales, both on a local, national and international level, and it is difficult to separate the two processes (Laursen 2009). The closer analysis of current transformation processes shows that the overall decline happens in an extremely differentiated way on a local scale, where growth and decline are situated close to each other. Looking at what could be considered an overall declining territory both growth and decline exist locally, and in that way growth and decline are interconnected. The same would be true in a generally growing area, where declining areas can also be found inside a growing territory (Laursen 2009).

Thus, growth and decline should rather be considered dynamic relational phenomena depending on multiple developments, e.g., at the political, socio-cultural, economical or technical level. This means that there are bigger and smaller territories suffering from shrinkage and bigger and smaller areas experiencing growth. This requires an awareness of the scale – that is, is it city, regional or metropolitan scale, city scale or city-district scale? Altogether, scale is an important element; because the particular scale determines the relationship between growth and decline. To eliminate territorial (physical) shrinkage as an isolated phenomenon is therefore not possible (Laursen 2009).

Thereby, cities are dynamic and changeable, and. therefore, a more network-oriented approach is required, which captures the fact that a greater transformation is happening which requires a differentiated and nuanced investigation.

The story of Berlin

But what does a shrinking city look like in real life? Berlin has been denoted a shrinking city (along with other municipalities) through the German Shrinking Cities project. In Berlin's case it is considered 'shrinking' because it suffers from a declining economy (Oswalt 2004).

In recent years the German capital has experienced shrinkage of its population and economy. The city has from the 1990s until 2008 experienced a minor decline in population (city population Berlin 2010). In addition, Berlin has a very high unemployment rate (16.5 per cent) and a low tax base (Der Regierende Bürgermeister von Berlin 2011). The high unemployment rate stands in stark contrast to other German cities; for example, Frankfurt am Main, which is one of the leading financial centers of Europe, has a more modest unemployment rate of 8,4 per cent in 2009 (Bürgeramt Frankfurt am Main 2009). This makes it obviously very difficult for Berlin to compete economically. And the economic problems of Berlin are evidenced by the fact that there is a lot of vacant office space, many newly constructed buildings are standing empty and there are areas which have fallen into disrepair and are in a very bad state, mostly in the former East German part of Berlin.

But despite this decline in population and economy at an overall city level there are districts which have experienced growth and where new development is taking place. This includes districts such as Treptow-Köpenick, Pankow, Friedrichshain, and Kreuzberg, which experienced growth in population in the period of 1995 to 2008 (city population 2010).

Berlin is considered to be one of the most interesting capitals in Europe and is a very popular city to visit. In 2006 alone, more than seven million people visited this German metropolis to experience an exciting and vibrant city (Der Regierende Bürgermeister von Berlin 2011).With its intriguing urban environment Berlin has a lot to offer to visitors and residents alike. Berlin is a city where history and heritage meets you wherever you go: old and new historical monuments, attractive buildings, and lively city quarters. There are countless cafes and restaurants, traditional as well as more untraditional such as the beach bars along the river Spree. Furthermore, the city is very green and has many parks and open areas that function as recreational spaces for the city. All of this provides room for a great cultural and ethnic diversity which makes Berlin ever-changing and a trendsetter.

Berlin has a vibrant art and music scene in a broad variety of genres from popular to underground music and art. On top of that, the cost for accommodation can be relatively low compared to other capital cities in Europe. Many Danish artists have discovered Berlin and have become a part of its cultural scene. The Danish Embassy has started an initiative, called *Berlinaut*, in collaboration with the Ministry of Foreign Affairs and the Ministry of Culture (BERLINAUT 2007). Berlinaut aims to support Danish artists who have either settled down in Berlin or want to participate in the dynamic cultural life of the city. The purpose of this initiative is to contribute to the internationalization of Danish culture and art and by long-term network-strategies helping professional Danish artists to establish themselves in Berlin or via Berlin (BERLINAUT 2007).

Berlin: a shrinking city?

From a cultural perspective, Berlin is a popular city. However, in terms of demographic and economic growth,

Berlin is considered a shrinking city. However, it is important to state that while Berlin is shrinking at a citywide level, at other scales the picture is different. For example, at a neighbourhood or district level, one district can experience growth in population (or growth in its economy), while another can suffer from shrinkage. In relation to this it might also be worth looking at suburbanisation as a factor for this development. Before the fall of the Berlin Wall suburbanisation was very limited, due to the city's position as a closed island without a relationship to its surroundings. But after unification there was an increase in suburbanisation (Reif 2002) which in the long term might have influenced the number of inhabitants within the city of Berlin. This out-migration to the suburbs has decreased since the end of the 1990s (Der Regierende Bürgermeister von Berlin 2011).

This means that Berlin is both a city with many cultural, recreational and social qualities, as well as a city with economic problems. And that dichotomy exists in spite of the fact that the German federal government has made major investments in Berlin since the reunification of Germany in 1989, when Berlin again became the capital of a united country. However, the reconstruction of Berlin as a new growth center with massive investment and the building of housing and office space have not had the desired effect of growing the metropolis' economy and residential population. The city has not yet become a growth center and the odds of that occurring seem unlikely.

The story told about Berlin is one of contrasts. These contrasts may make it difficult to determine whether to have a positive or negative picture of Berlin. But one thing is for sure, growth and decline seem to be interrelated in the German capital.

Growth and decline as parallel phenomena

The story of Berlin is, most certainly, not an unambiguous or simple story of decline. On the contrary, the example of Berlin suggests that a shrinking city may contain both positive and negative conditions and circumstances. It is not as simple as stating that growing cities (or urban regions) result in a high quality of life and declining cities are connected with collapse and decay (Beauregard 2005). The picture Berlin provides is much more nuanced. Here it becomes evident that it is not possible to look separately at either growth or shrinkage.

Berlin shows us that both growth and decline can be seen as an interactive within a complex organism characterized by an ever changing dynamic process. Thus, the phenomenon of growth and decline should not be designated as a dichotomy, but rather be seen as two aspects mutually dependent on each other. This means that depending on the scale and scope of views, decline can appear as an aspect of growth (or the flipside of growth). The growth of some urban territories in relation to population and economy might occur at the cost of others. This 're-distribution' can happen at a range of scales. At an international or national level, there can be clear distinctions between growth areas and no-growth areas, such as in Europe. It can also happen at a regional scale, where the inner-city areas shrink at the cost of increasing suburbanisation. Finally, this dynamic relationship between growth and decline can happen at a city level where some places within a city grow and other shrink.

Indeed, Berlin would indicate that the urban landscape is a polarized map of both growth and decline on a broad variety of scales spatially, economically and demographically (Laursen 2009). Thereby, shrinkage and growth co-exist side by side on an overall global scale, and the bipolar character of shrinkage and growth can also be observed within most countries and regions (Bundesinstitut für Bau, Stadt-und Raumforschung (BBSR) 2006). This shows that growth and decline are connected and relational e.g., shrinkage can only be understood when seen in relation to something else (growth) (Laursen 2009).

Berlin demonstrates that urban decline and urban growth are complex multiple scale conditions that occur locally with different spatial, social and cultural characteristics. Therefore, it is necessary to approach the urban with a broad approach.

Here at least four issues seem important. First we have to look at demographical development looking at the development in demography at a range of scales from national to city-enclave. Secondly, we have to look at economic development, also at a range of scales. The third issue is the socio-cultural aspects, and this category can be considered to cover 'everyday life' and represents the human side where social and cultural factors play a considerable role. And finally, there is the category of physical structures, where the spatial and physical aspects indicate the state of an urban territory and how it is coping. In the individual case these aspects are represented differently and not one urban territory looks the same as another (Laursen 2009). It therefore is necessary to talk about planning solutions that are prepared to look at the specific needs, characteristics and potential of a given territory.

Conclusion

In recent years a new shift in economy has occurred, moving from the industrial economy to a global knowledge based economy, which has also influenced settlement structures. The global society seems to engender a contemporary urbanity consisting of both growing areas *and* declining areas. Since the 1970s factors like globalisation and deindustrialisation have activated a restructuring of the urban fabric, producing both growing and declining urban areas and city regions. Parallel with these changes, deregulation of public administration towards an increased neo-liberalisation has taken place, contributing to increased polarization.

Thus, the emergence of a hybrid condition of growth and decline is not something new; however, the interesting and important thing is that an increased reorganization of the urban into growing city regions and declining areas is occurring (Laursen 2009). This development has led to the arrival of different urban terms trying to explain some of the urban development tendencies. The term shrinking city is one term that has appeared in recent years. This is a term that looks at declining cities, bringing the focus onto cities that suffer from decline in economy and population. However, the investigation of Berlin indicates that in order to make the term of shrinking cities more operative and to correspond more with the real life situation it is important to look at urban shrinkage at a variety of scales and not only look at city level; because within an overall shrinking city there are most likely to be districts of both growth and decline placed next to each other.

To conclude, growth and decline are in a dynamic relationship – this relational aspect is important to understand when trying to figure out what contemporary urbanity looks like. Growth and decline enter into a multidimensional, bipolar process where both urban concentration and de-concentration processes appear. This dynamic patchwork of growth and decline suggests a more network-oriented approach, which captures the fact that a greater transformation is happening which requires a differentiated and nuanced investigation.

It is important to have a scalar view when dealing with urban growth and decline, because there is a strong relation between the city and its region, urban and adjacent rural areas, and the city and its city-districts (i.e., neighbourhoods), where one place can be growing while the other is shrinking. Here the urban landscape is a field consisting of built-up and un-built areas connected through flow systems, as well as a field of urbanisation (growth) and de-urbanisation (shrinkage). This is a dynamic field that never stop changing, but will transform over time and this transformative landscape can accommodate both growth and decline. Furthermore, the physical demarcation between specific areas is more fluid in this urban landscape where the boundaries between areas are blurred, both in relation to growth and decline and to urban and landscape. This corresponds to what the case shows: urban growth and urban decline are situated next to each other and interact, so that urban growth and urban decline melt together – creating a dynamic, urban patchwork.

References

Allen, J., Massey, D. and Cochrane, A. (eds.). 1998. *Rethinking the region.* 1st Edition. London: Routledge.

Beauregard, R.A. 1993. *Voices of decline: The postwar fate of US cities.* 1st Edition. Oxford: Blackwell.

Beauregard, R.A. *Images of Renewal and Decline: paper presented at conference 'Beyond the Post-Industrial City,' Rutgers University-Camden, November 18, 2005.* [Online] Available at: http://invinciblecities.camden.rutgers.edu/papers/RobertBeauregard.pdf [accessed: 07 July 2011].

Berlinaut. *Danmarks Ambassade.* [Online] Available at: http://www.berlinaut.um.dk/da/Berlinaut.htm [accessed: 07 July 2011].

Bundesinstitut für Bau, Stadt-und Raumforschung (BBSR). *Growing and shrinking regions in Europe.* [Online] Available at: www.bbsr.bund.de/nn_23534/BBSR/...2006/2006.../2006_2.pdf [accessed: 07 July 2011].

Bürgeramt Frankfurt am Main. *Statistik und Zahlen: Labour market.* [Online] Available at: http://www.frankfurt.de/sixcms/detail.php?id=437171&_ffmpar[_id_inhalt]=258869 [accessed: 07 July 2011].

Der Regierende Bürgermeister von Berlin. *Zahlen und Fakten.* [Online] Available at: http://www.berlin.de/berlin-im-ueberblick/zahlenfakten/index.de.html [accessed: 07 July 2011].

Healey, P. 2000. Planning in Relational Space and Time: Responding to New Urban Realities. in *A companion to the city*, edited by G. Bridge and S. Watson. Oxford: Blackwell, 517–530.

Kaltenbrunner, R. 2006. The Future of Urban Redevelopment in Eastern Germany Seen in the European Context. in *Die anderen Städte: IBA-Stadtumbau 2010 = The other cities*, edited by Stiftung Bauhaus Dessau. Dessau: Stiftung Bauhaus, 38–41.

Laursen, L.H. 2009. *Shrinking Cities or Urban Transformation.* Aalborg.

Newman, P. and Thornley, A. 1996. *Urban planning in Europe: International competition, national systems and planning projects.* London: Routledge.

Oswalt, P. (ed.). 2004. *Schrumpfende Städte: Band 1: Internationale Untersuchung.* Ostfildern-Ruit: H. Cantz.

Oswalt, P. (ed.). 2006. *Atlas of shrinking cities: [an initial version of the atlas was presented at the Exhibition 'Shrinking Cities: International Research' KW-Institute for Contemporary Art Berlin September 4 – November 7 2004].* Ostfildern: Hatje Cantz.

Reif, H. 2002. Dynamics of Suburbanisation – The Growing Periphery of the Metropolis. Berlin 1890 – 2000. in *The European Metropolis 1920–2000: Proceedings*, edited by H. van Dijk. Conference at The Centre of Comparative European History, Berlin. Available at: http://publishing.eur.nl/ir/repub/asset/1020/Heinz%2BReif.pdf [accessed: 07 July 2011].

Soja, E.W. 2000. *Postmetropolis: Critical studies of cities and regions.* Oxford: Blackwell Publishers.

Solà-Morales Rubió, I. and Costa, X. 1996. *Present and futures: Architecture in cities.* [Barcelona]: Collegi d'Arquitectes de Catalunya; Centre de Cultura Contemporània de Barcelona.

www.shrinkingcities.com. *Shrinking Cities.* [Online] Available at: http://www.shrinkingcities.com/publikationen.0.html [accessed: 07 July 2011].

Chapter 6

The Importance of Strategic Spatial Goals for the Planning Process under Shrinkage Tendencies

Christian Strauß

Introduction

Dealing with urban shrinkage relies on town planning to guide spatial development. In response, a new set of instruments has been developed in Germany. This chapter examines the importance of these instruments in coping with demographic change and addresses the significance of strategic spatial planning objectives. With the local governmental authority being responsible for the advancement and regulation of urban development, attention is paid to the challenge posed by shrinkage within towns and cities.

Demographic change has had a major influence on spatial development in most local jurisdictions in eastern Germany, as well as increasing numbers in the west. This change has also altered the basic social structure in many areas. A number of components contribute to this change: on the one hand, the overall decline of the population due to the falling birth rate and migration to other places (from both adjacent districts and more distant locations), and, on the other hand, increasing life expectancy (Gans 2005: 1007). Taken together, these factors shift the population structure, resulting in the ageing of society (Birg 2005: 95).

The shrinking city as a new area for policy integration

The demographic change taking place in eastern Germany has resulted in 'urban shrinkage'. Shrinkage can be defined simply as 'interaction between social and spatial structures' which are particularly relevant in terms of urban sociology (Großmann 2007: 27). A more detailed definition of shrinkage states that it is a

'process of socio-spatial restructuring under conditions of a continuously declining population (…) in which social and physical spaces as well as their mutual interaction change and their mutual suitability decreases.' (Großmann 2007: 26).

In urban areas and regions in eastern Germany, these shrinkage processes are especially dynamic, because the trends of suburbanisation and long-distance migration overlap. They are also increasingly exacerbated by dwindling birth rates.

Of course, 'urban shrinkage' does not automatically involve the reduction of the built-up area's three-dimensional structure or its two-dimensional footprint. While demand declines, the boundaries and the area of the city remain the same size or in some cases even continue to be expanded (Kötter 2007: 30). It is perhaps more accurate to describe urban shrinkage as having the following:

- The unplanned emergence of derelict buildings or derelict land owing to buildings being demolished without their sites being reused (Genske, Hauser 2003)
- The conversion and alteration of the supply of property (Gatzweiler 2005)
- Buildings and land being put to temporary use (Dransfeld, Lehmann 2008)
- The under-utilization of technical and social infrastructure (Geyler, Prochaska 2007)

The reality of permanent abandonment has to be assumed, despite recent discussion of reurbanisation tendencies as an emerging trend. Then again, vacant buildings and derelict land need not be viewed as solely disadvantageous. After all, declining pressure coupled with falling property prices may enable new 'opportunity areas', the term for derelict land identified for redevelopment (see Davy, Kanafa 2004: 124, who borrow from Musil 1930: 16). These new spatial possibilities are accompanied by additional divergence of lifestyles and opportunities for new creativity (Liebmann 2003; Haller, Rietdorf 2003; Weeber, Kähler, Weeber 2005: 165; Huning 2006). Structural spatial changes do not take place evenly. Instead, heterogeneous changes can be made out in German regions (Bundesamt für Bauwesen und Raumordnung (BBR) 2005: 85) and even within cities (e.g., for Leipzig: Doehler-Behzadi, Lütke Daldrup 2004).

Consequences of demographic change and shrinkage for spatial control

The necessity of adapting space to changed circumstances begs the question of change in the control of spatial development, with cooperation between the public sector and other local actors growing in importance (Altrock 2005: 150). Three attributes of a new system of control under shrinkage conditions have been advanced: (1) the need for an overall approach instead of the planning of individual projects, (2) an integrated understanding of space, and (3) elements of strategic planning (Oswalt 2005: 17). At the same time, contradictions have been pointed out between foresighted planning and the unpredictability of future types of demographic change.

Shrinking cities (and urban regions) are above all forced by necessity to seek solutions for reorganising their existing urban structure in order to adjust supply to changed demand. Any system of control needs to be materially and formally geared to this approach by addressing the rights of property owners and infrastructure providers. Existing social neighbourhoods are also affected by urban redevelopment. Public control faces the challenge of dealing sensitively with the current state of affairs despite the need to make drastic changes to the spatial structure, in order to accommodate the significant population changes.

Following several shifts in conceptions by both practitioners and academicians over the past 20 years regarding the management of spatial development – ranging from cybernetics to muddling through – the current view is that of 'cooperative control'. Making use of various partnerships among key players demonstrates a 'communicative turn' (Healey 1997); it leads to a planning culture geared towards understanding (Naegler 2003: 23) and also to the so called jointed incrementalism (Ganser 1991).

However, this culture cannot necessarily change an area by itself. Instead, the public sector remains obliged to preserve order and often can use both protective and executive instruments. As a result, the understanding-based form of planning culture has augmented the traditional decision-based form and not replaced it. In contemporary spatial planning practice in Germany, a set of governing instruments with standardised procedures is used, as well as cooperative tools which are less prescriptive. In order to ascertain the contribution made by the new cooperative instruments, experiences of using this new set of instruments in eastern German planning practice are examined below.

State support for urban redevelopment in eastern Germany

Against the background of demographic change in eastern Germany, the political response to the considerable impacts of urban shrinkage has been carried out through the federal-regional joint programme Stadtumbau Ost ('Urban Redevelopment in Eastern Germany'). The Stadtumbau West programme for western Germany is not analysed here.

Stadtumbau Ost is used to support urban districts with considerable challenges in terms of urban development. It also accepts a change in the view of control in spatial planning. Federal legislative intent is for organisational power to be concentrated in urban districts. This requires a new, cooperative approach and a new culture of participation on the part of the relevant actors (Rietdorf 2001: 10ff.). Additionally, a new role is implied for the public sector. Local authorities are only granted funding under this programme if they can demonstrate that they have a system of integrated control through partnerships.

The aim of urban redevelopment is to take an integrated approach to spatial development and to break away from sectoral or departmental strategies. However, what originally prompted the beginning of the programme in 2001 was the need to consolidate the housing market and the high commercial risks in the housing sector. There are examples where these issues can be quite explicitly expressed in adopted urban development strategies (e.g., regarding the town of Wurzen: Büro für Siedlungserneuerung 2006: 42).

In 2004, the federal legislature recognised the long-term need to react to demographic changes in the planning of existing urban areas and introduced a new section into the federal building code (Baugesetzbuch). Under the code, urban redevelopment is subject to a physical-spatial concept, which generally has not integrated social dimensions of spatial development. Therefore the measures of federal building code focus on physical space. Ringing-in an 'urban development area' is now essential in order to receive subsidies under the federal-regional programme. This subsidy framework provides a de jure definition of the areas of a local urban or rural authority where 'considerable physical or functional deficits in terms of urban development' exist and where they do not.

The urban development programme as defined by Section 171b of the federal building code is the main instrument used to control urban redevelopment at a local level (Bundesamt für Bauwesen und Raumordnung (BBR) 2007: 65). The aims and measures of urban redevelopment must be formulated in the programme on the basis of a detailed analysis. In accordance with the code, urban redevelopment measures must serve the public good. Under Section 171a(2) of the federal building code, urban development structures must be sustainable.

In the view of federal and regional government, local authorities are to deal with space in a holistic manner in their urban redevelopment programmes, precipitating a marked increase in the importance attached to integrated approaches to urban development. The redevelopment of existing urban areas calls for many small steps and often lacks guidance from a model or vision based on sustainable urban shrinkage. Nevertheless, the approach when determining the issues at hand and the formulation of integrated goals and measures require a multi-dimensional tack. This enables them to meet more recent demands for an integrated urban development policy, such as in the Leipzig Charter 2007 and leads to concepts like more 'qualitative' than 'quantitative' growth or development (European Union 2007).

The importance of structural spatial objectives in urban redevelopment programmes

To manage urban shrinkage, an integrated view of the city as a whole is essential to attain a holistic understanding of the challenges stemming from demographic change. It is therefore logical to observe the development of the entire city and its individual areas. Conceptual planning is performed at all levels resulting in an integrative approach which combines broad and individual perspectives. After all, if the overall population is declining, stabilising one area would likely precipitate destabilising tendencies in other districts. In a shrinking city, demand is usually merely redistributed; only rarely is new demand generated (for example, by migration from outside or reurbanisation). Consequently, comparing districts is just as important as addressing the entire urban context and regional integration. The federal states ('Bundesländer') in contrast to national government have realised the relevance of taking a comprehensive, integrated view of urban redevelopment and therefore expect conceptual approaches encompassing an entire local authority.

Urban development is intended to restore sustainable spatial structures either by means of improvement or by demolition. Different strategies may be required in different districts and neighbouring local authorities. For example, if the population of a city is declining, retaining the structural and social density of each district could be unrealistic. Therefore, the overall socio-demographic, structural, economic and ecological situation needs to be analysed in each area.

The economic treatment of land is understood from the objective of sustainable spatial development and formulated as a political aim. Avoiding expansion into peripheral areas coupled with promoting development and intensified use of core areas is the preferred outcome. Therefore, one desired aim in shrinking cities is to identify new and revised land requirements within the existing urban area and to keep outlying areas completely free of new construction (Liebmann 2006). Preserving or restoring the balance between supply and demand under conditions of shrinkage is key to sustainable spatial development. The maintenance of a compact urban form takes into account:

- ecological requirements (no destruction of natural spaces, especially if there are redevelopment or infill sites),
- economic measures (a compact infrastructure used efficiently), and
- sociocultural requirements (preserving identity and the social community).

It can be deduced from this that both strategies to avoid expansion into outlying areas and strategies to redevelop existing urbanised areas need to be developed.

Generally speaking, the strategies for different urban districts vary depending on their location within the city. In inner-city areas, there is little sense in devising strategies to preserve or restore a structural and socio-cultural minimum density. Reasons for these strategies include the historical buildings frequently present, the sense of identity they provide, the good infrastructure, and the proximity to the city centre. If this strategy is adopted, the aims that can be concluded for districts on the outskirts include the demolition of buildings and urban withdrawal inwards. Social programmes are also needed to deal with 'temporary urban districts' (Beer 2002) which still exist at this moment but will be torn down in a few years. These strategies are pursued by federal and regional policy.

Indeed there are challenges. For one, the socio-spatial structures can still be stable in districts on the outskirts of a declining core. For example, these outlying districts can be peaceful, desirable areas with plenty of greenery. For another, high vacancies and a high need for renovation can prevail in inner-city districts. There can be additional obstacles, such as along arterial roadways, where there can be high levels of noise coupled with underutilized or even vacant buildings. These situations demonstrate the challenges of more traditional spatial planning aims.

Fresh inspiration needed for structural spatial visions

The debate about urban development models that seemed to rage in the mid-1990s between the vision of (1) a 'European city' and (2) a model of 'modern urban development' associated with corresponding east and west German ideologies has now died down. Residents' inclinations to remain in their familiar, inhabited prefabricated blocks of flats are accepted, while in addition the debate about urban development issues has given way to discussion of the fastest possible demolition of vacant or outdated structures. Even the need to protect designated historic buildings in preserved old-town cores, such as in Görlitz, received practical consideration. In other words, the treatment of built structures has become pragmatic.

In 2001, discussion of urban development was dominated by the term 'perforated city' (Lütke Daldrup 2001). Rather than being a vision, it is actually a reflection of the urban development process under conditions of shrinkage. The perforated city is associated with fear. It seems as if fear of losing the European city is tied to the fear of losing compact urban form (Akbar, Beeck, Krems 2006: 20).

The 'perforated city' should not become the model for shrinking cities, because it conflicts with sustainable urban patterns having negative physical, social and economic effects. However, until the mechanisms for rolling back the currently inflated urban structure to a compact form take effect for economic reasons, perforations and fragments will persist in eastern Germany. But there is still no standard model for the urban development of a shrinking city. This is due in part to the continuing dilemma between the will to structure a compact city and the sober, realistic assumption of perforation. Furthermore, it takes courage to adapt supply to declining – and simultaneously changing – demand. Even so, supply has been reconfigured and new urban development and architectural typologies have emerged (Goebel 2003).

Nonetheless, adaptation strategies need to be carried out not just on individual sites, but also in a comprehensive manner (Stimmann 2001: 25–26). In urban development, however, this applies not just to the built-up city, but also the city as it is 'lived' in terms of its social context (Läpple 1991). And it should not be overlooked that an integrated, cooperative approach in the shrinking city builds on the tradition of the European city as a place of civil society.

In the process of urban redevelopment, consensus on future urban development is essential and must be sufficiently concrete in order for it to be compulsorily implemented. The idea of the 'European city' is viewed not so much as a structural model, but more as a model for political and social order (Akbar, Beeck, Krems 2006: 21). However, understanding the 'European city' as only an element of civil society would be an oversimplification, for it is also defined via the genus loci.

Therefore, the actors in charge of the city are obliged to treat its architectural heritage conscientiously.

It is not possible to preserve all the buildings in a city – not even all those which have major significance for its character. Consequently, the culture of memory in the shrinking city, which is necessary to maintain its unique identity, will under certain circumstances have to make do without some of the structures that have contributed to its architectural heritage. The main objective of critical deference to the historical architectural elements of a European city should nevertheless not be abandoned; its identity must be upheld in order to leave future generations an urban structure worth living in.

New types of solutions are needed. Urban space has three levels of perception which are relevant to the qualification process in urban redevelopment: (1) the physical space in its narrow sense, (2) subjectively experienced space, and (3) the location of objective elements that communicate an awareness of social identity (Brenner 2005: 47).

Urban spatial qualification in the light of transformation processes is not just restricted to urban development or architecture. Instead, the term also encompasses an expectation of quality from the process. Together, the spatial and procedural or cultural dimensions produce a new form of urban culture: urban redevelopment culture. Urban redevelopment culture means a consensus regarding new spatial and social configurations. It combines the cultural with the spatial question. Accordingly, urban redevelopment culture ought to combine building culture in the narrow sense with the question of the quality of life in built, lived-in space (Haller, Rietdorf 2003).

The aim of compactness which intends sustainability requires new solutions

Following the goal of sustainability, the spatial planning aim for the shrinking city should continue to be to preserve or restore a compact urban structure. This means preventing a fragmented landscape (Sieverts 1997), preventing bad investments by private and public actors (as well as bad public-sector subsidies which work against sustainable development), and finally strengthening and improvement urban cores, centres of villages, and small market town centres.

However, problems can emerge in attempts to revitalize a city at its core. Inhabitants' preferences for living in green surroundings are easier to meet on the outskirts. Suppliers in the housing market have accumulated debts in the refurbishment of the building stock in peripheral areas. And small towns and villages in the surrounding area competing with the core city can be more interested in attracting new residents than a sustainable urban structure. These intentions of different actors show that a concept of compactness can not easily be implemented. Conflicts between these intentions have to be identified and to be solved.

What long-term spatial concepts would result from taking an incremental approach? To achieve sustainability requires the 're-editing of and adaption' to the vision of the community (Stimmann 2001: 18). Buildings and obsolete plan allocations should be reconsidered and if necessary adapted to current and future needs. Urban redevelopment should be pursued in a manner that builds on a city's architectural texture and settlement structure.

Conclusion

'Urban redevelopment' under shrinkage conditions has been tested in Germany as a new form of control since the early 2000s. New, informal instruments are being used to augment the existing set of formal tools. Even so, this collective experience of planning practice is too limited to ascertain whether a cooperative approach and clinging to a traditional vision will succeed. It is interesting that compactness is still discussed as the European way of spatial development, although in many urban regions the average density has been decreasing for decades. From a scientific angle, questions must continue to be raised, especially about dealing with the objectives of spatial planning (Strauß 2008).

In structural spatial terms, urban redevelopment means a strategic focus on urban and village cores under conditions of shrinkage. It boils down to urban qualitative improvement and the instruments which are available to achieve this. Spatial planning objectives are significant in this respect because they provide an answer to vacancies, derelict sites and declining density. Furthermore, the public sector needs to be the organiser of spatial planning within a planning culture geared to understanding. It must be borne in mind that the urban redevelopment culture under conditions of shrinkage does not have sufficient predecessors or examples it can make use of. The actors involved need to not be afraid of taking risks. New, flexible urban structures which contribute to changing demands could add a new dimension to spatial planning, because for the first time they would enable the reversal of spatial development – that is, reverting urbanised lands to non-urban uses.

References

Akbar, O., Beeck, S. and Krems, M. 2006. Schrumpfung – Herausforderung für die europäische Stadt. in *Die anderen Städte: IBA-Stadtumbau 2010 = The other cities*, edited by Stiftung Bauhaus Dessau. Dessau: Stiftung Bauhaus, 20–28.

Altrock, U. 2005. Stadtumbau in schrumpfenden Städten – Anzeichen für ein neues Governance-Modell? in *Jahrbuch Stadterneuerung*, edited by U. Altrock, R. Kunze, U. von Petz and Schubert D. Berlin, 149–70.

Beer, I. 2002. Wohnen und Leben im Wartestand. Ein Quartier in Schwedt zwischen Abriß und Aufwertung. *Berliner Debatte Initial,* 13(2), 49–56.

Birg, H. 2005. Bevölkerung und Bevölkerungsentwicklung. in *Handwörterbuch der Raumordnung*, edited by E.-H. Ritter. Hannover: Akad. für Raumforschung und Landesplanung, 89–97.

Brenner, J. 2005. Stadtumbaukultur – Paradigmenwechsel in der Stadtentwicklung. in *Tatort Stadt II: Perspektiven einer Stadtumbaukultur*, edited by G. Langenbrinck. Berlin: Jovis, 40–51.

Bundesamt für Bauwesen und Raumordnung (BBR). 2005. *Raumordnungsbericht 2005*. Bonn: Selbstverlag des Bundesamtes für Bauwesen und Raumordnung; Bundesamt.

Bundesamt für Bauwesen und Raumordnung (BBR). 2007. *5 Jahre Stadtumbau Ost – eine Zwischenbilanz: Zweiter Statusbericht der Bundestransferstelle*. Erkner.

Büro für Siedlungserneuerung. 2006. *Städtebauliches Entwicklungskonzept Stadt Wurzen (unveröffentlicht)*. Dessau.

Davy, B. and Kanafa, K. (eds.). 2004. *Die neunte Stadt: Wilde Grenzen und Städteregion Ruhr 2030*. 1st Edition. Wuppertal: Müller und Busmann.

Doehler-Behzadi, M. and Lütke Daldrup, E. 2004. *Plusminus Leipzig 2030: Stadt in Transformation*. Wuppertal: Müller + Busmann.

Dransfeld, E. and Lehmann, D. 2008. *Temporäre Nutzungen als Bestandteil des modernen Baulandmanagements*. 1st Edition. Dortmund: Forum Baulandmanagement NRW; [Inst. für Landes- und Stadtentwicklungsforschung].

European Union. *Leipzig Charter on Sustainable European Cities, Agreed on the occasion of the Informal Ministerial Meeting on Urban Development and Territorial Cohesion in Leipzig on 24 / 25 May 2007*. [Online] Available at: http://urbact.eu/fileadmin/corporate/doc/AppelOffre/Leipzig%20Charter%20EN.pdf [accessed: 30 June 2011].

Gans, P. 2005. Schrumpfung. in *Handwörterbuch der Raumordnung*, edited by E.-H. Ritter. Hannover: Akad. für Raumforschung und Landesplanung, 1004–11.

Ganser, K. 1991. Instrumente von gestern für die Städte von morgen? in *Die Zukunft der Städte*, edited by K. Ganser, J.J. Hesse and Zöpel C. Baden-Baden: Nomos-Verl.-Ges, 54–65.

Gatzweiler, H.-P. 2005. *Innovative Projekte zur Regionalentwicklung*. Bonn.

Genske, D. and Hauser, S. (eds.). 2003. *Die Brache als Chance: Ein transdisziplinärer Dialog über verbrauchte Flächen*. Berlin, Heidelberg, New York, Hong Kong, London, Milan, Paris, Tokyo: Springer.

Geyler, S. and Prochaska, C. 2007. Technische Infrastrukturen zur Ver- und Entsorgung. in *Die Kernregion Mitteldeutschland: Ein erster Überblick; Bevölkerung Finanzen Infrastrukturen Raumstruktur und Wirtschaft*, edited by J. Ringel, T. Lenk, K. Friedrich, R. Holländer and W. Kühn. Leipzig: Forschungsverbund KoReMi, 65–86.

Goebel, B. 2003. *Der Umbau Alt-Berlins zum modernen Stadtzentrum: Planungs-Bau- und Besitzgeschichte des historischen Berliner Stadtkerns im 19. und 20. Jahrhundert*. Berlin: Braun.

Großmann, K. 2007. *Am Ende des Wachstumsparadigmas?: Zum Wandel von Deutungsmustern in der Stadtentwicklung ; der Fall Chemnitz.* Bielefeld: Transcript.

Haller, C. and Rietdorf, W. 2003. *Positionspapier Baukultur Stadtumbau-Ost.* Erkner.

Healey, P. 1997. Discourse of integration. Making Frameworks for Democratic Urban Planning. in *Managing cities: The new urban context*, edited by P. Healey, S. Cameron and A. Madani-Pour. Chichester, New York, Brisbane, Toronto, Singapore: John Wiley & Sons, Ltd, 251–72.

Huning, S. 2006. *Politisches Handeln in öffentlichen Räumen: Die Bedeutung öffentlicher Räume für das Politische.* Berlin: Leue.

Kötter, T. 2007. Stadtumbau – Handlungsfelder, Strategien und Instrumente. in *Immobilienwertermittlung und Flächenmanagement beim Stadtumbau: Grundlagen und Praxisbeispiele ; am 6. und 7. März 2006 in Magdeburg*, edited by P. Porstendörfer. Augsburg: Wißner, 23–46.

Läpple, D. 1991. Essay über den Raum. in *Stadt und Raum: Soziologische Analysen*, edited by H. Häußermann, D. Ipsen, T. Krämer-Badoni, D. Läpple, M. Rodenstein and W. Siebel. Pfaffenweiler: Centaurus-Verlagsgesellschaft, 157–207.

Liebmann, H. 2006. *Stadtumbau Ost – Stand und Perspektiven. Erster Statusbericht der Bundestransferstelle Stadtumbau Ost.* Berlin.

Liebmann, H. (ed.). 2003. *Städtische Kreativität – Potenzial für den Stadtumbau.* Erkner, Darmstadt: Inst. für Regionalentwicklung und Strukturplanung; Schader-Stiftung.

Lütke Daldrup, E. 2001. Die Perforierte Stadt. Eine Versuchsanordnung. *Bauwelt*, 24(150), 40–45.

Musil, R. 1930. *Der Mann ohne Eigenschaften.* Hamburg: Rowohlt.

Naegler, D. 2003. *Planung als soziale Konstruktion: Leitbilder als Steuerungsmedium in Stadtplanungsprozessen.* Berlin: Ed. Sigma.

Oswalt, P. 2005. Einleitung. in *Schrumpfende Städte: Band 2: Handlungskonzepte*, edited by P. Oswalt. Ostfildern-Ruit: H. Cantz, 12–18.

Rietdorf, W. 2001. *Stadtumbau in den neuen Ländern. Integrierte wohnungswirtschaftliche und städtebauliche Konzepte zur Gestaltung des Strukturwandels auf dem Wohnungsmarkt der neuen Länder .* Berlin.

Sieverts, T. 1997. *Zwischenstadt: Zwischen Ort und Welt, Raum und Zeit, Stadt und Land.* Gütersloh, Berlin, Basel, Berlin: Bauverlag; Birkhäuser.

Stimmann, H. 2001. Das Gedächtnis der europäischen Stadt. in *Von der Architektur- zur Stadtdebatte: Die Diskussion um das Planwerk Innenstadt*, edited by H. Stimmann. Berlin: Braun, 11–27.

Strauß, C. 2008. Modelle, Ziele und Leitbilder zukünftiger räumlicher Entwicklung. in *Räumliche Konsequenzen des demographischen Wandels*, edited by P. Küpper, L. Küttner, J. Luther and C. Strauß. Hannover: Akad. für Raumforschung und Landesplanung, 14–20.

Weeber, R., Kähler, G. and Weeber, H. 2005. *Baukultur: Informationen – Argumente – Konzepte : zweiter Bericht zur Baukultur in Deutschland.* 1st Edition. Hamburg: Junius.

Chapter 7

Regional Land use Management under Shrinkage Tendencies in the Region Halle-Leipzig[1]

Anja Kübler, Christian Strauß, Barbara Warner

Introduction

Shrinkage and socio-demographic transformation are two worldwide trends, to which spatial development needs to react. Accordingly, the spatial consequences of shrinkage have to be considered in the planning process.

The planning process in a region is more complex than that of a city because far more public and private actors with different (and often contrary) intentions, different instruments and different powers are involved. As an example, the east-central region of Germany is currently undergoing a process of structural spatial change caused by a persistent trend of depopulation in most regions. This change is even more pronounced in polycentric agglomeration areas, impacting on the requirements of population and urban areas, regional development, environment and the (local) public financial system.

However, different spatial patterns can be identified in central Germany, making this region a good example of parallel tendencies of both shrinkage and growth. Consequently, a planning process in this region needs to distinguish between these parallel patterns. One possible solution would be to implement a sustainable system of regional land use management which is focused on the cities. The strategy follows the political principle of subsidiary and is aimed at cooperative instead of hierarchical forms of planning. Cooperation appears necessary not just to establish the strategy for further spatial development but also in order to analyse the spatial challenges, to find instruments for the implementation of the goals, and also for the process of evaluation. For all these parts of the planning process, a cooperative method of governance (bottom-up) seems to be more successful than a top-down-approach.

---

1   Parts of this chapter have been published in a former version as: Strauß, C.; Warner, B.; Kübler, A. 2011. Land use management under depopulation tendencies in the Halle–Leipzig region: Challenges for regional and local instruments. In: Journal of Town and City Management, Vol. 2 (1) (June-August), 32-43.

The content of this chapter explains the joint research project 'Objectives and Transferable Action Strategies for Sustainable Regional Land Use Management under Depopulation Tendencies' (REFINA KoReMi). The project is funded by the German Federal Ministry of Education and Research (BMBF) under the programme 'Research for the Reduction of Land Consumption and for Sustainable Land Management (REFINA)'. The project began in 2007 and was completed in 2010.

The interdisciplinary project KoReMi examined the aims of regional planning and local authority planning practice in regard to the designation of residential and commercial as well as industrial areas. The German federal government's policy of 'presaving open space' clashes with the fear of local authorities in the Halle-Leipzig region of suffering financial losses whenever zoning designation is withdrawn. However, there are a lack of sustainable concepts for dealing with the sometimes massive vacancies afflicting residential and commercial areas in this region, which is experiencing both shrinkage and growth. Steering approaches need to be found that strengthen the competence of regional and local authority planning equally. KoReMi is designed to empirically study and assess zoning practices and local authority instruments so that recommendations can be made.These recommendations combine aspects of population, urban areas and infrastructure as well as financial incentive mechanisms.

Motivation and Framework

Figures on the development of urban areas and transport infrastructure throughout Germany were first published by Germany's Federal Department of Statistics in 1992 (Statistisches Bundesamt Deutschland (DESTATIS) 2006). Since then, the 'consumption' (development) of greenfield land for these purposes has continuously accelerated, reaching 129 hectares per day between 1996 and 2000, and rising to as much as 131 hectares per day in 2004. Assuming this trend was to continue linearly, Germany would be completely paved over in about a hundred years.

The declining consumption of urban areas and transport infrastructure to 93 hectares per day in 2003 is chiefly attributable to the poor economic state of the construction industry (Umweltbundesamt (UBA) 2009; Deggau 2004) and not to progress made in presaving greenfield land. Indeed, additional greenfield development subsequently rose in 2004–07 to 113 hectares per day. One positive aspect is that the proportion of land used by buildings and open spaces has dropped while the share of recreational land has risen (although this is partly due to statistical adjustment). The transport sector must still be regarded as a major consumer of land.

In addition, the continuing designation of urban areas has led to a sometimes considerable change in existing development structures. This is compounded by the problem of depopulation and ageing, especially in eastern Germany, which is mainly due to the changing economic and social structures following German reunification in 1990. As a result, the average density of use (both in Germany as a whole and eastern Germany in particular) is falling in terms of both population density and land-based economic activities. The continuing development of urban areas and transport infrastructure also results in the loss of non-renewable resources and in changes to the landscape. Too much land is being earmarked for residential and commercial purposes without taking advantage of the existing (especially inner-city) potential. In other words, new areas are being set aside for development while inner-city areas are being left to fall derelict.

The declining density of areas is accompanied by a constantly increasing pressure to provide infrastructure and also continuously rising local authority budget deficits (for example due to reduced tax revenue), severely limiting local councils' scope of action. This pushes down land 'productivity' (such as ecosystem services) and raises the costs of existing spatial structures (for example costs of technical infrastructure, mobility costs).

This explains the need to encourage the sustainable use of land. This primary aim of protecting land follows the environmental quality goal of preserving natural resources and is also linked to other sustainability objectives. Furthermore, it is convergent (yet also partly divergent) with other aims of society such as ensuring a high quality of life and strengthening economic productivity.

Land policy (and hence the protection of natural resources) is essentially the responsibility of local government self-administration in connection with a local authority's area's planning supremacy enshrined in Article 28 of the German Constitutional Law. However, there is also a requirement to adapt to the aims and principles of environmental planning. Whereas under conditions of population growth 'healthy' competition between local authorities for potential demand through a policy of stockpiling land can still be justified as long as it is steered by a regional framework (e.g., the priority growth of central locations), under conditions of shrinkage this competition may become ruinous. Local authority investment will be in vain – which cannot be the point of either local or regional land policy. Yet local authorities do not pursue the aim of saving land per se; they do not assign land an intrinsic value but attach objectives to it such as contributing to the public good or even political aims. Under the New Political Economy, opening a new commercial estate will bring in votes and help keep the current local political leaders in office. On top of that, local authorities hope that by attracting businesses and residents they will be able to raise the additional trade and income tax needed to consolidate their budgets.

For these reasons, the effect of sustainable land policy currently appears inadequate under conditions of both population growth and demographic shrinkage. The main unhealthy competition is between the planning region and the local authority (the planning hierarchy), as well as between adjacent local authorities. These problems are exacerbated if land policy is impaired not just by local authority boundaries, but also regional borders (including between German federal states).

These implications and consequences of land consumption have prompted debate in Germany regarding sustainable land policy aimed at the economical, appropriate treatment of urban areas and transport infrastructure.

Germany's federal government has declared the problems of land use the subject of political interventions. Accordingly, in its National Sustainability Strategy published in 2002, it set the quantified target to limit the new development of additional greenfield land for settlement purposes and transport infrastructure to 30 hectares per day by 2020 (Bundesregierung 2002: 99). It has realized that too much greenfield land is being designated for development and that this non-renewable resource is being used up rapidly. However, the sustainable treatment of land currently remains one of those sustainability goals in which no significant progress has yet been achieved (Bundesregierung 2008: 15).

The federal government has put forward a development aim for land as an environmental resource containing both a quantitative target (reducing the consumption of virgin land to 30 hectares per day by 2020) and a more qualitative one (achieving a ratio between internal and external development of 3:1). As far as the planning hierarchy is concerned, the government intends to have these two national targets implemented at the planning tiers of the federal state, region and local authority. Above all, they are to be declared the basis of future local authority policy by planning departments. This indicates a normative objective to particularize land policy aims at the respective levels of control and to have them implemented by means of suitable instruments.

Scientific discourse and planning policy debates have taken place recently in an effort to operationalize the national sustainability strategy in Germany regarding land policy aims. Solutions for future sustainable land policy are to be elaborated in order to halt the mistakes outlined and to at least discuss the ambitious land policy aims put forward in planning practice.

The ongoing zoning of land for development contradicts the federal government's target of 30 hectares per day. Moreover, this increase in the volume of land used for urban areas and transport infrastructure contrasts with the general development of the population.

It was for this reason that the German inter-ministerial support programme REFINA was launched with the aim of conducting practical research to determine viable action. Practical recommendations for sustainable land policy are to be put forward and tested in order to advise policymakers. The project 'Aims and transferable action strategies for a system of cooperative regional land management under conditions of shrinkage in the core region of central Germany (KoReMi)' is part of the REFINA programme and is explained in more detail below in connection with the issues raised above.

The example of the core region of central Germany

The core region of central Germany, which comprises the two regional centers Halle (Saale) and Leipzig including their extensive suburbs as well as neighbouring rural areas; has been chosen as the example study area for the KoReMi project in order to examine the problems of increasing land use accompanied by a dwindling population. The region is subject to a process of structural change largely resulting from demographic shrinkage. In fact its structural transformation is severely altering the framework of conditions of development of the population and urban areas, regional development, the use of environmental resources and infrastructure, transport infrastructure and public finance. A feature of the study area is the border between the states of Saxony and Saxony-Anhalt, and also the boundaries of three regional joint planning groups. Land use policy coordination throughout the region hence poses many challenges for the administrative and political institutions.

In the first few years following German reunification, there was no legal framework in place for the local authorities in the east German region of Halle-Leipzig for the zoning of virgin land under west German law. Since there was a need for commercial, office and residential buildings but no zoning plans had been drawn up, the number of greenfield developments was high. The unresolved ownership in inner-city areas and the low land prices on the periphery led to the unbridled growth of development on cities' outskirts and in surrounding areas. Hopes of an economic upswing prompted many local authorities to invest in the necessary infrastructure at their own expense, frequently before specific enquiries had been received from potential investors. Exaggerated expectations led to too much land being reserved for development under planning regulations. Some of this is now part of unused land banks for which a binding land use plan was granted several years ago.

These unused sites are frequently located in areas which are geographically unsuitable or for some other reason not in demand. In a region suffering from population decline, not all areas can enjoy the same development prospects and instead a few islands of growth should be agreed, where development should be concentrated (e.g., favouring the strengthening of central locations over suburban areas). Under certain circumstances, examination of spatial development prospects may result in expectations of growth and commercial exploitation having to be abandoned. Therefore, dealing with unused land for which a binding land use plan has long been granted in shrinking regions entails examining the spatial development of towns and regions in terms of not just planning law but also from a broad political and social perspective.

Under the joint project KoReMi, possible strategies for a system of cooperative regional land use management in conurbations hit by demographic shrinkage are being developed and discussed by way of example in central Germany. The extent to which cooperation between local authorities and even federal states can contribute to steering land use is also being examined. With solo efforts by local authorities no longer sufficient for sustainable land use policy, the project is designed to encourage sustainable land use management – and hence contribute to cooperative forms of steering involving different institutions.

The existing planning requirements and expectations of different actors such as planning authorities and local authority policymakers are to be taken into account. The aim is to develop recommendations with which local authority and regional actors can find suitable instruments adapted to their areas of responsibility in order to reduce the use of virgin land.

The current situation in Central Germany

The core region of central Germany is on the one hand characterized by various forms of change, including technological and economic structural transformation (with for instance new types of labour organization and the requirements of globalisation intensifying competition among different locations). On the other hand, political and social change have taken place, accompanied by changing standards, the debate about safeguarding the public services, and the pluralisation of different lifestyles. Demographic change promotes spatial disparities, above all in the structurally heterogeneous study area. With the exception of Leipzig, all the districts in the region concerned (including the city of Halle) are characterized by continuing demographic shrinkage (Figure 7.1). This is occuring in contrast to the rising land use consumption.

First of all, it must be noted that the functional and administrative areas have very different ranges and intensities. This is partly reflected in the impact of the suburbanisation wave in the 1990s, which impeded the appropriate (i.e., sustainable) control of spatial development. This begs the question whether the 'autonomy of the region can be strengthened' by 'pursuing the autonomy of its parts' (Strauß 2007). The suburbanisation wave has since leveled off and reurbanisation trends are only to be observed in Leipzig. However, the trends of spatial and natural population development and demographic ageing overlay punctual positive development tendencies throughout the region (Warner 2007). For example, the costs incurred by local authorities owing to migration and ageing of the population exceed their revenue. Local authorities are being hit especially hard by the decline of their 'own' populations via the direct local authority equalization payments based on population size, while demographic transformation also leads to reduced tax revenue (Falken-Großer 2007).

By contrast, the development of urban areas and transport infrastructure is evidently not following the trend of demographic shrinkage and sluggish economic development. As a result, although it slowed down in 2004–05, the volume of development land is still growing from year to year in contrast to the dwindling population (Brandl, Gawron, Heilmann 2007, Figure 7.2).

Attention is also directed towards the structural parameters affecting the population-specific costs of the technical infrastructure in built-up areas (e.g., water supply and sewage disposal). For example, the degree of sewage disposal sometimes varies considerably from one local authority to the next, while the scope remaining for adapting infrastructure which has yet to be built to future trends of land development is comparatively limited (Geyler, Prochaska 2007). The situation for transport

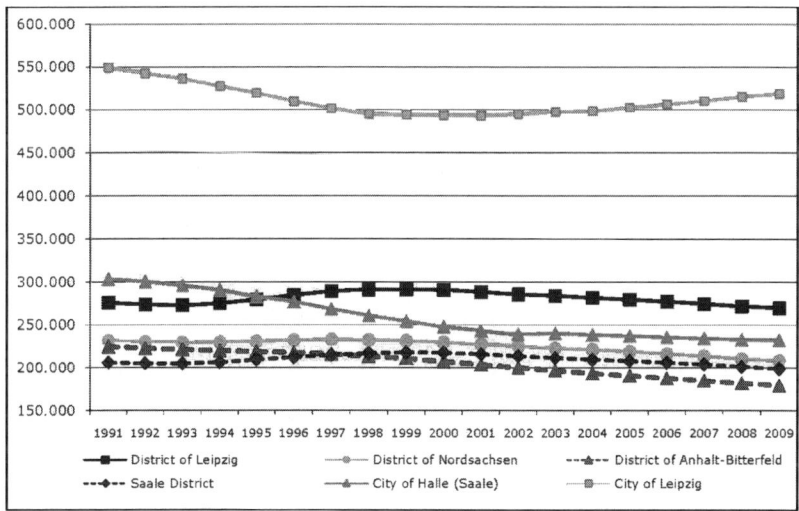

Figure 7.1 Development of the population in the study area (districts and two central locations), 1991–2009

Source: Saxony and Saxony-Anhalt Departments of Statistics (as shown in Warner 2007: 23).

infrastructure is characterized by the high concentration of roads and railways in the two urban locations Halle (Saale) and Leipzig (Winkler 2007).

Cluster analysis has identified six types of areas in the core region of central Germany (Geyler 2008): medium-sized cities, rural towns, surrounding municipalities, and three levels of rural areas (Figure 7.3). These types enable the complexity of structural spatial challenges to be reduced and also typical strategies for sustainable land use policy to be formulated.

A high proportion of the large number of sites designated for development prior to 2000 have not been used. This is typical of areas where the population is declining and results in a diversified demand for land use policy, which needs to target a sustainable reorganization of urban areas. Sometimes, it may be necessary to reduce the volume of built-up areas in order to rebalance supply and demand. Reducing the number and size of existing build-up areas will increase demand for the remaining locations and promote inner-city development as well as the revitalisation of derelict land.

To sum up, a sustainable land use policy in the core region of central Germany must address both shrinkage and the variety of boundaries and different municipality types. The first steps towards finding a solution ought to be a shift from 'supply planning' (land is offered for investors to consider) to 'demand planning' (first an investor asks for land, then the municipalities look for a suitable location) in response to shrinkage, cross-boundary approaches (cooperation or hierarchy) and cluster-specific proposals (different guidelines).

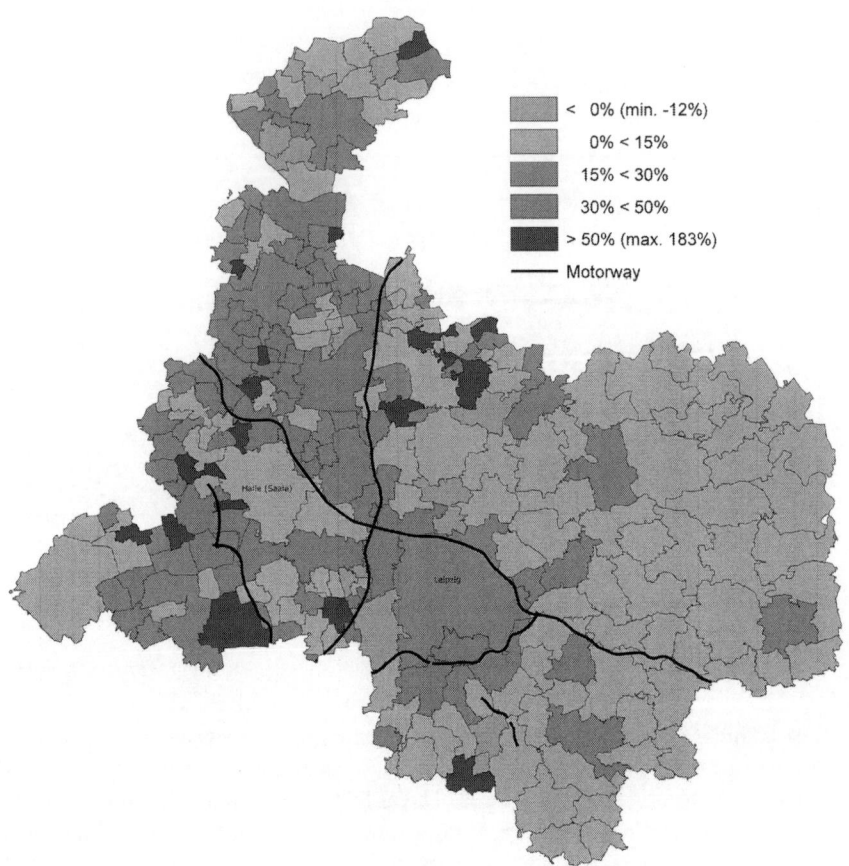

	< 0% (min. -12%)
	0% < 15%
	15% < 30%
	30% < 50%
	> 50% (max. 183%)
——	Motorway

Figure 7.2   Growth of land used for urban areas and transport infrastructure in the local authorities of the study area in the periods 1996–2005 (left) and 2000–2005 (right)

Source: Map based on the ATKIS digital landscape model; Saxony and Saxony-Anhalt Departments of Statistics (as shown in Brandl, Gawron, Heilmann 2007: 63).

Planning policy requirements and possible instruments

Although qualitative and quantitative land use targets were set in the German federal government's National Sustainability Strategy, Saxony and Saxony-Anhalt have so far failed to formulate binding land use aims. In line with Germany's federalist structure, each state is for the time being in charge of its own environmental planning, and according to recent studies, the federal government's competence when it comes to the implementation of its targets to preserve greenfield land is

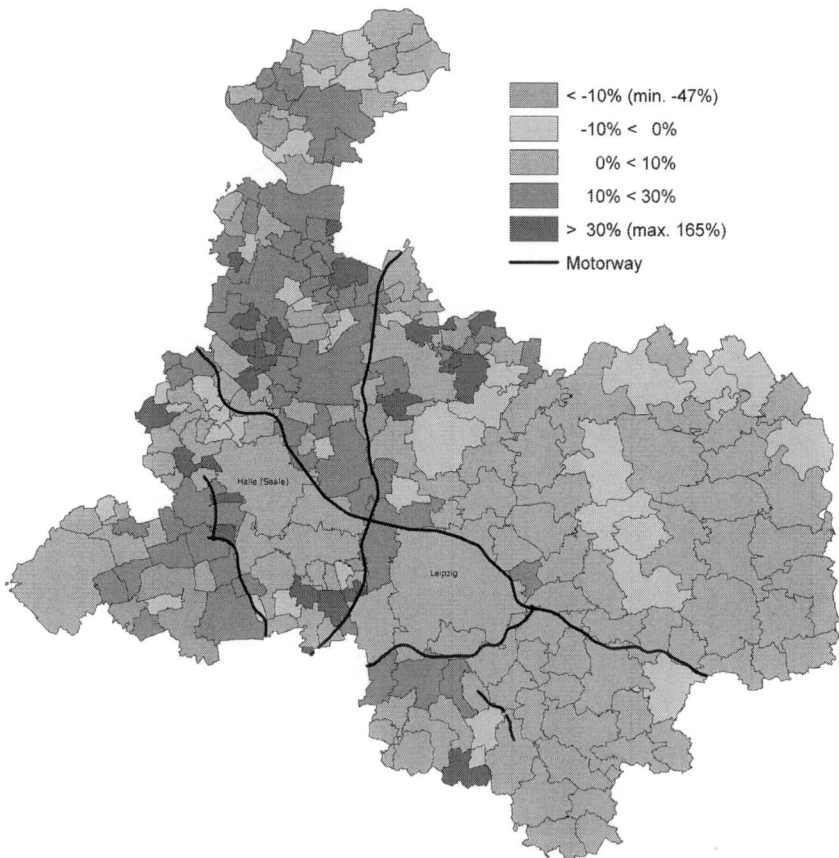

Figure 7.2   Concluded

poor (Siedentop 2008). Consequently, Saxony and Saxony-Anhalt are required to fix their own land use targets.

Although a strategy for preserving land is currently being prepared in Saxony, this has largely been left to the Ministry of the Environment and coordination with other ministries has barely begun. A new organization is going to be commissioned to strengthen land use policy in Saxony. Therefore a new policy program has been prepared. But at this moment it is still not clear how many of the measures will be implemented and how much the current land use policy will be changed in future. In 2010 in Saxony-Anhalt a new state development plan was set up (published 2011), but it contains no precise declarations for preserving land strategies. General regulations for land preservation in suburban areas and for vacancies (deconstruction and revitalisation) are defined, but are not underpinned with concrete aims.

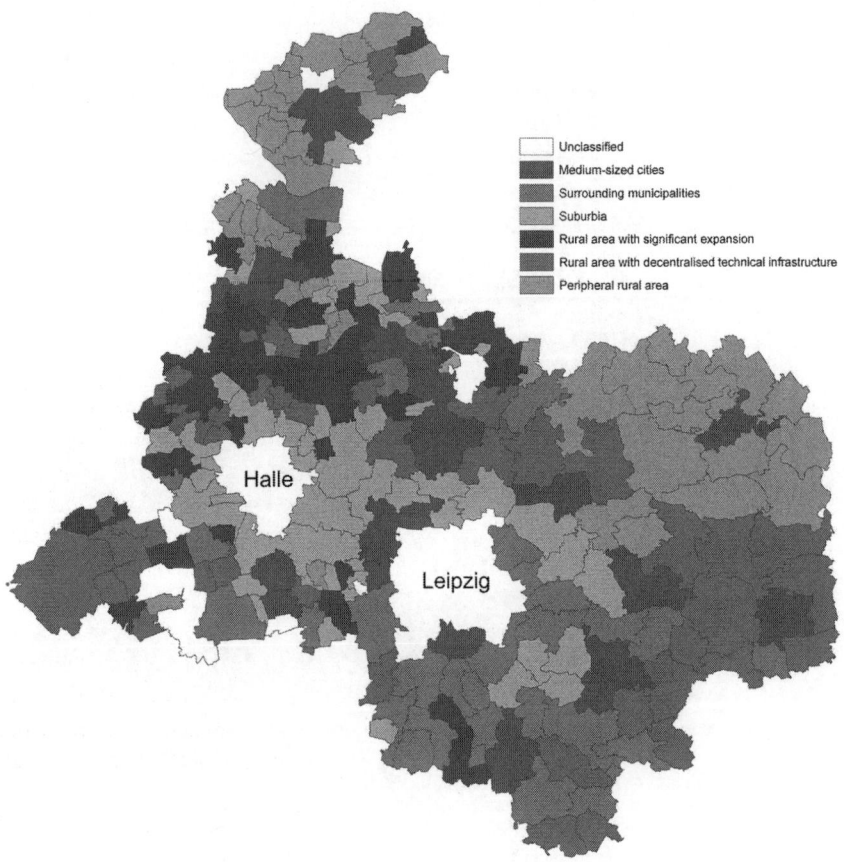

Figure 7.3   Classification of towns and other areas in the core region of central Germany

Source: Geyler 2008: 17

There is yet still no binding, coordinated land saving strategy in Saxony and Saxony-Anhalt. Therefore, the local authorities, who are responsible for development planning in built-up areas, have not been given any guidelines for the organization of an analogous local land use policy. And since no targets have been set by the German federal states, there is not yet a strategy in place to reach the federal government's 30 hectare per day aim.

Owing to the various functional connections spanning the administrative boundaries which divide local authorities, coordination within each federal state needs to be augmented by coordination across state boundaries. Traditional integrated planning is already subject to this requirement, with plans having to be coordinated between neighbouring federal states, regions and local authorities.

Although strengthening conurbations and reusing existing integrated locations are aims of municipal planning (and are geared to the objectives of federal state and regional planning), in practice this is often easier said than done. As a result, land is subject to massive demand despite the increasing amounts of unused residential and commercial land as well as the disproportionate infrastructure and transport systems. Consequently, the further use of virgin land is encouraged. At the same time, factors such as the additional costs of developing these new areas mean local authorities are increasingly strapped for cash.

Only in the two biggest cities of the region, Halle and Leipzig, is there a tendency of reurbanisation. This is due to new lifestyle trends, with people taking advantage of the opportunity to combine the quality of city life with the advantages of a shrinking city like cheap real estate prices and new open spaces within the inner city. It is therefore possible in both cities to realize new housing forms like detached houses, which combine the amenities of rural and urban living. Because of these new tendencies Leipzig has managed to stabilize and even to increase its number of inhabitants. Halle has gained an influx of population into its city districts because of a reurbanisation trend and an increasing number of students from other federal states. This progress is not as distinctive as in Leipzig but is becoming more important.

Furthermore, the sustainable development of an entire region is hugely impeded by the inter-state border (and hence uncoordinated federal-state and regional planning). There is no agreement concerning the necessary or possible compensatory mechanisms in the event of uncoordinated land zoning. Then again, the state development plan of Saxony makes provision for voluntary cooperation between local authorities of equal status designed to take the form of 'cooperation communities' consisting of cities, towns, municipalities and districts. In the new state development plan 2010 (published 2011) of Saxony-Anhalt, the necessity of cooperation between municipalities is established as a target ('The cooperation of municipalities for the stabilization of the development of subspaces has to be supported' (Landesregierung Sachsen-Anhalt 2011).

Additionally, cooperation within the metropolitan area consisting of Chemnitz, Dresden, Halle, Leipzig and Zwickau ('Saxony Triangle') has for many years been established in state development and regional plans.

Although the region lacks an integrated land use strategy, land use aims can be identified. However, these objectives are by themselves not enough to manage land use. In particular, they will need to be increasingly modified as demand continues to fall. A proposal for such modified targets is contained in the following list of aims compiled in coordination with the current debate (Table 7.1).

Table 7.1   Excerpt from the list of aims

Measures \\ Main aims	Measure 1: Economic development of commercial areas	Measure 2: Adapting the development of residential areas to demographic change	Measure 3: Promoting qualified development structure
	Steering commercial investments to existing locations	Balancing the designation of new building areas	(Joint) stabilisation of land use in central locations and development axes
Reduction of the additional development of greenfields			
Degradation of economic productivity			
Maintenance of the quality of life			
Integrated land use strategy: no new designation of land for development purposes			

Source: author's own illustration

Land use strategies under the main strategies identified in the project for implementing the land-saving aim (zoning of new sites, cancellation of existing status, strengthening conurbations and conversion) can be derived from the main aims, which in turn are connected to relevant instruments (Figure 7.4).

Cooperation as a contribution to sustainable land use management under shrinkage tendencies

The core region of central Germany is characterized by a variety of obstacles. The planning region of one federal state cannot regulate the local authority land use policy of another state – which is a particular problem in the case of overlapping suburbs of two central locations such as in the case of Halle-Leipzig. Local authorities, local institutions and also national actors therefore need to find new forms of cooperation in land use policy in this district, which accounts for a large part of the Saxony triangle Metropolitan region. Regional cooperation could aid in overcoming these boundaries. Three different types of cooperation would be conceivable (Figure 7.5): horizontal (between institutions of equal status) to overcome competition, vertical (between institutions at different levels) to

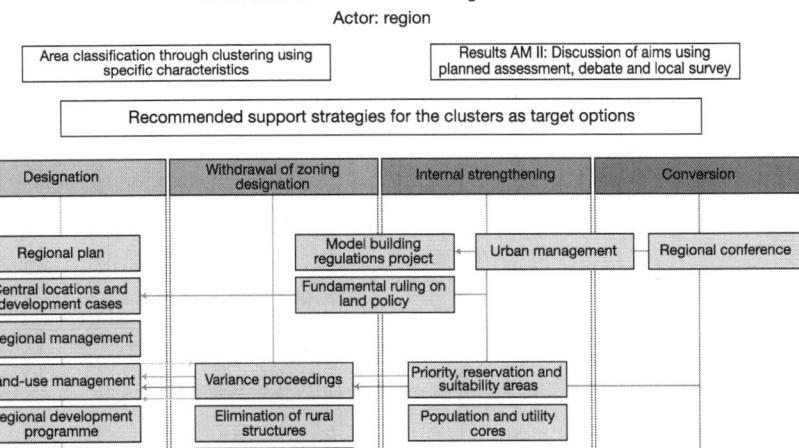

Figure 7.4   Example of the allocation of instruments for the levels of actors in the region

Source: Forschungsverbund KoReMi

overcome hierarchy, and across state boundaries in order to overcome institutional non-jurisdiction in overlapping suburban areas. This cooperation would address aims regarding spatial quality and action, which would be discussed with the competent actors in local authorities and higher tier planning bodies. The base of new cooperation projects is a greater quantity of information about demographic change and its correlation with land use and land use policy.

Although some promising, regionally restricted projects already exist, they are limited to the narrow region of the development area surrounding the airport. An example of a current project is the regional development programme for the 'Schkeuditzer Kreuz interchange', which encompasses 18 towns and municipalities in the vicinity of Leipzig/Halle Airport on both sides of the border between Saxony and Saxony-Anhalt. This alliance has launched a number of land related projects such as an analysis to gauge the potential for commercial estates and a regional living space analysis, but is not currently active.

Moreover, mechanisms for initiating and controlling cross-boundary cooperation between Saxony and Saxony-Anhalt were introduced by the agreement signed by the two states in 1994 and the Central German Initiative. New possible approaches for regional and inter-state cooperation in Central Germany are outlined below.

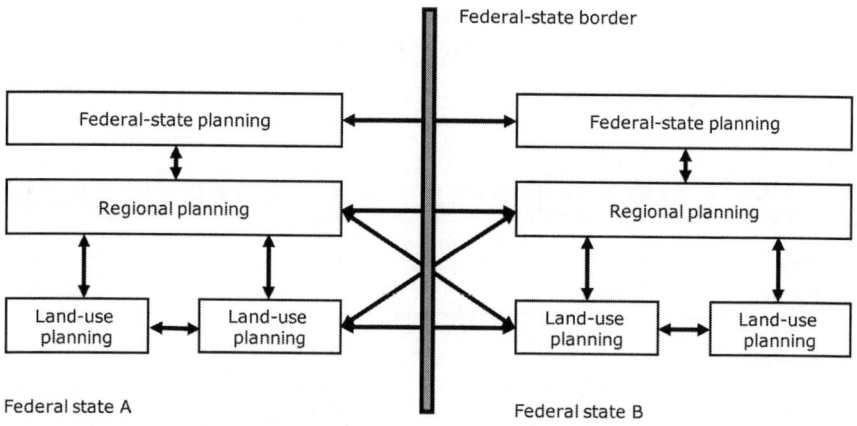

Figure 7.5   Coordination requirements between the individual levels of planning

*Source :*Forschungsverbund KoReMi

Only awarding subsidies for commercial investment on condition of cooperation

Currently, subsidy frameworks end at the border of the state ('Bundesland') to which they apply, which can lead to an oversupply of land allocations in areas near borders, even if the involvement of neighbouring local authorities and planning regions is prescribed. This situation is exacerbated by the fact that areas designated or developed using subsidies in the early 1990s have a holding period of 25 years, meaning that land allocations which are not in demand still need to be maintained. Connecting the award of subsidies to, for example, the requirement for cooperation between local authorities regarding the development of commercial estates, would be one way of steering land use policy and preventing the unbridled designation of new sites.

The regional planning authority acts as a mediator

If two neighbours have a dispute concerning their common boundary it may be necessary to enlist the help of a mediator on a regional level. Therefore it would be realistic to extend the responsibilities of the regional planning authorities towards a new agency for information management and planning dialogue. In opposite to that, the 'Saxony triangle' metropolitan region spanning the border between Saxony and Saxony-Anhalt is not suitable to act as a mediator, as land use policy is not part of the Saxony triangle's self-imposed range of responsibilities. Since economic prosperity is paramount in the metropolitan regions, steering correlations arise between companies' investment location policy, the local authorities' budget and infrastructure policy, and their land use policy. Therefore, the dialogue between the regional planning authorities must be improved, especially across the border between Saxony and Saxony-Anhalt.

Installing temporary utility networks

In connection with the duty to provide public services, the infrastructure must continue to serve the population of an entire region. This entails maintaining a decentralised supply network at important centres which has to be qualitatively and quantitatively adapted to the changed demographic structure. If necessary, temporary and even private installations must be used which, following a 'residual lifetime of demand' in peripheral rural areas, can be abandoned without financial loss. For a location like Halle-Leipzig, which faces international competition, investment also needs to be carried out in soft location factors such as regional innovation systems promoting clusters and 'milieus' (e.g., creative clusters).

These solutions outlined above focus on regional and federal-state issues that could also be relevant in other agglomerations and regions and are not limited to individual sets of conditions and circumstances in Central Germany. They emphasize the possibilities of cooperation between local authorities in a two-state region characterized by both shrinkage and growth.

Conclusion

In the Halle-Leipzig region new forms of cooperation are necessary, because apart from 'classical' combinations of competition and hierarchy the respective suburban areas and the most important areas of commerce and industry of the two central locations overlap. Promising forms of cooperation are necessary, which must mainly remain informal for constitutional reasons (with informal patterns of cooperation it is easier to follow individual and joint objectives).The framework for cooperation needs to be strengthened by the federal state governments, for example by means of incentives for cooperation as well as restrictions. The cooperation aim of the new state development plan of Saxony-Anhalt is formulated for municipalities in defined subspaces of the federal state, and does not specify any binding land-saving-targets. Moreover, neutral 'cooperation agencies' need to be set up (possibly with the regional planning authorities) which are recognized by the local authorities and that can provide advice on what shortcomings are emerging owing to a lack of cooperation, and what possibilities exist for cooperation within the strengthened institutional framework.

Taking this action could enable the land use policy on the border between the two federal states to be optimized to reflect the German government's land use target. As a result, the state's land use policy will also come into effect more strongly.

Moreover, closer cooperation can only be carried out on the basis of a more intensive land use policy debate within the respective state. The state must be aware of the proceedings in its own territory before negotiating with other actors, while on the other hand new aims regarding internal matters could be concluded from cross-border coordination.

Both states should improve their current policy activities. The newly discussed land use organization at the State level in Saxony is, institutionally speaking, too far away from the problems the municipalities have with land use management. Therefore new intra-regional forms of cooperative dialogue and management should be discussed.

Strengthening cooperation across boundaries between different administrative districts would hence optimize land use policy and generally make a valuable contribution to the further qualification of land use policy within Germany. Under conditions of shrinkage in particular, this would contribute enormously to sustainable development.

References

Brandl, A., Gawron, T. and Heilmann, J. 2007. Siedlungs- und funktionsräumliche Entwicklung in der Kernregion Mitteldeutschland. in *Die Kernregion Mitteldeutschland: Ein erster Überblick; Bevölkerung, Finanzen, Infrastrukturen, Raumstruktur und Wirtschaft*, edited by J. Ringel, T. Lenk, K. Friedrich, R. Holländer and W. Kühn. Leipzig: Forschungsverbund KoReMi, 55–61.

Bundesregierung. 2002. *Perspektiven für Deutschland: Unsere Strategie für eine nachhaltige Entwicklung; Nachhaltigkeitsstrategie für Deutschland.* Berlin: Presse- und Informationsamt der Bundesregierung.

Bundesregierung. 2008. *Für ein nachhaltiges Deutschland: Fortschrittsbericht zur nationalen Nachhaltigkeitsstrategie.* Berlin: Bundestag.

Deggau, M. 2004 *Zunahme der Siedlungs- und Verkehrsfläche : 93 ha/Tag.* [Online] Available at: http://www.innovations-report.de/html/berichte/statistiken/bericht-35820.html? [accessed: 07 July 2011].

Falken-Großer, C. 2007. Finanzen und öffentliche Haushalte. in *Die Kernregion Mitteldeutschland: Ein erster Überblick; Bevölkerung, Finanzen, Infrastrukturen, Raumstruktur und Wirtschaft*, edited by J. Ringel, T. Lenk, K. Friedrich, R. Holländer and W. Kühn. Leipzig: Forschungsverbund KoReMi, 38–49.

Geyler, S. (ed.). 2008. *Clusteranalyse der Gemeinden in der Kernregion Mitteldeutschland: Eine Typisierung der Region nach Entwicklungsparametern und Rahmenbedingungen.* Leipzig. Forschungsverbund KoReMi.

Geyler, S. and Prochaska, C. 2007. Technische Infrastrukturen zur Ver- und Entsorgung. in *Die Kernregion Mitteldeutschland: Ein erster Überblick; Bevölkerung Finanzen Infrastrukturen Raumstruktur und Wirtschaft*, edited by J. Ringel, T. Lenk, K. Friedrich, R. Holländer and W. Kühn. Leipzig: Forschungsverbund KoReMi, 65–86.

Landesregierung Sachsen-Anhalt. 2011. *Verordnung über den Landesentwicklungsplan 2010 des Landes Sachsen-Anhalt.* Freyburg: Freyburger Buchdruckwerkstätte.

Siedentop, S. 2008. Siedlungspolitischer Kontext des 30-Hektar-Ziels. in *Handelbare Flächenausweisungsrechte: Anforderungsprofil aus ökonomischer, planerischer und juristischer Sicht*, edited by W. Köck, K. Bizer, B. Hansjürgens, K. Einig and S. Siedentop. Baden-Baden: Nomos, 21–34.

Statistisches Bundesamt Deutschland (DESTATIS). *Zunahme der Siedlungs- und Verkehrsfläche: 114 ha/Tag*. [Online] Available at: http://www.destatis. de/jetspeed/portal/cms/Sites/destatis/Internet/DE/Presse/pm/2006/11/ PD06__492__85, emplateId=renderPrint.psml [accessed: 07 July 2011].

Strauß, C. 2007. Zum Umgang mit Grenzen in der Kernregion Mitteldeutschland. in *Die Kernregion Mitteldeutschland: Ein erster Überblick; Bevölkerung Finanzen Infrastrukturen Raumstruktur und Wirtschaft*, edited by J. Ringel, T. Lenk, K. Friedrich, R. Holländer and W. Kühn. Leipzig: Forschungsverbund KoReMi, 9–18.

Umweltbundesamt (UBA). *Daten zur Umwelt: Entwicklung der Siedlungs- und Verkehrsfläche*. [Online] Available at: http://www.umweltbundesamt-daten-zur-umwelt.de/umweltdaten/public/theme.do?nodeIdent=2277 [accessed: 07 July 2011].

Warner, B. 2007. Räumliche Merkmale der Bevölkerungsentwicklung. in *Die Kernregion Mitteldeutschland: Ein erster Überblick; Bevölkerung, Finanzen, Infrastrukturen. Raumstruktur und Wirtschaft*, edited by J. Ringel, T. Lenk, K. Friedrich, R. Holländer and W. Kühn. Leipzig: Forschungsverbund KoReMi, 21–38.

Winkler, C. 2007. Verkehrsinfrastruktur. in *Die Kernregion Mitteldeutschland: Ein erster Überblick; Bevölkerung, Finanzen, Infrastrukturen, Raumstruktur und Wirtschaft*, edited by J. Ringel, T. Lenk, K. Friedrich, R. Holländer and W. Kühn. Leipzig: Forschungsverbund KoReMi, 97–103.

Chapter 8

Germany's Post-War Suburbs: Perspectives of the Ageing Housing Stock

Stefan Fina, Simone Planinsek, Philipp Zakrzewski

Introduction

In former West Germany, more than one in three residential buildings are single-family homes built between 1949 and 1978, amounting to 22 per cent of all housing units. Today, considering the lifecycle of these buildings and current socio-demographic trends, their viability looks uncertain. As the population ages and birth rates decline, demand for single-family homes is waning. In addition, different lifestyle choices among the newer generations are leading them to prefer different types of housing.

The objective of this chapter is to assess the risks and challenges that post-war single-family home areas will face in the coming decade,[1] and to begin the discussion on how to deal with these issues. Strategies of revitalisation, conversion, or demolition are discussed, not only for the housing stock in question, but also for the areas they occupy.

Context

There is ample evidence that demographic change will affect all sectors of German society in the coming decades. In particular, the population of former East Germany is ageing and declining at such a high rate that vacancies in the housing sector have already become a serious issue. In response, the national government launched a 2.5 billion Euro programme to reconfigure urban structures (in German: 'Stadtumbau Ost') which took place between 2002 and 2009 (Bundestransferstelle Stadtumbau Ost 2009). It was specifically designed to stabilize the housing market by means of coordinated demolition and urban renewal measures (Häußermann, Läpple, Siebel 2008: 206).

During the period of the German Democratic Republic (GDR), private residential development was strictly limited. As a result, today's housing oversupply in the eastern states predominantly concerns large scale rental

---

1   In the context of this chapter, the term 'post-war period' refers to the years 1949 to 1978.

housing. In 'western' Germany (the area of the former Federal Republic of Germany), on the other hand, the single-family housing stock is largely privately owned. Furthermore, many of these regions still feel the effects of the population influx from the former East Germany and from abroad, as well as the higher birth-rates among immigrant populations. Despite this general population growth, socio-demographic change is still causing housing oversupply in some western German regions (BBSR 2008a). Consequently, from 2002 to 2007, the German federal government initiated a 30 million Euro western counterpart to its eastern urban renewal scheme (in German: 'Stadtumbau West') that triggered several pilot projects designed to deliver best practice solutions for western regions (Bundestransferstelle Stadtumbau West 2009).

The following data illustrates the factors that will contribute to the expected oversupply of low-rise housing: Assuming that first-time home buyers are usually between the ages of 25 und 45 (Palotz 2004: 25), those who bought their houses during the 1950s, 1960s and 1970s mostly belong to the birth cohorts 1905–35, 1915–45, and 1925–55. Assuming that owner-occupiers stay in their single-family home until the age of 85, periods of ownership change are due to take place between 1990 and 2020 for buildings constructed during the 1950s, between 2000 and 2030 for houses built during the 1960s, and between 2010 and 2040 for single family homes from the 1970s. At the same time, the generation of potential buyers is not only characterised by its relatively small size due to demographic change, but also by an increasing socio-cultural differentiation, expressed by a larger variety of living arrangements and family forms. The decline of the nuclear family and the corresponding growth of single person, single parent and so-called 'double-income-no-kids' ('DINK') households are generally less interested in detached single family homes compared to higher density urban dwellings particularly at central locations (Häußermann 2007). It can therefore be expected that the amount of second hand single family homes will exceed the number of potential buyers in the near future.

Nevertheless, prosperous regions will continue to experience housing shortages for the foreseeable future. There is a risk that certain single family housing areas will turn into segregated neighbourhoods with districts populated disproportionately with the poor and underprivileged. Structurally weak areas are also more likely to suffer from a drop in demand. These include old industrial or disadvantaged rural regions, which are already seriously affected by out-migration and an ageing population (BBSR 2008a). Particularly buildings in 'unfavourable' residential locations or neighbourhoods with image problems are at risk of long term vacancies, especially if they are poorly insulated and of low quality construction. Among other things, unfavourable locations are characterised by poor public transport connections, as well as a lack of job opportunities and community facilities (Hesse, Scheiner 2007).

A review of the relevant literature reveals how controversial the implications of socio-demographic change for single-family homes continue to be. Recent housing market outlooks present conflicting forecasts of medium term single-family home demand in Germany. On one hand, some urban analysts concluded that continuous household growth will result in high demand for single-family homes throughout Germany until 2020. In this view, the single-family home market would not become saturated until at least 2020 (Simons et al. 2006).

On the other hand, a real estate outlook for 2020 published by the Federal Office for Building and Spatial Planning (in German 'Wohnungsprognose 2020') expects decreased demand for single-family homes from 2010 onwards, due to demographic change (Bucher 2006). However, recent variations in real estate prices indicate that the level of demand varies between regions, and that these differences will become more pronounced in the future.

A range of journal articles provide a more general social sciences perspective. They focus on the effects of social change, as well as new family and living arrangements, on single- family home neighbourhoods. One author points out that families might prefer urban to suburban or rural living because of advantages like centrality, a wider variety of services and facilities, increased mobility with public transport, and the resulting efficiency gains. This is especially important for single parents and families where both parents work (Häußermann 2007).

According to other authors, automobile dependency will become a major disadvantage of suburban and rural single-family home areas in the future (Hesse, Scheiner 2007). With the population ageing, this phenomenon will be exacerbated. With old age, residents will suffer from reduced mobility and be less able to live in peripheral areas. Though advances in health and transportation are expected to extend the driving fitness of people to an older age in the future, the problems associated with ageing (loss of vision, limited mobility, decreasing social networking) will merely be postponed. In summary, suburban and rural life will eventually present marked inconveniences, in particular when access to services is purely reliant on automobiles (Oeltze, Bracher 2007). Other disadvantages are road traffic related air pollution and traffic noise – issues that used to be exclusively inner city problems but have been spreading into the suburbs for some time. Many wholesale retail shops, warehousing and office parks have moved to the urban fringe where accessibility by road is high and land prices are cheap. As a result, motorisation has continued to increase, and traffic loads are now high throughout the city region.

Risk areas at national and regional level

In terms of an empirical assessment of risk areas for the problems described above, Table 8.1 gives an initial overview of the total number of post-war buildings that will potentially be affected. For each of the former western German states it shows the number of buildings in 2005 (column 2), the number of single-family homes for the construction periods 1948–57, 1958–68, and 1969–78 (columns 3, 4, 5), their sum (column 6), and the proportion of post-war single-family homes of today's total building stock (column 7).

Table 8.1   Building statistics for former western German states (in thousands).

	Total Buildings 2005	Single family homes from 1948–57	Single family homes from 1958–68	Single family homes from 1969–78	Post war single family homes 1948–78	Share of Total
Baden-Württemberg	2262	187	307	289	783	35%
Bavaria	2834	223	401	410	1034	36%
Berlin	307	6	15	15	37	12%
Bremen	132	14	18	12	44	33%
Hamburg	233	26	33	15	74	32%
Hessen	1295	112	198	187	497	38%
Lower Saxony	2031	182	348	317	848	42%
North Rhine-Westphalia	3585	334	485	426	1244	35%
Rhineland-Palatinate	1097	86	150	134	370	34%
Saarland	295	42	45	33	120	41%
Schleswig-Holstein	724	63	107	102	272	38%
Germany (West)	14795	1276	2107	1939	5323	36%

Source: Federal Statistics Offices, compiled by the State Office of Statistics of Baden-Württemberg.

In terms of the former western Germany's total, the significance of post-war buildings and single-family homes is obvious: of 14.8 million buildings, 9.3 million are single-family homes. A further breakdown by building age shows that from these, 36 per cent were built in the post-war period from 1948 to 1978. Although the level of construction activities differs across the states, the general trend is that the construction of single-family homes intensified in the years after 1957.

The city-state of Berlin shows a striking difference. There, the post-war single-family homes comprise a significantly lower proportion of today's building stock (see column 'share of total'). This is certainly an effect of the unique development constraints Berlin experienced in that time.

A detailed analysis of municipality data using a multi-criteria assessment approach provides a detailed exemplary risk assessment (see Berke et al. 2006, Fina, Planinsek, Zakrzewski 2009) for four German states (Figure 8.1).

Table 8.2   Indicator development for risk assessment.

Topic	Indicators	Operationalisation	Year
Housing	Structure of the building stock	Percentage of post-war single home building stock (of today's buildings)	1987, 2004
	Household size proxy (pop / dwelling stock)	Number of people per dwelling	2004
		Change in household size proxy	1996–2004
Demography	Population	Population change	1996–2004
	Age structure	Percentage of people over 65	2004
	Migration	Balance of migrants aged 25–50, as a percentage of total population	2004
Land use	Density	Urban density (people per hectare of urban land)	2004
		Change in urban density (people per hectare of urban land)	1996–2004
	Centrality	Distance (driving time) to nearest high order central place* (over 100,000 people only)	2007

Note: *Central places as defined in the regional plans of the German spatial planning system (high order central places provide a set of important services to its hinterland, for example social infrastructure, cultural, administrative, or educational facilities).

Source: Federal Statistics Offices, Federal Office of Geodesy and Cartography, Federal Office of Building and Spatial Planning.

The criteria are built around the topics 'housing', 'demography', and 'land use' that represent the problem dimensions described in the 'context' section of this chapter: the ageing housing stock ('housing') in the context of demographic change ('demography') and the adverse effects of a suburban setting ('land use'). In the implementation process, a range of indicator values (see Table 8.2 for a detailed list) were compared to the average of their class (for example: urban density compared to the average urban density of all cells in the 'urban core' class). An indicator was considered to add to the risk when its value was above the average (land use and population variables) or below zero (migration balance). The rationale behind this approach is explained by the comparative nature of attractiveness: areas with above

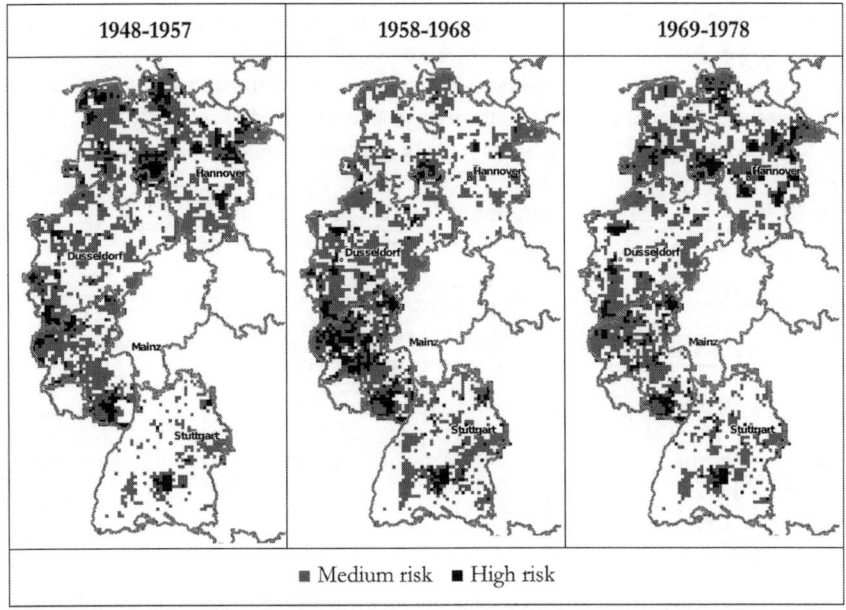

1948-1957	1958-1968	1969-1978

■ Medium risk ■ High risk

Figure 8.1   Risk assessment for Germany's post-war building stock

Source: Fina, Planinsek, Zakrzewski 2009

the average risk values are likely to be perceived as less attractive than the ones with below average values, at least within their own group.

A higher weighting (5x) was applied to the key variables 'share of post-war buildings' and 'share of single-family homes', since they are the focal points of this analysis. As such, the assumption is that risks are comparatively high where there are significant proportions of single-family homes of the post-war period in combination with risk factors like a suburban setting and demographic decline. The combination of all indicator results was then transformed to a uniform spatial scale (5 by 5 kilometre cells) where the values represent an accumulated risk, ranging from 0 to 20.

The visualisation of the multi-criteria assessment results uses three classes: high risk (values 15 and above, black), medium risk (values 10 to 15, grey), and low risk (lower than 10). An additional distinction was made for the post-war building periods (1948–57, 1958–68, and 1969–78) to allow for a differentiation of housing age for the calculated risk. A number of risk areas can be identified for all three periods, namely in south-central Baden-Württemberg (south of Stuttgart), in southern Rhineland-Palatinate, to a lesser degree in northern Rhineland-Palatinate (west of Mainz), north of Düsseldorf, and in the central area of Lower Saxony bordering North Rhine-Westphalia (east of Hannover). The northern parts of Lower Saxony show more risk areas with buildings constructed in the 1948–57 period, the north-eastern part also with buildings constructed during 1969–78 (north of Hannover). In contrast, Rhineland-Palatinate is generally more affected in the context of buildings constructed in the period 1958–68, indicating that suburbanisation processes were comparatively high in this time (east of Mainz).

In summary, the results show that the number of buildings that fall in the age bracket of post war single-family homes is considerable (roughly 22 per cent of all dwellings), and that their locations correlate highly with suburban settings. At the municipal level, a detailed risk assessment demonstrates that the complex interaction between housing, demography, and land use dynamics can add up to a configuration that is identifiable in a spatial sense.

Municipal and intra-municipal level – case study[2]

At the municipal and intra-municipal level, a model has been developed to predict the supply and demand of the post-war housing stock, and applied to a rural municipality in the federal state of Baden-Württemberg for which additional data was available. It is located in the northern part next to Mannheim and Heidelberg, with a population of approximately 5,000. Like many other rural municipalities in Baden-Württemberg, the case study does not rank as highly in the risk assessment as suburban areas at this point in time. However, due to the evidence presented here on the relationship between demographic change and dwelling oversupply, vacancies of peripheral single-family homes are likely to increase in the near future.

According to the developed model the ratio between dwellings and households in rural areas is about one-to-one. The corresponding ratios between people per dwelling and people per household are similarly balanced. This means that if there is an oversupply in dwellings, the ratio between households and dwellings becomes greater than one-to-one. The oversupply of dwellings compared to households serves as an indicator for unused living space (accommodation units).

Forecasts and missing data values (before 1986 and after 2007) are complemented by the extrapolation of data of previous years. Household growth is predicted as a minimum and a maximum variant, covering ambiguous assumptions for future household size. An important factor is whether the demand of a declining population is going to be offset by declining household sizes, or a higher number of households, respectively. The indicators average age, density and vacancy were implemented for the residential areas of the case study. Designations for residential areas can be found in legally binding land use plans (in German 'Bebauungsplan').

---

2   Methodology and data are excerpts from the dissertation of Dr. Simone Planinsek. It is about the development of suburban residential areas in the 1960s to 1980s in Baden-Württemberg (in German 'Die Entwicklung von Eigenheimgebieten der 1960er- bis 1980er-Jahre in Gemeinden des Umlandes und der Peripherie. Generierung und Analyse von Bevölkerungs- und Siedlungsstrukturdaten auf Quartiersebene durch Geocoding').

The risk assessment presented here focuses on peripheral residential areas of the 1960s to 1980s based on the date the legally binding land use plan came into force.

In 1961 there were 960 households, and in 2006 as many as 1625. Projections until 2025 predict a range between 1,300 to 2,000 households. The number of people per dwelling (ppd) in 1961 was 3.98. This number steadily and consistently decreased over the last 45 years and is now at 2.79 ppd (2006). If the recent trend of shrinking household sizes continues, the average household size for the municipality will go down even further, to about 2.21 ppd. Taking this household size and the population forecast of 4,330 inhabitants in 2025, the number of dwellings (1959) will be close to the predicted dwellings forecast of the modelled minimum variant (Figure 8.2). With respect to these figures it can be assumed that there will be no additional demand for dwellings until 2025. This is also visualised by the ratio between households and dwellings in Figure 8.2, which shows an oversupply of dwellings if the amount of households declines. In case the number of households follows population trends, oversupply will increase. Additional living space that is being developed to meet short term demand now will add to the oversupply in the long run. As a consequence, the destabilisation of the residential market is highly likely.

There is currently no indication that building activities will slow down in the near future. Local government still exercises a supply-oriented competition for new residents with the development of new greenfield areas, the latest one being from 2007. As a consequence, there will be an oversupply of buildings constructed during the 1990s and 2000s in residential areas or at potential building sites.

Figure 8.3 shows selected structural data for the case study (main district). The map in the first column identifies the vacancies of the residential building stock and location of residential areas of the 60s-80s (highlighted). Vacancies in single-family home residential areas of the 60s-80s are lower compared to the municipal centres, which is mainly a result of higher average age (see column 2). The average age of the population in the main district is 46.5 years which is a comparatively high figure for Baden-Württemberg with an average age of 42 years (Krentz 2008). The main district is therefore likely to have a higher share of elderly people. At the same time, residential areas with high average age are usually lower density neighbourhoods. This typically occurs because parents will remain in their home into their old age, though it is designed to accommodate a full family.[3] But renewal is already underway in some areas in the north and in the centre – however, new housing areas are developed in the southwest (rightmost column; light grey colour).

The case study illustrates an initial approach of supply and demand analysis using modelling techniques with indicators like density, average population age, and vacancy rates. In summary, it shows that single-family homes of the post-war period are certainly not neglected in terms of occupancy rates at this point in time.

---

3   This is called the 'remanence effect', a term widely used in German terminology ('Remanenzeffekt').

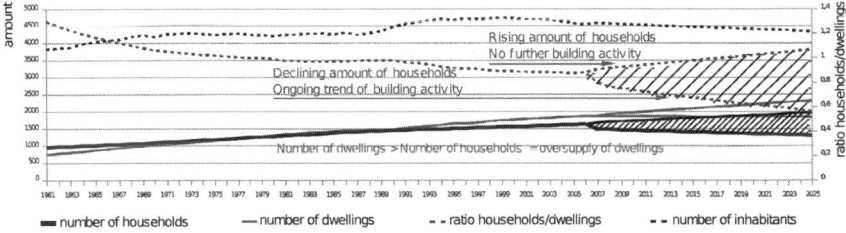

Figure 8.2   Scenarios of households and dwellings based on the present case study

Source: author's own illustration

However, there are clear signs of ageing and question marks around ownership succession and future maintenance. As in many rural areas of Baden-Württemberg, a future mismatch between the amount of housing that is available in the suburban settings of the post-war era and declining demand is clearly evident.

In general, the results of the empirical analysis show that the number of buildings that fall into the age bracket of post war single-family homes is considerable (approximately 22 per cent of all dwellings), and that their locations correlate highly with suburban settings. On the municipal level, a detailed risk assessment demonstrates that the complex interaction between housing, demography, and land use dynamics can add up to a configuration that is identifiable in a spatial sense. The case study illustrates an initial approach of supply and demand analysis using modelling techniques with indicators like density, average population age, and vacancy rates. The results help to identify development options as discussed in the following section.

Potential strategies

The main challenge in strategy development is the communication of theories and results from empirical research into the planning practice of local government. Usually, indicators such as the ageing of the residential population, population density and land use are not monitored comprehensively in small municipalities. Thus planners in local government are often not fully aware of the problems demographic change holds in store for the future. It is therefore timely and prudent that local authorities redefine their role in this context. Planners need to take on a leadership role and proactively get involved with new planning policies that address the realities of demographic change. The policies need to be coordinated with long-term sustainable development objectives, and strategic opportunities to plan for an ageing population need to be seized upon as and when they occur –

■ Vacancies (residential buildings)
■ Occupied residential buildings

Residential areas of the 60s-80s and vacancies

■ 0,0-30
■ 30,00-40,00
■ 40,00-50,00

■ 50,00-60,00
■ 60,00-70,00

Average age of residents

Figure 8.3   Examples of geocoding; visualising the present case study

Source: author's own illustration

whether for new communities or existing ones (Department for Communities and Local Government 2007).

However, as the case study demonstrates, the situation is spreading where ageing and low residential density correlate. 'Empty nesters'[4] and widows often stay in their oversized homes (Clark, Deurloo 2006). In consequence, living space per capita, as well as operating expenses per capita, increases accordingly. The most effective solution from a planning perspective would be to pursue a densification strategy. However, ownership structures and social aspects are significant barriers (Gräf 2007).

From a theoretical point of view, there are three basic options to deal with ageing single-family home areas at risk of decline: revitalisation, conversion and demolition. All measures aiming at the continuity of residential use fall in the category of revitalisation. Quality improvement strategies that target specific groups become increasingly important, since the living requirements of different household types vary widely (BBSR 2008a). Even the needs of families and young couples – being the traditional first-time home buyers – have changed significantly since the period when the houses were built. Tiny rooms and cramped layouts, for example, are characteristic of small houses from the 1950s, but do not meet today's standards.

The only way to maintain residential use in neighbourhoods at risk of vacancies is to attract a wider range of household types to reside within these areas. However, the lifestyles and needs of 'new' target-groups like the elderly, students or singles differ from those of the original residents. On the one hand, it is crucial to adapt homes and neighbourhoods to meet the needs of an ageing population (e.g., Feifel 2007, de Temple 2005). On the other hand, it can be fairly complicated to adapt these homes to the needs of aged or disabled persons, since most houses are two storey buildings. Furthermore, 'lifetime neighbourhoods' must provide accessible local amenities such as the built environment, infrastructure, public transport, services and shared social space (Department for Communities and Local Government 2007).

Faller (2001) suggests an alternative option, where new housing for the elderly within residential areas is developed. These new buildings are designed to attract elderly home-owners to move from their single-family home into locally assisted living facilities. Another possibility would be that medium-income households, which were previously not able to buy a house, move into the neighbourhood. Due to housing oversupply and the resulting drop of property prices members of this group, often with an immigration background, can easily get onto the 'property ladder' (e.g., BBSR 2008b, de Temple 2005). At this stage, property owners unable to find a buyer will be required to put their houses onto the rental market (BBSR 2008b)).

Irrespective of the improvement strategy one chooses – the prevalent reconstruction backlog requires investment in the housing stock in almost every

---

4   Parents whose children have moved out of the family home.

case. Prior to the 1973 oil price shock, building energy-efficient houses was fairly unusual[5]. According to present-day standards, most of the 1950s-70s buildings are therefore characterised by insufficient thermal insulation. Thus comprehensive modernisation to improve energy efficiency will be essential.

Nevertheless, in many cases it will not suffice to simply improve the buildings. Neighbourhood-related issues such as neglected public space or a lack of infrastructure, amenities and services have to be addressed as well. If these disadvantages can be overcome, there is a good chance that image problems or stigmas related to the neighbourhood will change.

In contrast, when the lack of demand indicates that the original residential use of several buildings cannot be sustained, there are two remaining options: firstly, former residential buildings could be converted for other purposes such as shops, cafes, offices, or community centres, essentially turning the neighbourhood into a mixed use quarter. The former residential area might even become a paradise for the 'creative class', if it is possible to attract innovative start-ups, artists and creative practitioners to relocate, for example, by renting out workspace at cost price (Florida 2002). Although this may be among the more complex options to implement, it is the one that offers the best chance of being effective. Unfortunately, on this route, planners and developers will have to overcome obstacles such as an unfavourable location, resistance of the residents, or a municipality not willing or not able to support this kind of innovative strategy.

Secondly, the systematic depopulation and demolition of single-family homes is the last alternative to prevent an endangered neighbourhood from dereliction (Adam, Ginzel, Weidner 2006). Even though such a strategy would be very unpopular (and extremely difficult to implement), there are additional positive effects associated with it. For instance, if other areas of a community are at a comparable risk of vacancies, the demolition of dwellings in peripheral locations would certainly help to stabilise population levels in the centre.

Conclusions

Demographic change is going to cause fundamental changes in the way we live in and plan our residential areas in the future. The top-down study methodology clearly demonstrated that the problem is national, but has very specific aspects at the local scale. Conflicting interests on the local level are often not visible at the regional or national scale since they balance each other out. It is therefore important to monitor the situation within municipalities and settlements, as the case study has shown. Although the dimensions of the problem are generally undisputed, some local decision-makers persist in ignoring the potential (and in some places the

---

5   The Thermal Insulation Ordinance (in German 'Wärmeschutzverordnung') which became effective on November 1, 1977 established energy saving building regulations for the first time in Western Germany.

present reality) of an oversupply of residential buildings, and its effect on the real estate market. The political motivation to enter a competition for migrating young families, and to promote the image of a young, dynamic, and thriving community is often in stark contrast to the realities of decline. Although there are some areas that will manage to maintain the economic and social balance in the future, most areas will have to rethink the way they manage their housing stock.

The performance of the residential property market is a reliable indicator for the attractiveness of locations and regions. However, it might already be too late for counteractive measures once house prices begin to fall and resale difficulties become common. At this point the question arises as to whether action should be taken at all, or whether the private housing market should be left to the devices of the free market.

There are several reasons to pursue planned, proactive arrangements in the best interest of the public, and to avoid a failure of the housing market. The slow death of suburban or rural single-family home areas is particularly problematic for municipalities, as population decline implies a loss of tax revenue. Furthermore, the efficient use of public infrastructure will be undermined, and the public perception of the affected communities' image will be damaged. Additionally, it would go against the public interest, if on the one hand the existing housing stock is facing increasing vacancies and on the other hand new residential buildings are being constructed elsewhere at the same time. Balancing supply and demand will therefore become a major housing policy challenge.

This chapter has identified risk areas for the ageing single-family home housing stock and discusses some potential strategies to deal with these issues. The limitations associated with applying these strategies within the complex ownership structures of private residential developments are recognized. The task to develop adequate solutions is not just the exclusive domain of experts – it is also a right and duty of civil society.

References

Adam, B., Ginzel, B. and Weidner, S. 2006. *Szenarien und Modellrechnungen für eine virtuelle Stadt.*

Berke, P., Godschalk, D.R., Rodríguez, D.A. and Kaiser, E.J. 2006. *Urban land use planning.* 5th Edition. Urbana: University of Illinois Press.

Bucher, H. 2006. *Raumordnungsprognose 2020/2050: Bevölkerung, private Haushalte, Erwerbspersonen, Wohnungsmarkt.* Bonn.

Bundesinstitut für Bau, Stadt-und Raumforschung (BBSR). 2008a. *Einschätzung der Marktchancen von Reihenhäusern, Einfamilienhäusern und kleinen Mehrfamilienhäusern aus den 1950er und 1960er Jahren.*

Bundesinstitut für Bau, Stadt-und Raumforschung (BBSR). 2008b *Umgang mit Bestandsobjekten im europäischen Ausland*

Bundestransferstelle Stadtumbau Ost. 2009. *Bund-Länder-Programm Stadtumbau Ost.*

Bundestransferstelle Stadtumbau West. 2009. *Allgemeine Informationen.*

Clark, W.A.V. and Deurloo, M.C. 2006. Aging in place and housing over-consumption. *Journal of Housing and the Built Environment,* 21(3), 257–70. Available at: 10.1007/s10901-006-9048-3.

Department for Communities and Local Government. 2007. *Towards Lifetime Neighbourhoods: Designing sustainable communities for all: A discussion paper.* London.

Faller, B. 2001. Hemmnisse der Wohneigentumsbildung. *vhw Forum Wohneigentum,* (5), 269–76.

Feifel, J.G. 2007. *Entwicklungsperspektiven und kommunale Strategien zur Attraktivitätssteigerung von Nachkriegssiedlungen dargestellt am Beispiel Esslingen am Neckar.* Stuttgart: Institut für Geographie der Univerisität.

Fina, S., Planinsek, S. and Zakrzewski, P. 2009. Suburban Crisis? Demand for Single Family Homes in the Face of Demographic Change. *Europa Regional,* 17(1). Available at: http://www.ifl-leipzig.de/1329.0.html.

Florida, R. 2002. *The rise of the Creative Class: And how it's Transforming Work, Leisure, Community and Everyday Life.* 1st Edition. New York (NY): Basic Books.

Gräf, B. 2007. *Der demographische Wandel in Deutschland – Auswirkungen und Handlungsalternativen.* Prag.

Häußermann, H. 2007. Suburbia im Umbruch – Das Einfamilienhaus im Grünen wird neu bewertet. *archithese,* 37(3), 28–31. Available at: http://www.baufachinformation.de/zeitschriftenartikel.jsp?z=2007069011210.

Häußermann, H., Läpple, D. and Siebel, W. 2008. *Stadtpolitik.* Frankfurt a.M: Suhrkamp.

Hesse, M. and Scheiner, J. 2007. Suburbane Räume – Problemquartiere der Zukunft? in *Im Brennpunkt: städtische Mobilität und soziale Ungleichheit,* edited by K.J. Beckmann. Berlin: Difu, 35–48.

Krentz, A. 2008. Was heißt hier 'alt'?: Zur Entwicklung des Durchschnittsalters in Baden-Württemberg. *Statistisches Monatsheft Baden-Württemberg,* (12), 7–12. Available at: http://www.statistik-bw.de/Veroeffentl/Monatshefte/PDF/Beitrag08_12_02.pdf.

Oeltze, S. and Bracher, T. 2007. *Mobilität 2050: Szenarien der Mobilitätsentwicklung unter Berücksichtigung von Siedlungsstrukturen bis 2050.* Berlin: Difu.

Planinsek, S. 2012. Die Entwicklung von Eigenheimgebieten der 1960er- bis 1980er-Jahre in Gemeinden des Umlandes und der Peripherie : Generierung und Analyse von Bevölkerungs- und Siedlungsstrukturdaten auf Quartiersebene durch Geocoding. Fallstudien aus Baden-Württemberg. Karlsruhe. Available at: http://digbib.ubka.uni-karlsruhe.de/volltexte/1000024512.

Simons, H., Braun, R., Pfeiffer, U., Schmidt, M. and Metzger, H. 2006. *Wirtschaft und Wohnen in Deutschland. Regionale Prognosen bis 2015. Wohnungsmarktentwicklung bis 2030.* Berlin.

Temple, N. de, 2005. *Einfamilienhaussiedlungen im Wandel Eine Untersuchung zum Generationswechsel vor dem Hintergrund des soziodemografischen Wandels am Beispiel der Stadt Dortmund.* Berlin.

Chapter 9

The Housing Market in Growing and Declining Regions – Political Implications for Housing Policy and Urban Planning

Christian v. Malottki, Joachim Kirchner, Holger Cischinsky

Introduction

The future development of housing demand is one of the key factors that influence decisions in urban planning. Furthermore, the stability of housing demand is a vital presupposition for protecting the value of the existing housing stock. This chapter looks at the impacts of the parallel patterns of growth and decline on the housing market and related political actions. In Germany a main focus of policy is the coordination of energetic modernisation and integrated urban development – especially in neighbourhoods of the 1950s and 1960s. We assume that both urban planning and housing policy will have to intensify these efforts in the future.

Housing demand in growing and shrinking regions

Germany – as many major industrialised countries – is a country where the processes of physical and/or demographic shrinkage and growth take place simultaneously and are spatially closely interrelated (Bundesamtes für Bauwesen und Raumordnung (BBR) 2005). The spatial concentration of labour markets and rising transportation as well as commuting costs stimulate these processes. This chapter draws special attention to the situation in the German state of Hesse, which includes a great variety of regions ranging from the boom region around Frankfurt / Wiesbaden and the northern area around Kassel where there has been a noticeable decline in population. The forecast of population in Hesse (van den Busch 2007) – which depends on demographic parameters and the migration balance – confirms the strong difference between the southern and the northern areas. This pattern is overlapped by the temporal aspect that shows an overall decrease of the rates of population change. This trend will intensify in future years.

Housing demand – the variable of interest– is not necessarily directly linked to overall population development, but to household formation. As the size of households shows an enduring decline, the negative demographic 'housing demand shock' is not as pronounced as the population forecast may lead us to expect. The

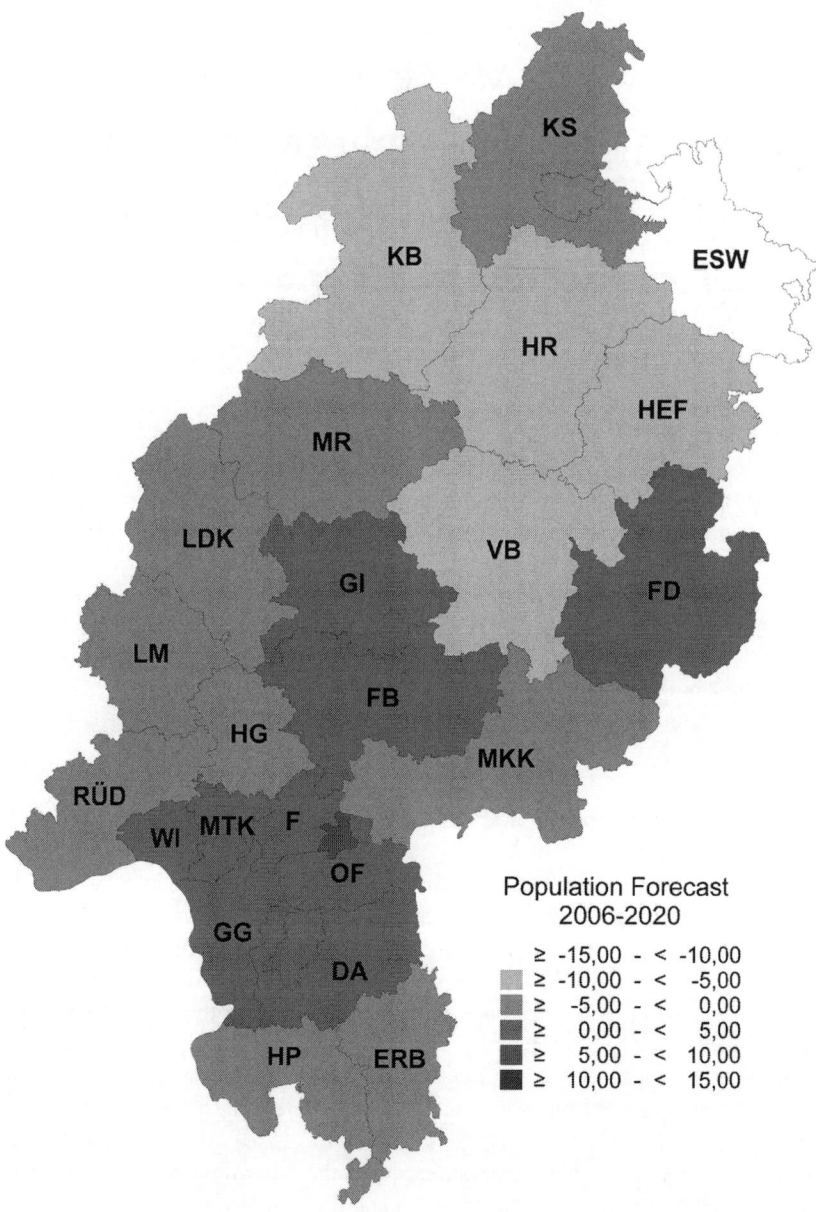

Figure 9.1   Population forecast, household forecast, required new dwellings and difference between needs and extrapolated completions ('housing shortage forecast') in Hesse until 2020

Source: (Kirchner, Rodenfels 2008)

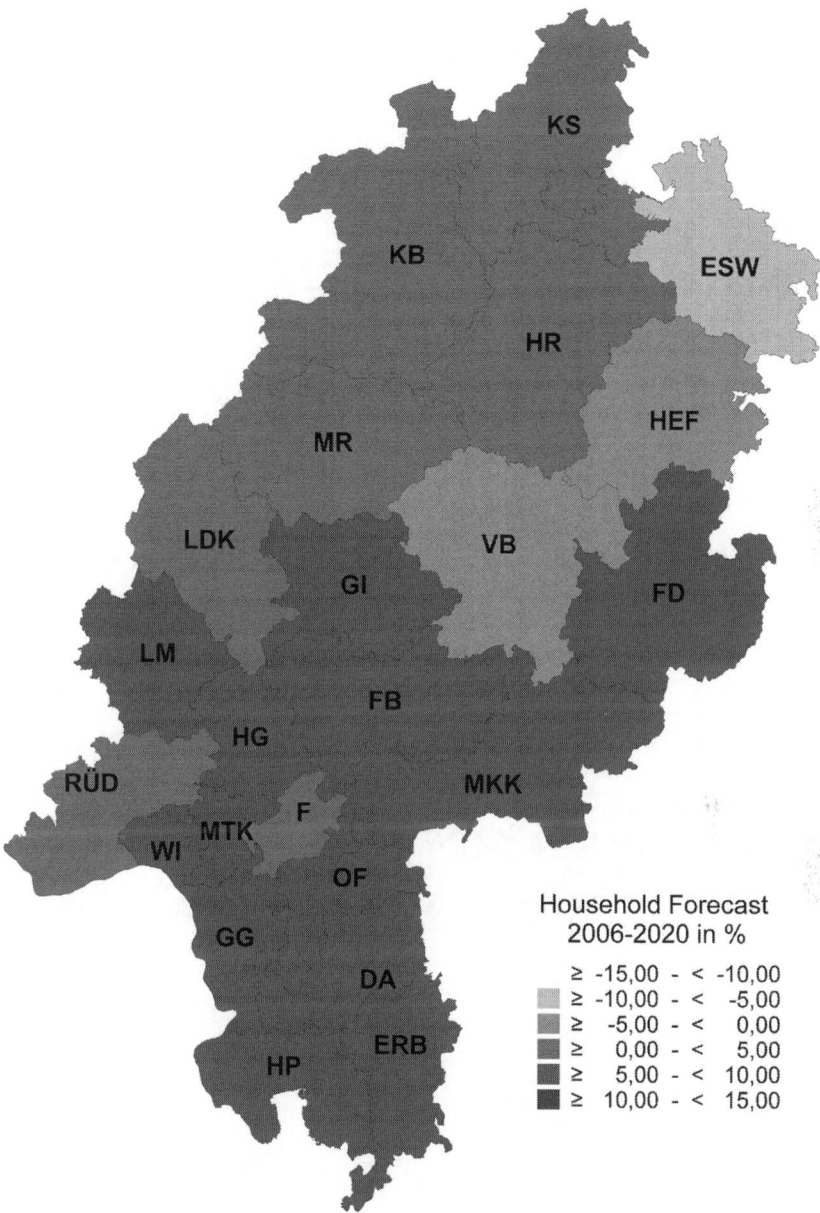

Figure 9.1   Continued

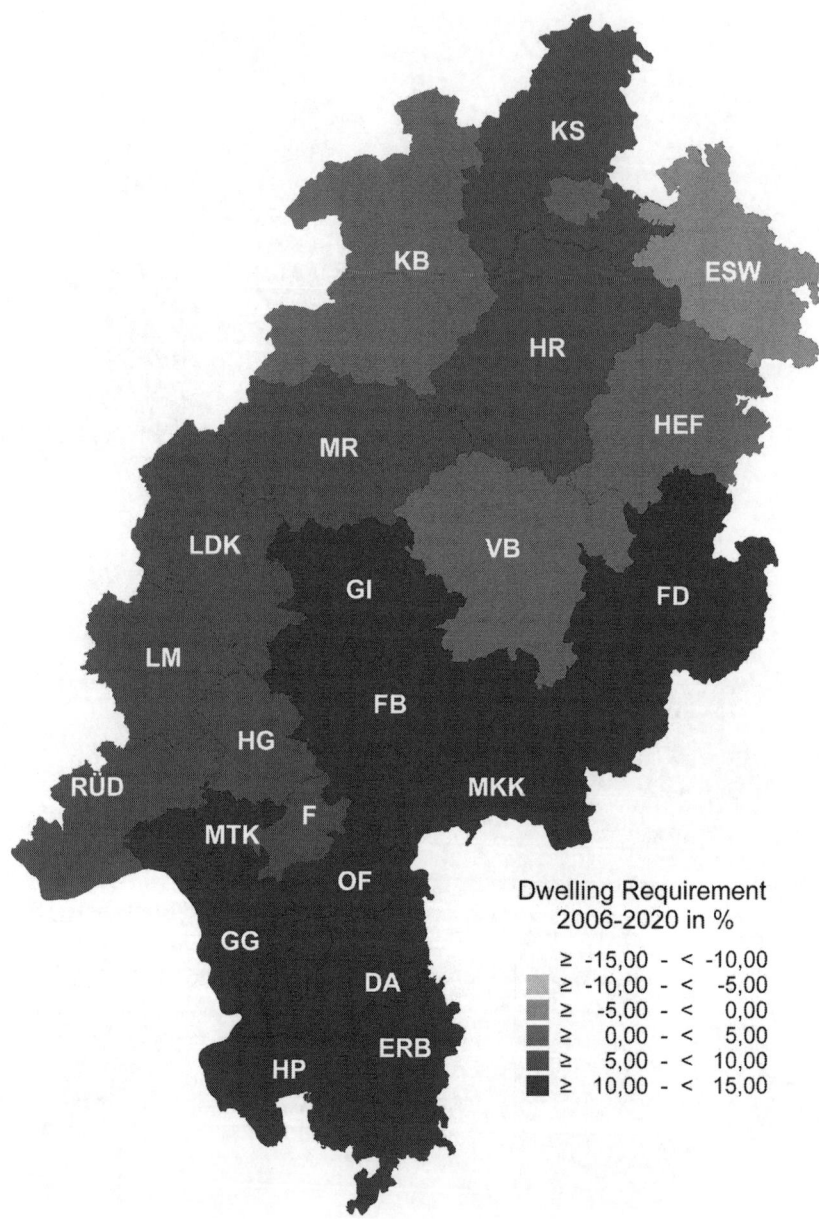

Figure 9.1   Continued

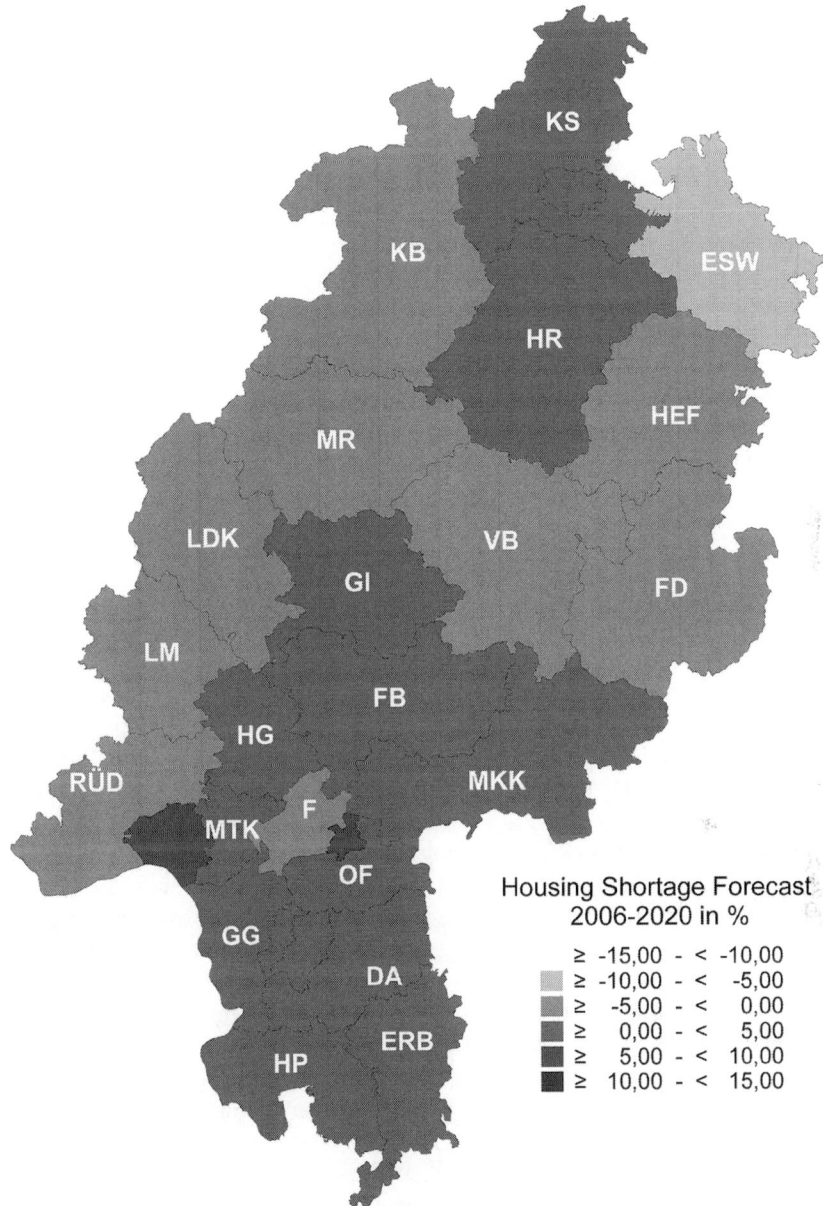

Figure 9.1   **Concluded**

household formation model, that provides the basis for the estimation of housing demand, works with the extrapolation of the rates of persons per age group whom are heads of a household. As the decline in household size slows down in the core cities and continues in rural regions, these ratios are modified. They are then matched with the age-specific population forecast (Kirchner, Rodenfels 2008).

The need for new dwellings is still higher than the number of new households (Figure 9.1). In this context supply shortages have to be reduced and the demolition of sub-standard buildings has to be considered. Figure 9.1 shows that the reduction of population does not cause a vacancy or dereliction problem across the whole of the state. Until 2020, the problem of negative housing need is mainly limited to a small north-eastern part of the state.

This result seems to be quite unspectacular and may allow us to draw the conclusion that no specific interventions into the housing market of, for example, housing policy or urban planning may be necessary. But we should also consider the supply side.

On the one hand, the fourth map in Figure 9.1 demonstrates that the completion figures of new dwellings are higher than the need, especially in the shrinking counties. The reason is a shift in preferences towards the kind of building typologies and dwelling sizes that are not offered by the market in sufficient quantity and quality – mainly single family homes. This supply surplus will lead to filter effects and vacancies in the context of specific building typologies.

On the other hand the housing land shortage and the resulting high level of land prices lead to a situation in which the dwelling completions per year fall far below the projected need in the metropolitan area around Frankfurt. The consequence is a rent increase that starts to get visible. Interestingly Frankfurt plays a special role in Figure 9.1 because of an actual urban extension that will be completed soon. Similar to the shrinking regions, the preferences of (prospective) home owners are changing. Winners and losers within the housing stock belong almost to the same building typologies than in the peripheral (shrinking) regions. Recently, several German research institutes started a discussion about whether the new attractiveness of the inner city as a place to live can be considered as the end of suburbanisation and as a trend back to the city (Jekel 2010). In fact, the preference for good living quality and centrality did always exist. It was (and is) the price of real estate that forced many families out of the cities. The effect of a rising population returning from outside the cities is now statistically significant in some middle-sized cities in rural regions of Hesse, where housing land or existing dwellings are available. In the metropolitan areas the return to the city is a socially perceived phenomenon in the context of gentrification and rising prices in central 'desirable' neighbourhoods, but it is not relevant in the quantitative dimensions of population increases. In the growing regions the strong segregation and the resulting social problems justify and require public intervention.

Figure 9.2 illustrates that the development of the demand side also has an interesting temporal dimension. While the north-eastern counties will face negative development overall, and the southern part will have no problems until 2030, there

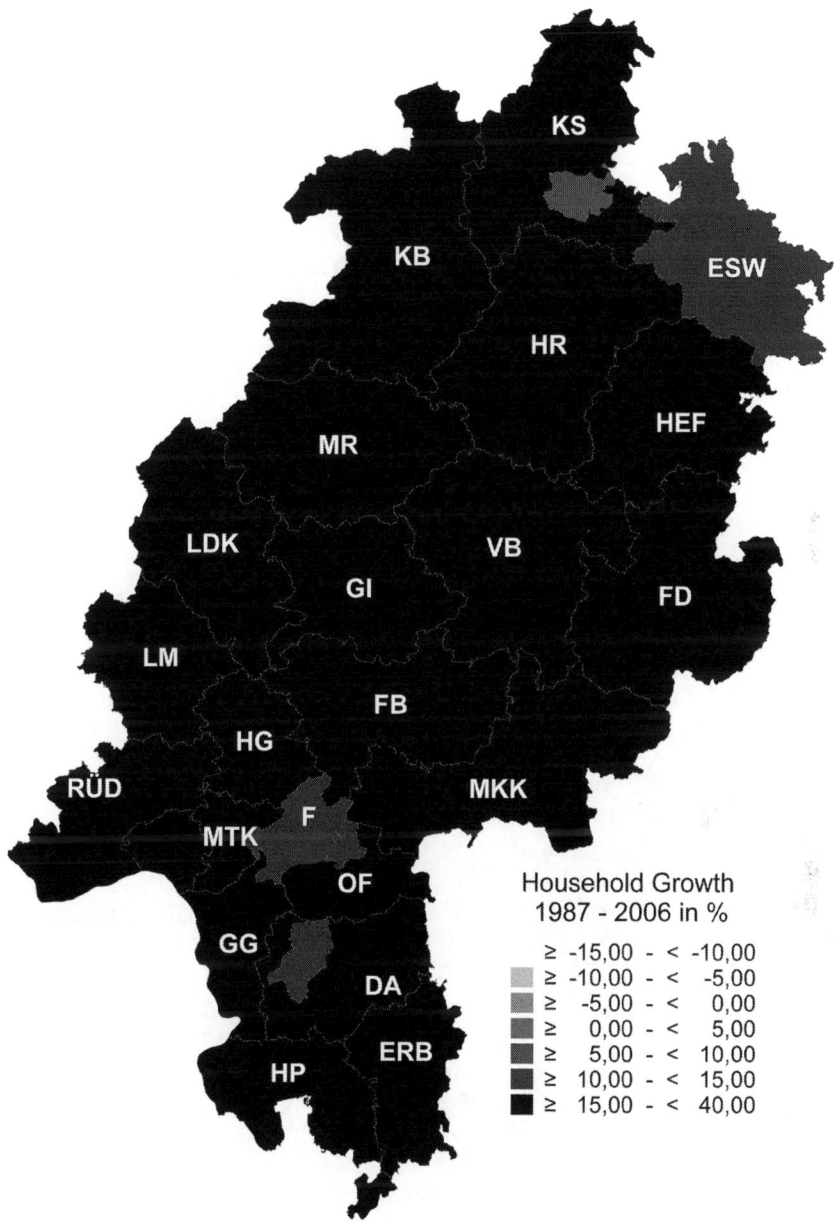

Figure 9.2 **Growth of household numbers in the periods 1987 – 2006, 2006 – 2020 (forecast) and 2020 – 2030 (forecast)**

Source: (Kirchner, Rodenfels 2008)

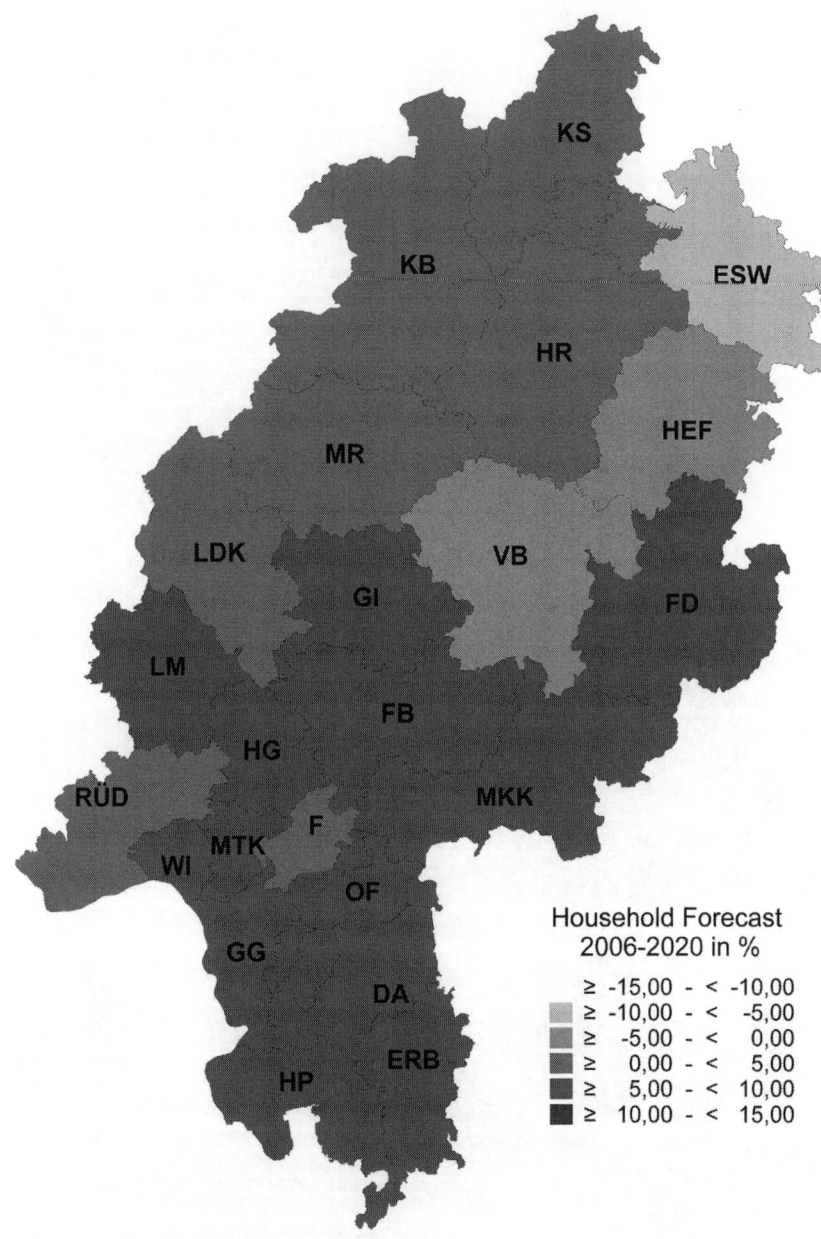

Household Forecast
2006-2020 in %

≥ -15,00 - < -10,00
≥ -10,00 - < -5,00
≥ -5,00 - < 0,00
≥ 0,00 - < 5,00
≥ 5,00 - < 10,00
≥ 10,00 - < 15,00

Figure 9.2   Continued

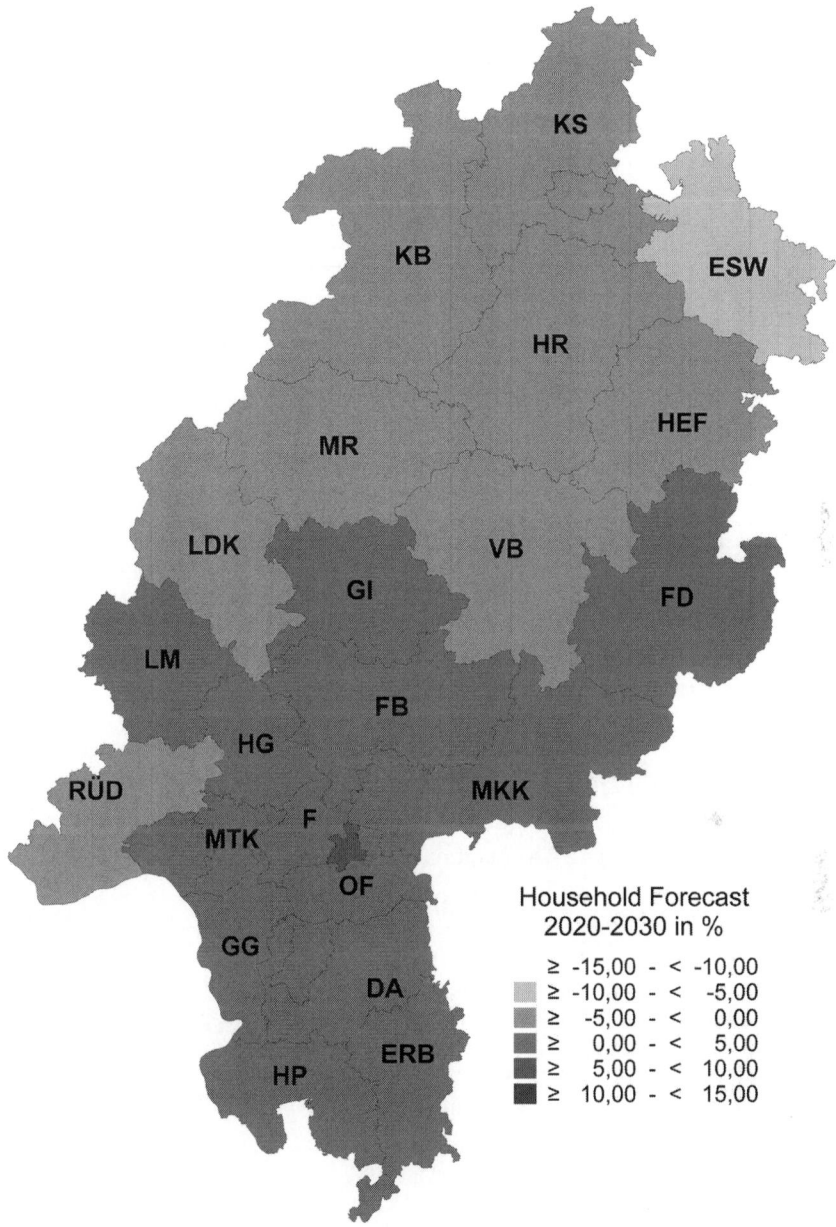

Figure 9.2   Concluded

are some diverging trends in the intermediate regions. There, the housing market has to manage a demand increase in the next years which will be followed by a demand reduction afterwards. It has to be assumed that private landlords (with long term interests) will avoid investments in those areas even if a factual demand exists today.

Table 9.1   Exemplary allocation matrix for household sizes and dwellings sizes (for the city of Fulda)

Household	Households in % 2020						
Size	in flats with ... rooms (the kitchen is a room)						Sum
	1	2	3	4	5	6	
Scenario 2: declining dynamics							
1	3,6	12,6	29,8	25,9	15,3	12,8	100,0
2	0,2	2,4	12,2	28,3	26,9	30,0	100,0
3	0,0	0,9	4,0	18,6	28,9	47,6	100,0
4	0,0	0,5	1,5	9,5	25,6	62,9	100,0
5	0,0	0,2	1,2	4,7	13,9	80,0	100,0

Source: (Kirchner, Stercz 2007)

Note: The shaded cells indicate the significance of older couples that remain in their single-family home long after their children have left.

Besides the spatial and temporal dimensions demand is also shifting between different sizes of dwellings. The traditional approach to housing needs projections based on the equation 'number of household members = number of rooms' is not valid any more. In particular, many older homeowners keep occupying the same number of rooms which they occupied when their children were living with them in the family home. In spite of this, the recent years were characterised by a strong increase in the demand for small flats. It was generated by the diminishing average household size in the segment of welfare recipients. The reforms of the German social welfare system (Hartz-IV-reforms) began to force smaller households dependent on social welfare into smaller flats.

These two effects can be joined into allocation matrices describing the percentage of each household size that occupies a specific flat size (see Table 9.1 as an example for the city of Fulda, the detailed version works with specific matrices per age group of household heads). The subsequent housing demand model developed by the Institute for Housing and Environment for this city shows that there is a particular lack of dwellings with one room plus kitchen and also with four or five rooms plus kitchen (Kirchner, Stercz 2007).

Market players and housing stock

Compared to other countries the supply side of the German housing market shows some specific and interesting characteristics.

Firstly, the ratio of owner-occupied housing is one of the lowest in the world. Only 42 per cent of the dwellings are owner-occupied (compared to rates of about 80 per cent in the US – mainly single-family housing – and Spain – mainly condominiums). A high percentage of the German owner-occupied dwellings is single-family housing.

Secondly, the German stock of social housing is very low compared to other countries with low ratios of owner-occupation (e.g. Austria, the Netherlands). In recent years, the volume of social housing stock has declined further. The welfare regime shifted its focus from so called 'object-oriented' or 'brick-and-mortar' subsidies to 'subject-oriented' subsidies (see section 4). In parallel to this, former social housing units were taken out of legal rent constraints and were subsequently let at market level rents or sold into owner occupation.

German housing stock is still dominated by the allocation to the rental market. Individual private landlords concentrate on stock constructed before 1914, on higher quality stock and the property which achieves higher rents. Their counterpart is the professional sector, who concentrates on cheaper buildings of the post-war period. Figure 9.3 marks the relevant sectors in the German building stock typology – this was originally elaborated for the purposes of an energetic building assessment at the national level (Diefenbach, Born 2007) and the EU level (www.building-typology.eu).

Most of the professional landlords are housing associations who are owned by the public sector – but act like private companies in the rental market. Many municipalities possess their own housing company. After some spectacular transactions in the early 2000s, public opinion turned against selling off publicly owned housing stock. The most important discussions centre on the question of how to measure the profits of public companies – so called 'city yields' and how to deal with the results. Further to this, the question arises how positive effects, e.g. the accommodation of households who are discriminated against, can help to inform decisions about which part of the stock should stay public and which part should be privatized (Spars, Heinze, Mrosek 2008).

Strategies of landlords

Figure 9.3 shows that a substantial part of the German building stock was constructed in the post-war period. These buildings have currently reached a point where major refurbishment is necessary. The most frequent refurbishment activities are energetic improvements of façades, the retrofitting of balconies, the amplification and modernisation of bathrooms and the renovation of stairways and other communal areas. Floor plan modifications, accessibility improvements – e.g.

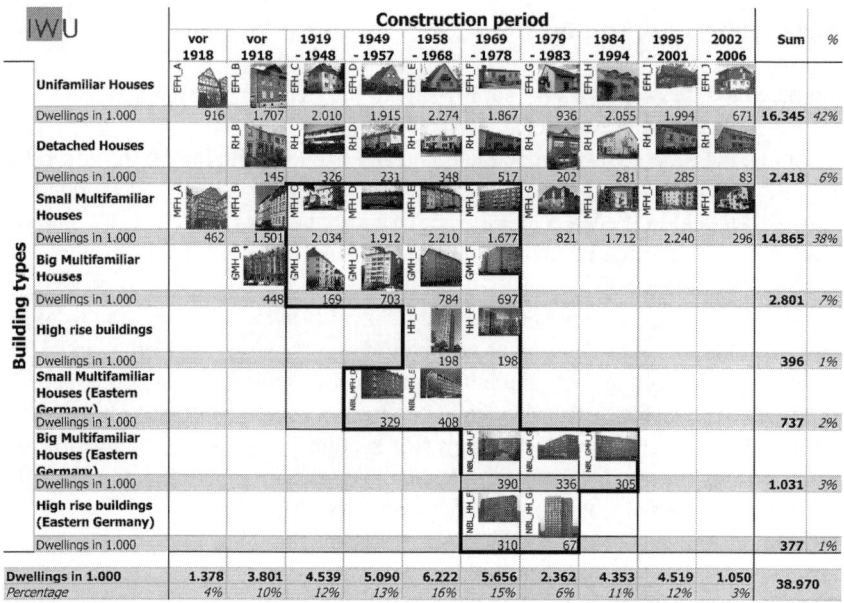

IWU		Construction period										Sum	%
		vor 1918	vor 1918	1919 - 1948	1949 - 1957	1958 - 1968	1969 - 1978	1979 - 1983	1984 - 1994	1995 - 2001	2002 - 2006		
Unifamiliar Houses													
Dwellings in 1.000		916	1.707	2.010	1.915	2.274	1.867	936	2.055	1.994	671	16.345	42%
Detached Houses													
Dwellings in 1.000			145	326	231	348	517	202	281	285	83	2.418	6%
Small Multifamiliar Houses													
Dwellings in 1.000		462	1.501	2.034	1.912	2.210	1.677	821	1.712	2.240	296	14.865	38%
Big Multifamiliar Houses													
Dwellings in 1.000			448	169	703	784	697					2.801	7%
High rise buildings							198	198					
Dwellings in 1.000						198	198					396	1%
Small Multifamiliar Houses (Eastern Germany)													
Dwellings in 1.000					329	408						737	2%
Big Multifamiliar Houses (Eastern Germany)													
Dwellings in 1.000							390	336	305			1.031	3%
High rise buildings (Eastern Germany)													
Dwellings in 1.000							310	67				377	1%
Dwellings in 1.000		1.378	3.801	4.539	5.090	6.222	5.656	2.362	4.353	4.519	1.050	38.970	
Percentage		4%	10%	12%	13%	16%	15%	6%	11%	12%	3%		

Figure 9.3   Housing stock in Germany differentiated into age classes and building typologies

Source: (Diefenbach, Born 2007)

wheelchair access – and the merging of smaller units into larger dwellings or vice versa are expensive and therefore rare strategies. If these investments do not take place the building stock is very likely to be less marketable.

Such refurbishment strategies only work when the investment can be refinanced by commanding an appropriate level of rent. The German rental legislation plays an important role as a general framework. It limits the possible rent augmentation to 11 per cent of the refurbishment costs per year (§ 559 of the German civil code). The law prohibits the expulsion of the inhabitants and therefore also prevents rapid gentrification.

As most buildings of the fifties and the early sixties in Germany were planned and constructed at low densities, the modernization can be combined with new construction projects including densification by means of infill or replacement housing. Concrete measures include the construction of a second row of buildings on sufficiently deep building plots or in loft conversions or even adding additional storeys on existing buildings. Figure 9.4 shows an exemplary penthouse addition in Darmstadt.

The project has the advantage that it fosters the social mix in the dwellings adding solvent tenants who wouldn't usually opt for this kind of building type. It is obvious that this strategy is limited to those metropolitan areas with a projected

Figure 9.4   Densification in Darmstadt, disinvestment in Kassel and energetic retrofit in Berlin

Source: Photographs: IWU

Figure 9.4 Continued

demand increase and to good, accessible locations. The latter also applies to appropriate locations in peripheral cities. In the case of new buildings as well as in the case of additional storeys the planning authorities must act by adapting the planning documents in a way that allows these higher densities. The refurbishment can be linked with remodelling of the green spaces, so that a higher proportion of

Figure 9.4   Concluded

private gardens and a higher quality of the residual (semi-)public areas increase the value of amenities – and the willingness to pay – for everyone.

As the large scale transactions of housing companies are expected to decrease the small scale privatisation of individual dwelling units remains a useful strategy. Units which fit this strategy are for example the penthouses mentioned earlier.

However, a substantial part of the housing stock is not suitable for a transfer to higher market segments (and it is politically important to maintain a sufficiently large affordable segment). In numerous districts the percentage of elderly people is very high. They are often a stabilising factor in the neighbourhoods. Therefore professional landlords are interested in keeping them in the neighbourhood even when they become dependent on external help. A recently evolving strategy includes offering additional services. Exemplary projects of innovative housing companies include: a task force team against noise in the neighbourhood, a shopping and home delivery service, personal emergency call functions and collection of medical data in individual homes. The service strategy also works for other target groups and can help to resolve typical problems which can arise between landlords and tenants. For example, the problem of rent arrears can be reduced by offering an external social consultancy service which helps the tenants to get back into a position of solvency (Behr et al. 2008).

In some cases all of these strategies are either impossible to finance or the owner is not interested in investing. The latter phenomenon seems to be concentrated in the stock of private non-professional landlords who are often quite old. A research project at the Institute for Housing and Environment will clarify the structure and the strategies of this group. The disinvestment 'strategy' is dangerous. Its negative external effects start within individual buildings but can spread to an entire neighbourhood. In the latest evaluation report of the Hessian subsidy programme for at risk neighbourhoods, the Institute for Housing and Environment identified three types of buildings that are especially at risk (von Malottki, Kirchner, Altschiller 2010):

- Large condominiums dating from the seventies, where the elderly flat owners die or leave the building and their heirs let the dwelling without consideration of a stable social structure in the building. An additional problem can arise in cases of multiple ownership, when the complete refurbishment of a building is quite an impossible process, due to the structure of different interests within the assembly of owners.
- Owners of decaying buildings with demolition costs which are higher than the land value and that are let exclusively to discriminated tenant groups. (see the remark about discrimination above).
- Buildings subject to repeated portfolio transactions, where the buyers do not have a long-term interest in a stable neighbourhood and search for the 'greater fool' to buy the dwellings.

Policy implications and the link between housing policy and urban planning

The above analysis and discussion proves that there are several strategies which can help to restore the attractiveness of the existing housing stock. Given a market condition without demand decrease and housing stock in a good location, the measures can be financed within the framework of the private housing market.

However, the market fails under certain circumstances which are mainly influenced by the overall quantity of demand and the changes in the preference structure. In this context it is not only important to look at the German housing policy but also at the policy in the field which has consequences for housing, social segregation, filtering processes and the number and location of new build (Kirchner 2006). In this context, spatial and urban planning plays a major role for a coordinated urban policy.

Object-related subsidies, social housing, demolition funding and land supply

Object-related subsidies are paid to owners that erect or renovate dwellings. Even in the metropolitan regions the new construction of social housing projects has fallen dramatically. The solution can be to shift the allocation of affordable or social housing from one building to another within a larger pool of dwellings. The advantage for the owner consists of the possibility of letting the newly built dwellings in higher market segments. The main question is under which circumstances this shifting process has positive or negative effects on the social composition of neighbourhoods and on the profitability of new housing projects.

Urban planning can act as an object-related subsidy in a very problematic way. In shrinking regions it is extremely problematic to bring large amounts of suburban housing land into the market. It speeds up filtering out the at risk stock and increases the vacancy rate. One could argue that public policy should not act against the housing preferences of the population. However, the preference for suburban single-family housing and the subsequent augmentation of the vacancy rate in the problematic stock causes substantial negative external effects for the public purse. High rates of vacancy are problematic because they attract vandalism and do not contribute to the maintenance of public infrastructure. Additionally, even the simple maintenance of the building can no longer be financed. Given the weakness of regional planning authorities the increase of allocated suburban housing land is difficult to avoid.

In this context, the demolition of problematic stock could free up land for reuse as single-family housing in appropriate locations, thereby helping to avoid (additional) greenfield development. This strategy could also help to refinance the demolition costs. The advantage of the existing infrastructure and the stabilisation of the spatial structure of the city may even justify public subsidies to help with demolition costs. With regards to spatial and urban planning new flexible instruments and planning processes have to be developed to meet both challenges shrinkage and reductions of density as well as densification of existing neighbourhoods in areas where growth management is required to avoid negative external effects of development pressures.

One could also argue that large portfolio owners of partly vacant buildings should pay for the demolition themselves. But the consequence of this would be a rent augmentation for the remaining occupied dwellings – and an even weaker position of the stock on the market. (It could be argued that when landlords have to pay for demolition themselves, they will never do it because they will weaken the position of their remaining stock in relation to competitors). The situation is definitely more complex in case of the multiple ownership of (partly) vacant buildings within the same neighbourhood. This constellation could lead to a 'free rider' problem if one owner demolishes part of the stock and the other owners benefit from this correction of the market without bearing demolition costs themselves. In this case a moderation process and/or public funding may be necessary. The parallel patterns of growth and decline may lead to the paradoxical situation that the public sector may have to provide subsidies for construction and for demolition at the same time.

Subject-related subsidies and social welfare system

In addition to the object-oriented subsidies and the influence of spatial planning, the German housing market is strongly influenced by subject-related housing subsidies that are paid to the welfare recipients themselves. The relevant effects emerge from social welfare system reform in 2005. The so called 'Hartz-IV-reforms' (named after the main architect of this system) merged social welfare and long-term unemployment subsidies. They also include a housing benefit element. Since 2005 the rent subsidy of the long-term unemployed is limited to a so called 'limit of adequate housing costs' determined at a regional level. As a consequence, households with a rent level above the limit have to relocate. A specific characteristic of welfare recipients is their small household size with the share of one-person households above the population average. Especially in suburban regions the need for small, cheap flats is not met because there is a lack of such small units (the social housing programs of the past decades were made for larger households) and the aforementioned subsidies (including the housing benefit element) are not high enough to cover the rents of newly erected buildings. The spatial consequences of the new regulations have not been exhaustively evaluated yet. Although the new welfare agencies do not have the interest or competence to govern the housing market, it is very likely that the definition of the 'adequate' market segment for certain households will have direct consequences for the housing market and the social pattern within cities or regions. The first evaluations show that the limit of adequacy is a very critical variable (Jacobs 2009). Fixed at too low a level, the welfare recipients are forced exclusively into cheap areas of a city or region, which offer a lower quality of life and fewer opportunities for upward social mobility – negative segregation is likely to rise. Fixed at too high a level, owners may develop a strategy of giving welfare recipients priority over other low-income groups who in turn may find it more difficult to find adequate accommodation. Beside the high costs to the public purse, a gentrification strategy relying on students or creative industries may be impeded. The problem can only be solved with very detailed market surveys and the definition of spatially differentiated 'levels of adequate housing costs' (von Malottki, Berner 2010). Hedonic price models improve the analysis of the price structure. Good management of these parameters may help to create stable social structures and may increase the success of urban regeneration measures that are usually carried out in the problem areas mentioned above. Again, a coordinated approach of urban planning and housing policy may improve the quality of the results.

References

Behr, I., Cischinsky, H., Malottki, C. von and Greiff, R. 2008. *Neue Soziale Fragen des Wohnens*. Darmstadt.

Bundesamtes für Bauwesen und Raumordnung (BBR). 2005. *Raumordnungsbericht 2005*. Bonn: Selbstverlag des Bundesamtes für Bauwesen und Raumordnung; Bundesamt.

Diefenbach, N. and Born, R. *Basisdaten für Hochrechnungen mit der Deutschen Gebäudetypologie des IWU*. [Online] Available at: http://www.iwu.de/fileadmin/user_upload/dateien/energie/klima_altbau/Flaechen_Gebaeudetypologie_07.pdf [accessed: 18 July 2011].

Jacobs, T. 2009. *Kosten der Unterkunft und die Wohnungsmärkte: Auswirkungen der Regelungen zur Übernahme der Kosten der Unterkunft auf Transferleistungsempfänger und Kommunen;*. Berlin, Bonn: BMVBS; BBSR.

Jekel, G. (ed.). 2010. *Stadtpolitik und das neue Wohnen in der Innenstadt*. Berlin: DIFU (Deutsches Institut für Urbanistik).

Kirchner, J. 2006. *Safeguarding target-groups-specific housing supply, A European comparison: Final Report*. Darmstadt.

Kirchner, J. and Rodenfels, M. 2008. *Wohnungsbedarfsprognose Hessen 2030: Endbericht*. Darmstadt.

Kirchner, J. and Stercz. 2007. *Vorbereitende Untersuchung für kommunale Wohnraumversorgungskonzepte in der Stadt und im Landkreis Fulda – und – Ergänzende Untersuchung zu einem kommunalen Wohnraumversorgungskonzept für den Landkreis und die Stadt Fulda*. Darmstadt.

Malottki, C. von and Berner, B. 2010. Grundsicherungsrelevante Mietspiegel unter Berücksichtigung der Verfügbarkeit. *(NDV) Nachrichtendienst des Deutschen Vereins für öffentliche und private Fürsorge*, (08), 349–54.

Malottki, C. von, Kirchner, J. and Altschiller, C. 2010. *Wohnraumversorgung in Soziale-Stadt-Gebieten: Leitfaden für die Fortschreibung der Integrierten Handlungskonzepte im Themenfeld Wohnen*. Darmstadt.

Spars, G., Heinze, M. and Mrosek, H. 2008. *Expertise: Stadtrendite durch kommunale Wohnungsunternehmen*. Bonn.

van den Busch, U. 2007. *Bevölkerungsvorausschätzung für die hessischen Landkreise und kreisfreien Städte bis 2050*. Wiesbaden.

Chapter 10

Sustainable Suburbia through the Perspective of Lower Density and Shrinkage: The Case Study of the Nagoya Metropolitan Region in Japan

Kiyonobu Kaido, Tsuruta Yosiko

Overview

This chapter focuses on old suburban residential areas, developed mainly for commuters of Japan's Nagoya metropolitan area in the 1970s and 1980s. The focus here is how to evolve these areas into more sustainable urban districts as they continue to experience a decrease in population. The study consists of four parts: (1) a concept of sustainable suburbia, (2) the spatial structure of the Nagoya City region and the characteristics of suburban housing estates, (3) characteristics and views of residents of suburban housing estates, and (4) the sustainability of suburban housing estates.

The resiliency of the city and its greater urban region affects the sustainability of suburban housing estates. Some suburban housing estates are changing to become more localized communities in their own right, rather than bedroom suburbs for long distance commuting. Many, but not all, suburban housing estates have the possibility of becoming more sustainable with positive benefitsand more supportive of adopted public policies. Even if compact city development is most suitable and more desirable for achieving overall sustainable urban form, urban areas also benefit from having various types of homes and housing areas, including those in more vibrant suburban districts.

Background and purpose

Japanese society is now faced with a reduction in population after a period of growth that continued for about 100 years, starting in the second half of nineteenth century (Figure 10.1). Some new characteristics of urbanisation in Japan began to emerge after the 1990s: (1) a rapid decrease in population and disappearance of rural villages in remote areas; (2) population reductions and lower densities in small and medium-sized cities and towns; (3) large urban areas that attract many customers

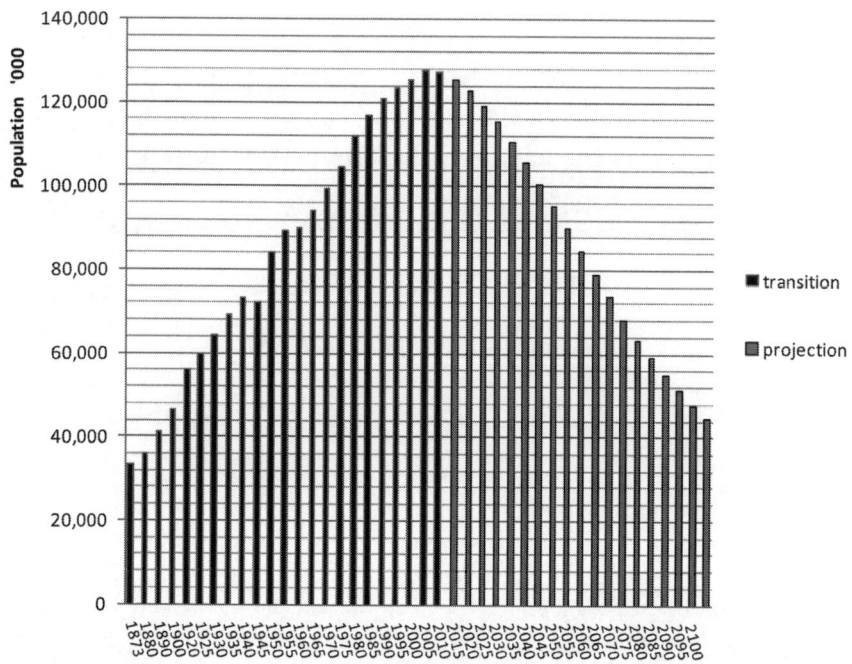

Figure 10.1 Population transition and projection in Japan, 1873–2100

Source: Illustration by authors with data from the national census (transition) and National Institute of Population and Social Security research (prediction)

for retail and entertainment; (4) ageing population and lower densities in suburban residential areas or 'new towns'; (5) a hollowing out of city and town centres in most local cities and towns; (6) population decrease and ageing in inner city areas; (7) shifting land uses from industrial sites to multifamily housing areas or shopping centres; and (8) population growth or recovery and construction of many apartment houses in metropolises or large city centres and around rail stations.

These new characteristics of today's urbanisation in Japan seem different from the conditions in other countries, such as the United Kingdom, but it is accepted that they both are preceding in a similar direction of unbalanced development of a mature society(Ravetz, Roberts 2000).

The old suburban residential areas in the Nagoya metropolitan region consist of detached houses developed by private companies. They were first developed mainly as homes for commuters to metropolitan business centres. Today, the residents are ageing and many housing areas have a reduced population, mainly because the younger generation has moved out in order to find a job, proceed to higher education or to marry. Some suburban housing areas may become less sustainable. In any case, various policies, planning tools, urban design concepts and activities are needed to make them more sustainable and to promote the 'smart shrinkage' of suburbia.

Recently, many cities and urban regions in Japan have established the concept of the compact city as their future city vision. The national government has amended legislation about town planning law in order to allow local governments to control development with their own policies in response to local conditions. However, special efforts are needed to make cities more compact in a society with a shrinking population. Suburban residential areas are one of the most important problems to understand and address with sufficient research and study. Many suburban residential areas are confronting population reduction and the ageing of their residents. The average 'life-span' of Japanese houses is about 30 years –much shorter than their European or American counterparts. Decreasing population and shrinking urban regions are new and serious problems in Japanese society.

What are sustainable suburbs?

What are suburbs?

Suburbs should be viewed as an organic and related part of an urban region, with a relationship to the inner city or urban centre. It has been said that suburbs are the 'forgotten dimension' within governmental urban policy (Boland, Simpson 2007: 1–2).In Japan too, urban policies concerning suburban residential areas have only recently emerged as a concern for central government and local governments.

Suburbs can have a broad range of characteristics. A report by The Civic Trust summarizes them briefly as

> 'traditionally associated with a medium/low density residential area, with homes and gardens of similar size and type, adjacent to the city but dependent on it for employment, services and trade.'(Gwilliam 1998: 5)

That report also shows the traditional perception of suburban houses as primarily favoured by and for families, mainly owner occupied, often with green public spaces, and often detached or semi-detached houses. But suburbs are much more diverse. A report (Office of the Deputy Prime Minister (ODPM) 2005) points outs what the issues are and what we should do about them:

- The difficulty in precisely defining suburbs;
- Existing suburbs are changing;
- The need to improve the sustainability of suburbs; and
- The need to retain or improve quality of life in suburbs.

The characteristics of suburbs and suburban housing estates in the European and North American settings are similar to Japan, although there are also significant distinctions.

Criteria of sustainable housing development

The Commission for Architecture and Built Environment developed a useful set of sustainability criteria in a study titled'Building for Life.' Among the criteria, it mentions (1) environment and community, (2) characters, (3) streets, (4) parking and pedestrianisation, (5) design and construction.(Commission for Architecture and Built Environment (CABE) 2002) Similarly, a recent report prepared in the United Kingdom on sustainable communities also provides a number principles that should be taken into account:

> 'consider the context; improve environmental sustainability; improve existing housing stock; improve sustainable travel; protect and promote appropriate suburban employment; reinforce the role of local centres; improve infrastructure and services; improve the quality of design and the public realm; and ensure social inclusion and community safety.' (Office of the Deputy Prime Minister (ODPM) 2005: 15)

In yet another set of guidelines for sustainability, the following factors are offered: (1) maximize proximity to facilities and public transport and to encourage walking and cycling instead of the use of cars,(2) safeguard the existing ecology and improve the natural habitat,(3) minimize energy consumption, (4) conserve water resources and reduce its consumption, and (5) recycle materials and reduce waste. As for mixed use developments, non-residential uses, including offices, shops, and services should be incorporatedinto residential facilities(see the discussion of the *Essex Design Guide* by Moon 2005).

Looking once again at lessons from the United Kingdom, one of the primary objectives of the country's housing policy is to provide for adequate housing through the development local and community-based plans and planning decisions.

> 'Planning shapes the places where people live and work and the country we live in. It plays a key role in supporting the Government's wider social, environmental and economic objectives and for sustainable communities'. (Department for Communities and Local Government 2006: front cover)

The specific outcomes of the planning system should include:

- High quality housing that is well-designed and built to a high standard.
- A mix of housing, both market and affordable, particularly in terms of tenure and price, to support a wide variety of households in all areas, both urban and rural.
- A sufficient quantity of housing taking into account need and demand and seeking to improve choice.
- Housing developments in suitable locations, which offer a good range of community facilities and with good access to jobs, key services and infrastructure.
- A flexible, responsive supply of land – managed in a way that makes efficient and effective use of land, including re-use of previously-developed land, where appropriate.

Suburban housing estates in Japan

Japan's criteria for housing development do not focus as clearly on the concept of sustainability to the same degree as in the United Kingdom and other countries. There is very little guidance for creating a more sustainable future for the country's suburban housing estate developments. The population of Japan is predicted to decline through the twenty-first century. The Nagoya area will also lose population. Old suburban housing estates were developed 20 or 30 years ago mainly for nuclear families commuting into central Nagoya. Now most residents are ageing and their children are leaving the nest. New housing development in the suburbs is almost at a standstill and there is a new wave of people moving back to the city. The change is slow but steady. Some forward-thinking community and voluntary groups have begun to form to resolve problems in their own neighbourhoods. The national government and most local governments in Japan have not yet established clear policies for declining suburban housing areas.

The following questions are posed regarding the sustainability of suburban housing estates where the population is ageing or declining in numbers.

- Are ageing residents who hope to remain in their current homes able to live in safety and security, especially without using private cars?
- Can communities support healthy and attractive housing?
- If depopulation continues, how will spatial conditions change and will vacant lots and houses increase and damage the character of the community?
- What will be the impacts of increasing costs to supply and manage public services because of decreasing density?

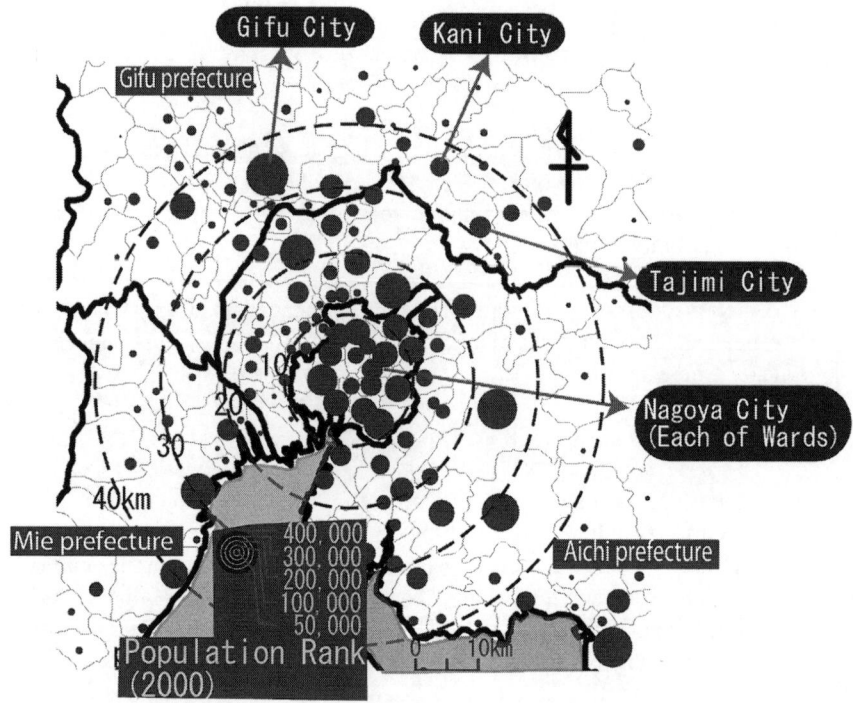

Figure 10.2   Population location in Nagoya City region and the location of three cities

Source: Illustration by authors with data of census 2005

The spatial structure of the Nagoya City region and the condition of the suburban housing estates

The Nagoya City region includes three prefectures: (1) Aichi, (2) Mie and (3) Gifu. The area is the third largest urban region in Japan. The radius is about 40 kilometres and the population is about eight million (Kaido, Kwon 2008). The central city is Nagoya City which had a population of approximately 2,260,000 and approximately 1,020,000 households in 2010. The spatial form of the Nagoya City region shows a polycentric pattern with both historic cities and newer municipalities. The population density is lower and automobile transportation is more popular than in the Tokyo and Osaka metropolitan regions. Three cities in the Nagoya City region were selected as the subject of the study: Gifu City, Tajimi City and Kani City. They are each located about 30 to 35 kilometres from the center of Nagoya, but each city has different characteristics (Figure 10.2).

Gifu City, which had a population of approximately 420,000 and 170,000 households (in 2010), is the governmental centre in Gifu prefecture with its own

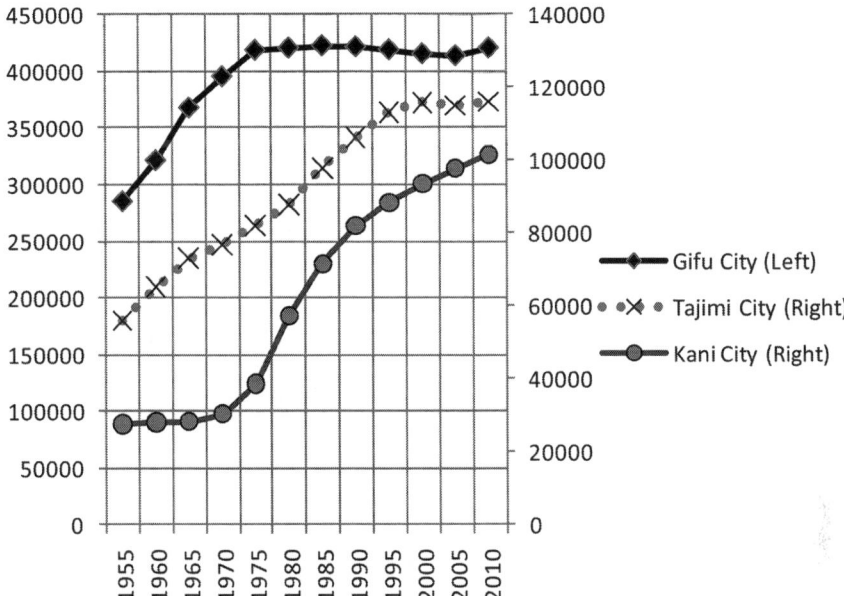

Figure 10.3   Transition of population of Gifu, Tajimi and Kani City

Source: Illustration by authors with data of census by areas of administrative districts in 2010

city region, industries, history and culture. Its characteristics as a suburban city of the Nagoya city region have recently become more pronounced. It is very close to Nagoya station, only 18 minutes by train. Tajimi City, which has a population of 116,000 and 44,000 households, has strengthened its characteristics as a suburban commuter city with the recent siting of a major ceramic industry facility. The commuting time from Nagoya station to Tajimi station is 30 to 40 minutes. Kani City, which has a population of 102,000 and 39,000 households, shows characteristics of both an industrial and commuter area to Nagoya city region. The commuting time to Nagoya station is 45 to 55 minutes.

The short history of the development of three cities

Many housing estates have been developed in the three cities, but significant new housing estates have not been constructed since 2000. The timeline and scales for each city are different (Figure 10.3). In Gifu City, the population had been steadily growing by about 10 per cent for every five year period between the late 1950s and the 1970s; and the number of households grew about 15 to 30 per cent during that period.

In *Kani City*, the population grew by about 60 per cent and the number of households by 70 per cent from 1975 to 1985. Kani City's population growth rate was the highest in all Japanese cities during that period. Tajimi City shows a different growth pattern, with a more steady growth rate at about 10 per cent for every five years between 1955 and the early 1990s; and about 10 to 20 per cent increase in the number of households during that period. Detached housing estates developed in hilly areas by private development companies in each of these cities. Since 2000 the development of many small apartments on what had been farmland began to increase in Kani City. In Tajimi City population growth levelled off after the late 1990s.

In *Gifu City* 57 housing estates were larger than one hectare with about 8,600 houses. In Kani City, there were 48 housing estates with about 12,000 houses. *Tajimi City* had 84 housing estates with about 11,300 houses. The average number of homes per housing estate is 150 houses in Gifu, 450 in Kani and 220 in Tajimi. The housing estates are generally larger in Kani where 500 houses or more are common. In Tajimi and Gifu housing estates with 100 houses or fewer are more typical.

The characteristics and main types of suburban housing estates

Suburban housing estates in the Nagoya City region have been developed primarily by private development companies, except for a few large 'new towns' developed by the public sector. The key characteristics of these housing estates are:

- Type of houses – detached houses and home ownership. (Note: Both developed and undeveloped lots are sold)
- Average lot areas–about 150 to 210 (or 300) square metres (Note: larger lots are more common further from main city centres)
- Quality of houses – average by area
- Land uses — single use housing areas, not mixed-use
- Quality of housing environment – few amenities or facilities, especially in smaller scale housing estates
- Daily life – highly dependent on car use for shopping and other daily needs
- Original lands for development – new development in hilly areas
- Transport – poor accessibility to rail stations and bus services

Three different types of suburban housing estates are found within the Nogoya urban region (Figure 10.4).

Type A is mainly for commuters to central Nagoya, as well as closer to rail stations. Type B is not only for commuters to central Nagoya, but also to neighbouring local cities. Type C is mainly for commuters to neighbouring areas by means of private automobile.

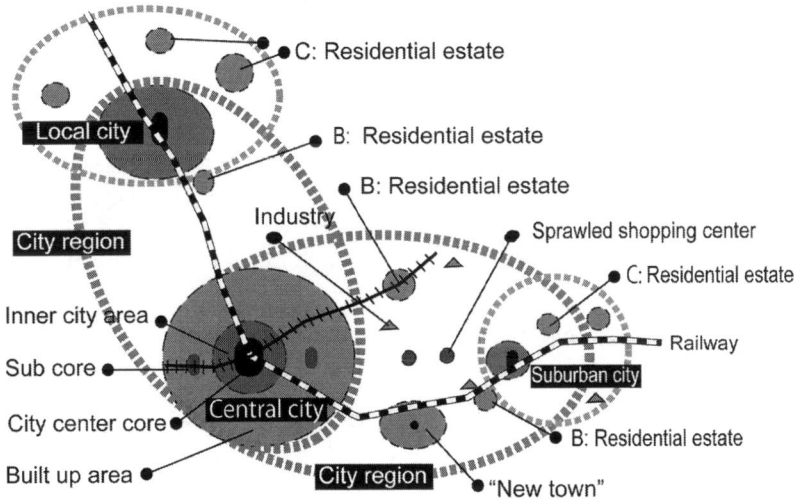

Figure 10.4   Three types of suburban housing estates in the Nagoya City region

Source: Illustration of authors

Lives and thoughts of inhabitants of suburban housing estates

Basic conditions of each housing estate type

Three different housing estates were selected as the subject for further investigation in this portion of the study: (1) *Tajimi-E* is located in Tajimi city as type A, (2) *Kani-E* is located in Kani city as type B, and (3) *Gifu-E* is located in Gifu city as type C. They were each developed by different private companies about 25 years ago and occupy a larger than average area for their housing estates than in the region as a whole. Most houses are detached houses. **Table 10.1** provides detailed information on the characteristics of each of these housing estates.

Table 10.1   Outline of the characteristics of each of housing estates

Item/ Each estate	Gifu-E	Tajimi-E	Kani-E
Initially inhabited (year)	1975	1981	1973
Development area (hectare)	54.1	120.3	98.0
The number of housing lots (Initial plan)	2,040	2,479	1,618
Population (#**)	5,133	7,547	3,783

Item/ Each estate	Gifu-E	Tajimi-E	Kani-E
Households (#**)	1,984	2,348	1,456
Ratio of vacant lots (%**)	3.8	3.5	10.8
Ratio of vacant houses (%**)	3.0	0.8	4.1
Average lot size (m2**)	204	213	278
Number of rail stations within 3 km radius	0	2	1
Number of bus runs in one working day (#**)	51	71	38
Rate of commuters to Nagoya City (%*)	4.7	50.2	36.2
Rate of commuters within the City (%*)	48.5	9.1	14.2
Rate of car commuting (%*)	84.5	46.0	58.8
Commuters who takes more than one hour to get to work (%**)	14.1	42.4	31.9
Moved from within the same city (%**)	71.4	7.7	4.5
Purchase of new house and lot (%**)	26.6	68.9	36.0

Source: Illustration by authors with data of the governmental office of Gifu Prefecture and original research by authors, *survey at 2005, **survey at 2007

Age composition, transition and projection of population

Many of the older housing estates in the three cities have experienced a reduction in the number of residents, but the total number of household has not decreased. However, household size is shrinking. Kani-E provides an example of the shifting age composition (Figure 10.5). The population was 3,900 and there were about 1,000 households in 1985, when most lots were occupied with a single house. The graph of ages displays two peaks around the ages of 35 to 44 (for parents) and the ages of 5 to 14 years (for children). The number of senior persons (ages 65 and over) is only four per cent.

The population peaked in 1997 at 4,289, and after that began to decrease. The population in 2010 was at 3,894. The average size of households has dropped from 3.67 in 1985 to 2.59 in 2010. The shrinking of the population has also been accompanied by an ageing of the population. The percentage of senior citizens has increased from 4.5 per cent in 1985 to 16.9 per cent in 2005.

Kani-E has lost about 1200 from its peak year (1997). It is forecast to have a population of only 2,945 by 2025 with 48.3 per cent of the population being senior citizens. Unless younger families with children begin to move in, the trend

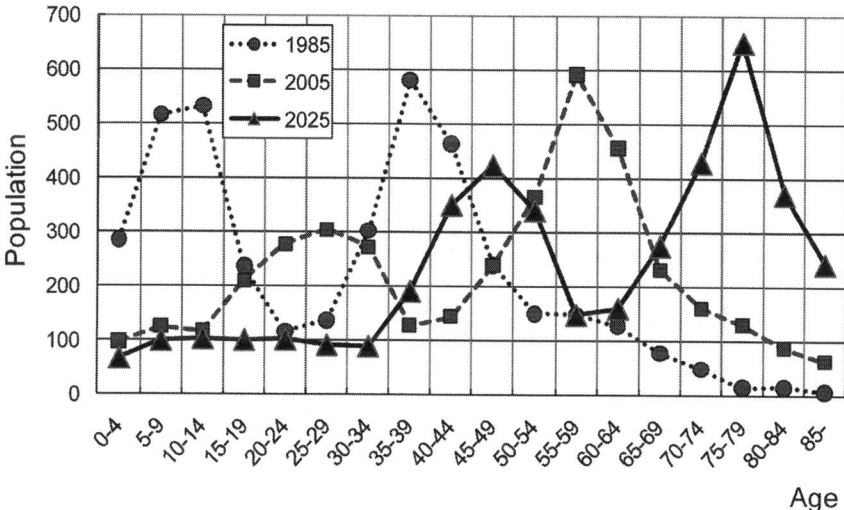

Figure 10.5 Transition and prediction of age composition of inhabitants in Kani-E

Source: Illustration by authors with data of census and original forecast

of population decrease and rapid increase in the percentage of senior residents is expected to continue.

Lifestyle of inhabitants

Ownership and use of private cars
The ratio of automobile ownership is almost 100 per cent and about 60 per cent of residents own two or more vehicles. The means of transportation for daily shopping is 80 to 90 per cent by car. It is lower in Kani-E where a supermarket is located in the estate. Private car use is essential for daily life in these suburban estates.

Main reasons for selecting the estate and the house
The main reasons (multiple answers) for selecting a particular estate and house to live in are (1) 'adequacy of house price' (50 per cent or more in Gifu-E), (2) 'excellent townscape' (the most common reason in Kani-E), and (3) 'excellent transit' (high response in Tajimi-E). Thesee answers reflect the unique characteristics of each estate. 'Excellent nature' and 'adequate size of site' also received high responses overall.

More than 40 per cent of residents feel dissatisfied with the street environment for walking, and with the accessibility to rail stations, shops, and medical facilities. In general, accessibility to shops and medical facilities ranked the highest. The second most important aspect is safety. Many inhabitants feel fairly satisfied with the natural environment, community activities and townscape – however these factors did not rank as high.

Lifestyle desires and expectations
Many inhabitants in Kani-E desire a typical life in suburbia and feel that they have achieved this goal. For example, they enjoy maintaining a home and garden, and get along well with their neighbours. They enjoy both concerts and shopping, although there are actually relatively few opportunities. Community involvement and volunteer work are slightly lower preferences for the residents and there are also few opportunities.

Evaluation of living environment
The degree of satisfaction with the overall living environment is higher in Kani-E. The total number of respondents for 'quite satisfied' and 'rather satisfied' is 57 per cent, compared to only 18 per cent in Gifu-E. In Kani-E, 78 per cent of the respondents intend to continue to living in the community, but only 68 per cent in Gifu-E and 61 per cent in Tajimi-E. Inconveniences in daily life, such as limited accessibility to shops or medical facilities, are a significant reason given for wanting to move out. The desire to live in a more urbanized area ranks at 20 per cent in Kani-E. These results show that the main reasons for wanting to move out come from dissatisfaction with suburban living.

Inner structure and sustainability characteristics of the suburban housing estate

The condition of vacant lots and vacant houses

The condition of vacant lots and vacant houses in all of the old housing estates (1 hectare or more in area) which were developed 20 or more years ago in the three cities were researched in 2006 and 2007. In Kani City, 19 estates with a total of about 12,600 lots were analysed. In Tajimi City 31 estates with about 10,400 lots were analysed, and 58 estates with about 8,600 lots in Gifu City. The rate of vacant lots and vacant houses were 15.1 per cent and 1.5 per cent respectively in Kani City, 9.2 per cent and 0.8 per cent in Tajimi City, and 10.6 per cent and 2.7 per cent in Gifu City. Most vacant lots had never been built on. In other words, vacant lots resulting from demolition of older structures are relatively few. Depopulation in these older housing estates results in a shrinking of household size, but has not resulted in an increase of vacant houses.

The rate of vacant lots varies significantly difference between the estates. Two estates in Kani City and one in Tajimi City had a rate of vacant lots at more than 40 per cent. In Kani City six estates had a vacancy rateof more than 20 per cent of the lots, with seven in Tajimi City and six in Gifu City. The use of vacant lots for parking ranges from 20 to 30 per cent and the use for community gardens is at

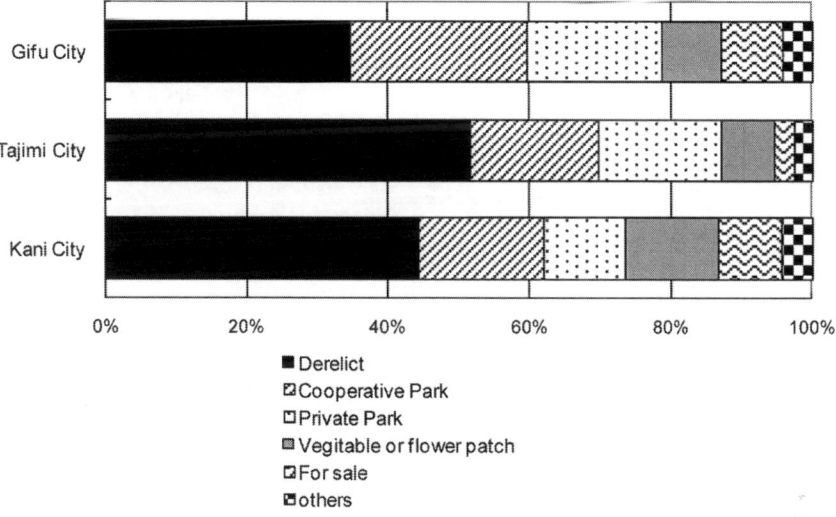

Figure 10.6   Condition of vacant lots

Source: Illustration by authors by original research

about 10 per cent. While the ratio of vacant houses is only one to two per cent, most are in a derelict condition (Figure 10.6).

The characteristics of new housing estates

If old housing estates can attract new housing demand, the sustainability of these communities will increase. The neighbouring housing estates, K-estate and H-estate in Kani City, have been managed by a private company since the late 1990s and many new residents have moved in recently.

K-estates: People started moving in 1994 and it has the population of 1,100, and 370 households in 2008. All houses are of a detached housing type and the average lot size is 320 square metres. The average age range per household is between 30 years old to 50 and their income levels are generally high. Only 20 per cent of the locations to which people commute are within Kani City and Nagoya City. The main reason for selecting an estate is 'good townscape'. Other reasons include large lots and a nice natural environment.

H-estate: People started moving in 2005 and it has a population of 650 and 200 households in 2008. All houses are detached and the average lot size is 210 square metres. The main age range of residents is narrower, with most residents being in their early 30s. Their income levels are not as high. Around 35 per cent of the residents commute within Kani City and 13 per cent to Nagoya City. The main

Figure 10.7   Main reasons for not purchasing an existing home (multiple answers)

Source: Illustration by authors by original research

reason for selecting the estate is suitable house prices. Residents also like that the development is new.

The residents of both estates strongly depend on the private automobile for daily life. They think that accessibility to shops and medical facilities and safety are very important. On the other hand, in H-estate the distance to a primary school is 3 kilometres and hardly any services are located in the estate. Many residents in H-estate think that neighbourliness is very important. Residents perceive new houses to be 'beautiful and friendly' and view existing homes as 'uncomfortable' (Figure 10.7). Improving the quality of existing homes and new housing in old estates may be helpful in order to attract new housing demand.

Main characteristics of researched housing estates

The main findings of the research are:

- Old housing estates which were developed for the rapid growth of population and households are now beginning to show the stages of rapid ageing, shrinkage of household size, and decrease in population.
- The degree of overall satisfaction with the living environment and the

desire to remain in the current residence are correlated.

- Daily life in suburban housing estates strongly depends on the use of private cars. The important factors for residents are accessibility to services and facilities, as well as crime safety. Services and facilities are especially important for senior citizens.

- Most suburban housing estates do not have comprehensive services for daily life. The opportunity for employment and the convenient access to services or facilities within the city region are essential for people to stay in the community. However, people who prefer to live in more convenient areas and have greater economic potential may move to more urbanized areas.

- The reduction in the number of households in most housing estates has not yet become an issue. The quality of existing old houses is generally not very high. The value of existing homes is declining (note-1) and new occupation rates are not very high.

- The increasing number of vacant lots and vacant houses accelerate the decline of housing estates where the number of households is decreasing.

- The characteristics of suburban housing estates in the era of urban expansion have been reproduced in new housing estates where the factors of new development and homes at low prices have attracted initial residents. However, commuting to nearby employment is on the rise.

- Support for community activities is weakened because of an ageing population and decrease in number of residents.

Sustainability of suburban housing estates

The study demonstrates that there are many challenges for the sustainability of suburban housing estates in the Nagoya City region. **Table 10.2** shows the conditions, difficulties or possibilities of sustainability of suburban housing estates.

Table 10.2   Conditions and difficulties or possibilities of sustainability of suburban housing estates

Aspects	Conditions	Difficulties or Possibilities
Inhabitants and Community	Ageing, population reduction; Homogeneous age structure and social class; Few newcomers; Increase in moving in with blood relatives or commuters to closer areas; Neighbourhood association is participated in by most neighbours	Lower density; High ratio (close to 100%) of membership of neighbourhood association; Loss of community vitality by ageing neighbours; Increasing risk of crime Weakened human connection; Indication of mutual cooperation activities
Daily life and Location	Loss or lack of day service facilities and work places; Separated job locations Awkward public transit and car dependency;	Inconvenient daily life without using a car; On- street parking in narrow neighbourhood road; Keeping a private garden; Roomy detached house for single or two persons household;
Development or environment	Unplanned, dispersed and small in size; Greenfield development; Hilly areas development	Difficulty in walking on steep streets; Expensive and inefficient infrastructure management; Close to nature; Wide range of housing environments
Housing market	Shrinking; Mainly owner occupied houses; Mainly detached houses; Uniform size of lots; Large or small ratio of vacant housing lots and houses	Lack of diversity of housing; Weak response to change of needs; Price slump of lands and houses; Abandonment of maintenance of vacant lots or houses; Abilities to reuse vacant lands

Source: Illustration by authors

Both sides of the sustainability of suburban housing estates

The sustainability of suburban housing estates has two sides. On the one hand, they can exist as stable and fully contained housing areas in themselves. On the other hand, they are positioned to become a part of a sustainable city or urban region. In other words, if the compact city is a sustainable urban form, then the continuation of sprawling and low density suburban housing estates of poor quality impacts the sustainability of the entire city and/or the greater urban region.

Eight factors are necessary to enhance the sustainability of housing estates:

- Residents who continue to live in the same housing estate
- A certain number of new residents moving in
- Diversity of age groups, family types and income levels of inhabitants
- Keeping house and land prices stable
- Accessibility to daily needs and services, such as shopping or medical facilities
- Safety and security from crime and environmental pollution
- Low environmental impacts and a rich natural environment
- Positive self-governance by residents

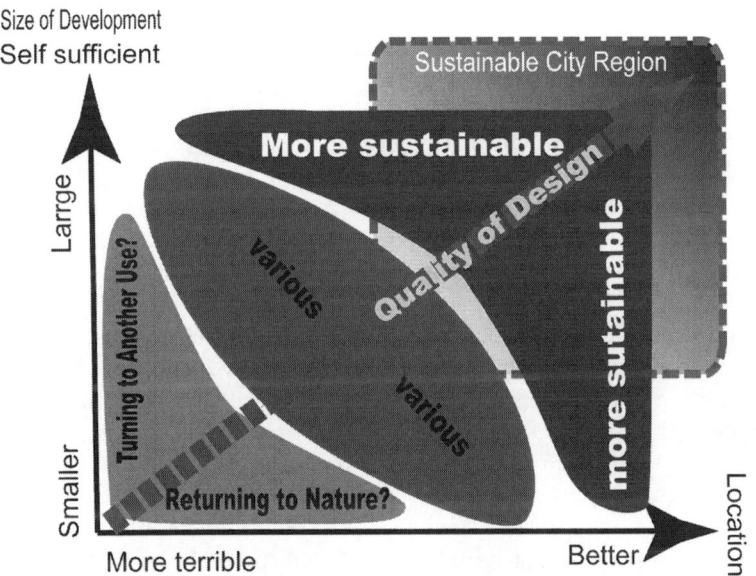

Figure 10.8   Sustainability and future scenarios of suburban residential estates

Source: Illustration by authors

Figure 10.8 shows some patterns of sustainability and future scenarios of suburban residential estates. Sustainability of suburban housing estates depends on basic characteristics, such as location and transportation, self-sufficiency and mixed land uses, the size of the development and its distribution, and the quality of the spatial condition and design. The sustainability of a city and urban region strongly affects the sustainability of suburban housing estates within it. One possible scenario is to convert housing estates with insufficient sustainability to another land use or back into natural areas. However it be possible that small housing estates with poor locations can be sustained as low density housing areas or rural communities, perhaps as leisure homes.

Conclusions

Policies and planning methods to enhance the sustainability of suburban housing estates

Today's Japanese cities are facing a new phase of urban development after a period of rapid urban growth. If suburban housing areas where 70 to 80 per cent of all urban area residents now live are to be able to enhance sustainability as a whole rather than declining, then a broad range of residential demand need to be satisfied.

The findings of this study indicate that the sustainability of cities and city regions can be enhanced by diversifying housing types to attract residents of all age groups. This includes improving the quality of homes, through better renovation and reconstruction. It is important to address vacant properties and derelict lots as suburban districts experience a loss of population. This can be in the form of cooperative management of vacant lands or other forms of property management regulation.

Suburban areas should be enhanced, with adequate parks and gardens, improved public spaces, a better mix of land uses, and the use of design guidelines. A broader array of community activities also contribute to sustainability and the well-being of residents, including the provision of meeting spaces, the establishment of community associations and neighbourhood organizations, and the creation of communication networks to offer news and information to residents. Mobility and accessibility should also be enhanced by providing community-based taxi, buses, and ride-sharing services.

It would be most advantageous for each housing estate to establish its own process for identifying which planning tools and approaches to sustainability are best suited for its context. That is important for ensuring that the residents themselves are investing their own talents and time to create long-term sustainability for their communities and generations to come.

References

Boland, L. and Simpson, J. 2007. *State of the suburbs: An economic, social and environmental analysis of the English suburbs.* London.

Commission for Architecture and Built Environment (CABE). *Building For Life: The 20 criteria.* [Online] Available at: http://webarchive.nationalarchives.gov.

uk/20110107165544/http:/www.buildingforlife.org/criteria [accessed: 29 June 2011].

Department for Communities and Local Government. 2006. *Consultation on Planning Policy Statement 3 (PPS3): Housing.* London.

Gwilliam, M. 1998. *Sustainable renewal of suburban areas.* Layerthorpe, York: YPS for the Joseph Rowntree Foundation.

Kaido, K. and Kwon, J. 2008. Quality of Life and Spatial Urban Forms of Mega City Regions in Japan. in *World cities and urban form: Fragmented, polycentric, sustainable?*, edited by M. Jenks, D. Kozak and P. Takkanon. Abingdon, Oxon ;, New York: Routledge, 161–74.

Moon, E. 2005. *The Essex Design Guide.*

Office of the Deputy Prime Minister (ODPM). 2005. *Delivering Sustainable Communities: The Role of Local Authorities in the Delivery of New Quality Housing.* Wetherby, West Yorkshire.

Ravetz, J. and Roberts, P. 2000. *City-region 2020: Integrated planning for a sustainable environment.* London: Earthscan Publishers.

Chapter 11

Population Growth and Change in Non-Metropolitan Coastal Australia

Nicole Gurran, Barbara Norman, Elisabeth Hamin

Overview

This chapter examines the processes of urban and social change experienced by regions undergoing dramatic population shifts in peri- and non-metropolitan areas of coastal Australia. It focuses on population movements associated with a process known as amenity migration, whereby relocation is motivated by lifestyle aspirations, rather than to improve income or employment prospects. In this chapter we focus on the process of amenity migration as it has affected a sample of 67 coastal communities of Australia. There has been much policy concern about the environmental and social implications of amenity migration – or sea change as it is known in Australia. However, to date the emphasis of this concern has been on managing continued processes of rapid growth. Drawing on population data (1991–2006), we contend that the defining feature of amenity migration in much of non-metropolitan coastal Australia is instability, which includes periods of rapid growth but is often followed by growth stagnation and in some cases rapid decline. Understanding that popular amenity destinations are likely to experience a range of population movements – from sudden influxes of newcomers to equally rapid departures, or a constant turnover of residents, requires a far more nuanced set of social and physical planning responses. Referring to data on the broader demographic and economic trends characterising our sample of 67 coastal destinations in Australia (household formation rates, ageing, income and employment, housing characteristics), we outline the key planning challenges and approaches to managing change in high amenity regional settings. Overlaying our analysis are the implications of responding to such population instability within a context of high physical exposure to climate change impacts, particularly associated with sea level rise and storm surge.

Introduction

Rapid urban migration and consequent rural depopulation raise major issues for planners and environmental policy makers. However, equally significant issues arise when large numbers of people shift in the opposite direction – away from the city and towards peri or non-metropolitan areas. Often they gravitate to locations characterised by attractive natural scenery or productive farmland, so threatening important agricultural landscapes or fragile native ecosystems. The social and economic consequences of urban-rural migration may also be problematic. While some migration towards declining rural areas represents a welcome injection of new population for struggling country towns, newcomers compete with existing residents and tourism operators for new housing and infrastructure, often generating house price inflation and exacerbating underlying problems of rural unemployment and regional disadvantage.

This chapter examines these issues with specific reference to coastal Australia. Coastal amenity migration, or sea change, as the phenomenon is colloquially described in Australia, has been a defining concern of Australian regional and coastal planning since the mid-1970s (e.g., Burnley, Murphy 2004, Essex, Brown 1997, Sant, Simons 1993). To date the policy and planning emphasis has been on managing processes of rapid growth in coastal locations, with the expectation that such growth would only continue, bringing new jobs and economic opportunities to compensate for inevitable environmental change (Australian Labour Party (ALP) 2006, Greene 2005, Resource Assessment Commission (RAC) 1993). However, new research suggests that instability, rather than a steady growth trajectory, defines the experience of amenity migration in non-metropolitan coastal Australia. In this chapter we explore these themes of growth and change in coastal amenity regions of Australia using longitudinal data for a sample of 67 coastal communities. As well as population and migration trends, household formation rates, ageing, income and employment, and housing characteristics are reviewed over three national census periods (1991, 2001, 2006). We use this analysis to argue that amenity driven population change in Australia is associated with the emergence of several distinct features: instability associated with fluctuating migration and visitation; a sharpening chasm between wealthy newcomers, long-time residents, and welfare migrants; an unbalanced demographic profile tipping towards the frail aged; service oriented economies; and the emergence of suburban, rather than new urban patterns of coastal growth. We argue that these distinct features of Australian coastal amenity communities are likely to resonate in other amenity regions around the world, with specific implications for urban and environmental planners.

The first part of the chapter provides a brief overview of the international literature on amenity migration. Secondly we introduce the phenomenon of coastal amenity migration in Australia. Thirdly we present key data on demographic, housing, income and employment trends characterising our sample of 67 Australian coastal amenity destinations between 1991–2006 (Gurran, Squires 2008).[1] Finally we highlight the key policy and planning implications of amenity driven growth and change for affected regions in Australia and internationally.

---

1   Data presented here is sourced from the report Meeting the Sea Change Challenge: Sea Change Communities in Coastal Australia: Update Report and Data Supplement 2008.

Amenity migration

The profound social, technological and economic changes of the late twentieth century have provoked new patterns of urban and regional development. Despite an almost centrifugal population shift towards the major urban conurbations, some regions, particularly those distinguished by high quality natural landscapes and amenities, have experienced a new renaissance. Beyond the well-known 'sun'n'fun' destinations such as Florida in the United States, the Sunshine Coast in Australia, or the Costa del Sol in Spain, many formerly low key fishing and farming regions are experiencing new population pressures from those seeking a new life within an attractive natural setting.

Various theoretical frameworks are used to describe and explain such processes of growth and change beyond the major population centres. The term counter-urbanisation provides a broad description for major population shifts away from metropolitan areas, but usually implies a simultaneous process of regional growth and urban decline (e.g., Dahms, McComb 1999, Sant, Simons 1993). Sant, Simons 1993 emphasise that counter-urbanisation usually results in social change but not necessarily economic change and that it may not affect all potential 'source or destination areas' in the same way. They also argue that counter urbanisation can operate at the same time as other migration processes. Hence, an exodus of lifestyle aspirants to selected regional destinations might not necessarily disrupt overall patterns of international and domestic migration to major population centres.

Some use the more specific term population turnaround to describe the reversal of rural depopulation in selected non-metropolitan locations in nations such as Australia and the United States, the United Kingdom, and parts of Europe, where the rate of growth exceeded the major cities during the 1970s (Burnley 2005). Explanations for counterurbanisation processes or rural population turnaround include production-based (people moving for jobs) and consumption-based migration (people moving for lifestyle) (Sant, Simons 1993, Walmsley, Epps, Duncan 1998). In summary, post-fordist forms of production have allowed some industries to disperse, and new industries relating to culture, tourism, and leisure to emerge (Esparza, Carruthers 2000, Jones et al. 2003, Marcouiller, Clendenning, Kedzior 2002). Secondly, social, economic, and demographic changes of the late twentieth century have allowed a cohort of people not tied to a particular place for work – including retirees, pre retirees, and those on welfare benefits, as well as those willing to downshift -- to relocate to attractive, lifestyle oriented settings (Hamilton 2003, Hugo 2005, Marshall 2003). Terms used to describe these migration processes include retirement, welfare, and lifestyle migration (Haas, III, Serow 2002, Rodriguez, Fernandez-Mayoralas, Rojo 2004, Gurran, Blakely 2007, Marshall 2003). Thirdly, a parallel cultural shift towards leisure and tourism has created new jobs in tourist destinations, largely in retail and commercial sectors, with consequent job creation in health and personal services associated with retiree migration (Burnley 2005). Internationally, a phenomenon known as transnational retirement migration describes the emergence of wealthy retirees (predominantly from the United Kingdom, Northern Europe, and North America) shifting to warmer destinations in Southern Europe, South America, and, increasingly, parts of South East Asia (Gustafson 2001, Marcouiller, Clendenning, Kedzior 2002). These transnational retiree migrants typically spend summers in their country of origin, and winter in their second home.

While such migration processes may extend and reinforce ongoing patterns of seasonal visitation and second home tourism, when combined with increasing permanent migration of lifestyle residents and retirees, the cumulative impact can represent a profound social and environmental transformation. Describing processes of lifestyle migration in Southern Appalachia, Haas, III, Serow 2002 observes the impact of 'green migrants', who seek a lifestyle closer to nature and the 'rural frontier' (Haas, III, Serow 2002: 222), but create significant impacts for rural communities and their environments, including a need for new infrastructure (and higher local taxes, rates, and house prices), competition for farmland and consequent conversion to residential and rural residential development, soil erosion, riparian damage, habitat loss, water pollution and so on (Haas, III, Serow 2002). In responding to such pressures, it is important to recognize the unique processes of amenity led development and to plan in ways that focus specifically on the distinctive features of affected communities, rather than applying suburban solutions for accommodating growth on the edge of central cities (Marcouiller, Clendenning, Kedzior 2002). Metropolitan style approaches to accommodating growth not only extend suburban development further into untouched natural landscapes or the rural hinterland; they also seriously undermine the appeal of destinations reliant on tourism income. In particular, increasing numbers of retirees not only present a marketing challenge for resort towns striving for a glamourous tourism identity (Dredge 2001), but also transform the demographic profile of an area – requiring more intensive health care and community services to cater to the needs of the frail aged (Skelley 2004). On the other hand, equity concerns emerge when growth management solutions focus on restricting numbers of new residents, therefore exacerbating house price escalation and reducing opportunities for lower income people to access affordable accommodation (Green 2001).

Ironically, many of these social and environmental problems emerge as a result of deliberate strategies to recognise the value of natural assets and to preserve them through a strategy of promotion (Green 2001). Many rural populations actively seek retirement migration and tourist development to improve their economic prospects, particularly following changes in agricultural industries. However, the literature contains little evidence of lasting economic improvement arising from amenity driven migration. While some movement to amenity regions relates to new job opportunities associated with growth itself (largely in temporary or unskilled sectors like construction, retail services, and aged care), by definition, amenity migrants move for lifestyle, not jobs (Beyers, Nelson 2000; Casado-Diaz 1999; Dahms, McComb 1999; Green 2001; King R., Warnes, Williams 1998; Marcouiller, Clendenning, Kedzior 2002). So, aside from artisans, entrepreneurs or workers in the new economy, who are able to telecommute, partially commute, or establish niche production away from the major markets, employment opportunities for long-term residents as well as amenity migrants of working age are often extremely limited.

In summary, we use the term 'amenity migration' to describe a migration process that fits loosely under the broader conceptual framework of counter-urbanisation. Unlike some processes of urban – rural migration, however, amenity migration is driven largely by lifestyle aspirations or economic disadvantage, rather than economic opportunity, and long term economic outcomes for amenity destinations are often disappointing. Amenity migrants include retirees, pre-retirees, workers able to commute or partially commute to the major cities, entrepreneurs and workers in cultural and niche industries, downshifters, and those reliant on welfare payments unable to afford urban life. While the economic impacts of amenity migration are ambivalent at best for affected regions, the social and environmental consequences are particularly significant. These features of amenity migration, and the implications for planners and environmental policy makers are explored further below with specific reference to the experience of amenity migration in coastal Australia over the past two decades.

Amenity migration within coastal Australia

Amenity migration processes occur within the wider context of domestic migration and settlement patterns. Australia, established as a British penal colony in 1788, is characterised by a small number of primate population centres along the fertile coast. Today, more than 60 per cent of its population is concentrated in its six State capital cities and surrounding hinterlands. Apart from a ribbon of coastal settlements extending from the capital cities of the south-east, population density is sparse. For most of the last century, Australia's population primate capital cities (Sydney, Melbourne, Brisbane, Adelaide, Perth and Hobart) attracted the greatest share of population growth, while the proportion of people living in rural areas declined (Australian Bureau of Statistics (ABS) 2003).

The 1950s and 1960s saw an intensification of job loss in rural areas corresponding with the manufacturing boom in the cities. At the same time, the growing prevalence of the motor car and an increasing interest in leisure supported the growth of coastal tourism destinations, particularly in proximity to the major cities. Analysts describe this period as the first expression of coastal sprawl in Australia Marshall 2003. As in many nations, the 1970s brought deindustrialisation (arresting population growth in Australia's manufacturing centres) while an agricultural downturn, particularly in the dairy industry, made rural land attractive and accessible to those in search of an alternative lifestyle.

The population share between urban and regional areas over the past 25 years has been fairly stable at around 36 percent, but at the regional level, there are distinct and simultaneous patterns of growth and decline (Australian Bureau of Statistics (ABS) 2003). While many inland rural areas have continued to lose residents, popular coastal areas and strategic inland regional centres have grown (Burnley, Murphy 2004). Although the major cities are again the main focus of population growth largely due to international immigration and natural increases, at different points over the past twenty years coastal areas beyond these centres have recorded rates of population growth that equal or exceed metropolitan areas, driven by net gains in internal migration (Australian Bureau of Statistics (ABS) 2004; Burnley, Murphy 2004; Hugo 2005). The following sections explore this growth and associated demographic, social, economic and environmental changes in more detail.

Study approach

This chapter draws on commissioned research for Australia's National Sea Change Taskforce (Gurran, Squires 2008). We refer to a sample of 67 non-metropolitan and coastal local government areas across the six Australian states of New South Wales (NSW), Victoria, Queensland, South Australia, Tasmania, and Western Australia. The smallest administrative unit in Australia, known as local government areas, are the basis for analysis because environmental and land use plans are prepared and enforced at this jurisdictional level. The local government areas were selected on the basis of their membership in the National Sea Change Taskforce. According to their website, 'the National Sea Change Taskforce was established in 2004 as a national body to represent the interests of coastal councils and communities experiencing the effects of rapid population and tourism growth. The Taskforce now has more than 68 member councils from around Australia. Collectively, these councils represent more than four million residents. The role of the National Sea Change Taskforce is to provide national leadership in addressing the impact of the 'sea change' phenomenon and to provide support and guidance to coastal councils attempting to manage the impact of rapid growth' (National Sea Change Taskforce Inc. 2011). Membership in the Task Force represents about half of all of the non-metropolitan coastal areas in Australia and captures all regions experiencing significant growth and change; for this reason, it is an effective sample universe.

We use data from two main sources; the national Australian Bureau of Statistics (ABS) census for 1996, 2001, and 2006 (Australian Bureau of Statistics (ABS) 2007a); and its annually updated 'Estimated Resident Population' data (projections based on census counts of usual residents, plus other local sources of information) (Australian Bureau of Statistics (ABS) 2007b). Census data is collected during the southern winter month of August providing a good basis for analysing the characteristics of the permanent resident population. However, it fails to capture the massive seasonal fluctuations in visitors and semi-permanent residents experienced during the summer months.

The impact of population growth and change for particular communities is affected by their underlying characteristics. Even a small increase in population – a single new residential development – can have a significant impact for very small settlements, while larger tourism destinations are already accustomed to waves of newcomers and development pressure. To distinguish such differences we refer to a baseline typology of Australian coastal amenity communities (Gurran, Squires, Blakely 2005).

This typology uses two critical criteria—distance from state capital cities and population size—to differentiate community types in coastal Australia. As shown in Table 11.1, Coastal Commuters are settlements that are already, or are becoming, contiguous with major metropolitan areas, up to a 1.5 hour commuting radius; Gosford near Sydney in New South Wales a key example. Coastal Getaways have less than 100,000 residents and are within a three hour drive of the state capital (a standard distance for weekend tourism in Australia). Coastal Cities are secondary cities with populations of more than 100,000 and represent a combination of traditional tourism destinations like the Gold Coast in Queensland, and former industrial cities, like Newcastle in New South Wales. Coastal lifestyle destinations are situated more than a three-hour drive of the state capital, have less than 100,000 residents, and attract lifestyle migrants, domestic, and international tourists. Coastal hamlets have populations of less than 15,000 residents, and their distance beyond three hours of a state capital means that they have been largely protected from significant development pressure to date. Here the terminology 'hamlet' reflects the relatively small size of the local government unit in the Australian context, but the settlement typology contained within this category might range from a fishing village with a few hundred permanent residents, to a small resort town of up to 15,000 inhabitants.

Table 11.1   Typology of Australian coastal amenity communities

Settlement Type	Population Categories	Distance Categories (Time)
Coastal Commuter	>15,000 people	0–1.5 Hour drive from State Capital City
Coastal Getaway	15,0000-<100,000 people	< 3 Hour drive from State Capital City
Coastal Lifestyle	15,0000-<100,000 people	> 3 Hour drive from State Capital City
Coastal City	>100,000 people	> 1.5 Hour drive from State Capital City
Coastal Hamlet	<15,000 people	> 3 Hour drive from State Capital City

Source: (Gurran, Squires, Blakely 2005)

We turn now to the review of population trends in these communities, focusing on five themes of amenity migration: population instability associated with fluctuating migration and visitation; a sharpening chasm between wealthy newcomers, long-time residents, and welfare migrants; an unbalanced demographic profile tipping towards the elderly; the emergence of service oriented economies at the expense of agriculture and productive industries; and resultant patterns of urban change and coastal suburbanisation.

Instability associated with fluctuating migration and visitation

In international terms, Australia has a highly mobile population, with households moving on average every seven years (Hugo 2005). However, levels of mobility and population fluctuation appear even more pronounced in coastal amenity settings. Growth trends for the period 1991–2006 show that while population growth along Australia's non-metropolitan coast has been a theme since the late 1980s, the focus of growth has shifted over this period. During the early 1990s, the New South Wales north coast, and much of southeast Queensland, absorbed the most dramatic population increases, but by 2006, growth along the New South Wales coastline had arrested and in some cases begun to decline. In 2006, the fastest growing coastal local government areas are generally located in close proximity to the Queensland and Western Australian state capitals (Brisbane and Perth), with annual rates of growth between 2001–2006 ranging from 8.4 per cent (Capel, a coastal getaway community south of Perth) to 7.5 per cent (Wanneroo, a coastal commuter to Perth's North) and 4.1 per cent in Caloundra on Queensland's Sunshine Coast. Queensland's famous Gold Coast sustained a rate of over 3.5 per cent per annum for the ten year period between 1996–2001 (Gurran, Squires 2008).

Overall figures of net population growth mask the internal mobility or turnover of residents. We examined evidence of population turnover by referring to a basic indicator included in the national census, which records the numbers of residents who had moved to the local area over the past five years (Australian Bureau of Statistics (ABS) 2007c). As expected, our sample communities generally had higher proportions of recent movers than their respective State averages. Large Coastal Cities and Getaways in Queensland such as Gold Coast, Maroochy, Caloundra and Townsville as well as the rapidly growing Coastal Commuters in Western Australia attracted the most significant proportions of recent movers from outside of the LGA (up to 41 per cent in Queensland, compared with 31 per cent for the state, and 46 per cent for Capel in Western Australia, compared to 25 per cent for the state). However, census figures are limited to final net movements over the past five years, with intercensal shifts not recorded. The literature (e.g., Beyers, Nelson 2000, Stimson, Minnery 1998), and our own discussions with elected officials in Australian sea change communities, suggests that up to 35 per cent of populations in amenity destinations may turn over in a single year, as employment prospects fall through, or newcomers fail to establish binding social connections, but such fluctuations are not captured by existing census data.

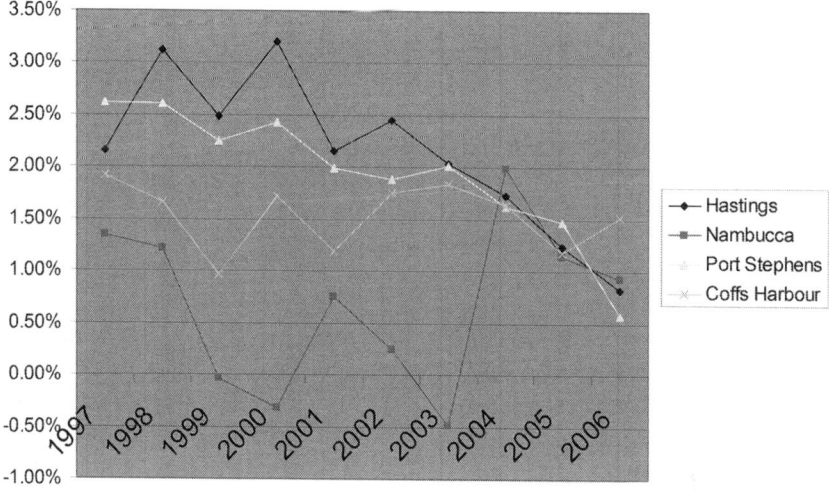

Figure 11.1   New South Wales North Coast Selected Population Trends (1997–2006)

Source: Australian Bureau of Statistics (ABS) 2007b, Gurran, Squires 2008

Some insight into such growth volatility is gained by analysing yearly changes in population growth patterns using regional population estimates, as shown in the graph below for selected communities in New South Wales.

As shown in the graph, significant annual fluctuation is perceived across these popular holiday and retirement destinations although again these estimates are based on net trends rather than individual household movement patterns. This instability is exacerbated by the spectrum of seasonal visitation (holiday makers) and residence (second home owners, seasonal workers) that characterises these holiday destinations.

An unbalanced, ageing demographic profile

We now provide a brief overview of the demographic profile of Australian coastal amenity communities. The most distinctive demographic feature of the majority of communities included in our sample is their residents' age profile. Coastal amenity communities in Australia are typically characterised by a greater proportion of people aged 65 years and over and lower proportions of children (aged less than 15 years) and people of working age (15–64 years) compared with state averages.

Newer migrants to very high growth amenity areas (particularly in Queensland and Western Australia) tend to have a lower age profile than Australians overall, perhaps reflecting the new growth in employment associated with tourism, leisure and retiree development (Australian Bureau of Statistics (ABS) 2004). However, as they are moving to locations already characterised by an ageing demographic, younger amenity migrants are doing little to dilute the overall profile of amenity regions. Indeed, the majority of communities in our sample are not only older, but are ageing at a faster rate than Australia overall. The rate of ageing actually intensified between 2001–2006 in many communities within our sample, with median ages remaining higher than state and national medians and accelerating more quickly. For example, South Australia coastal amenity areas have median ages of up to 53 years compared to the overall median age of 38 for the State. The change in median age in the decade to 2006 in South Australian coastal areas ranged from an increase of four years (in the community of Robe), to an increase of 8 years (in Victor Harbor), in comparison to the state rate of three years.

Catering to such an ageing population profile raises significant social, economic, and physical planning issues. Opportunities for economic diversity are limited when much of the population is no longer part of the work force (Skelley 2004). At the same time, a concentration of retirement developments tends to be inconsistent with the tourism appeal of coastal destinations, thus further limiting economic opportunities. The social needs of ageing residents are complex and often beyond the means of local authorities, particularly when faced with the task of servicing small and relatively remote population settlements. Older people are often less able to travel independently, yet public transport facilities are generally non-existent in Australian coastal amenity areas. Similarly health facilities are limited and dispersed. Finally, it is unclear whether retirement migrants will remain in their new locations or will return to the city when a partner dies or when they become too frail to maintain independent living. If so, a new wave of return migration may be looming, with further issues for local planners and policy makers.

Consistent with their ageing populations, some distinct household characteristics are emerging in Australia's amenity regions, particularly those beyond the peri-urban commuting rim. While Australian household sizes have shrunk overall, this trend is particularly marked in amenity regions, with incidences of smaller households characterized by lone persons, couples without children, and single parent families, increasing faster than the nation overall, and proportions of couples with children declining at much greater rates in comparison to State and national figures (Australian Bureau of Statistics (ABS) 2007c). These trends have particular implications for planning and housing policies within these communities, as discussed further below.

A sharpening social chasm between wealthy newcomers, long-time residents, and welfare migrants

Amenity migrants often move to places where average incomes are lower than their places of origin. Indeed, often, relatively affordable housing and lower living costs are part of the appeal of an amenity destination. This is particularly so for affluent retirees able to capitalise on higher housing values in their city or country of origin (Casado-Diaz 1999). Newcomers competition for housing with existing residents can have an inflationary impact on house prices (Rodriguez, Fernandez-Mayoralas, Rojo 2004). So-called welfare migrants, unable to find work or afford to remain in a major city, also compete with existing residents for lower cost housing on the local market (Squires, Gurran 2005). The results are an intensification of existing levels of social disadvantage, combined with increasing cleavages between wealthy newcomers, often able to colonise the most attractive and accessible locations, and lower income residents, who are often forced into more remote and inaccessible hinterland areas.

Regional coastal Australia has lower income levels than the Australian population overall. Only 14 of the local government areas included in our sample currently exceed the National median household income of AU$1,025 per week, and the highest of these (Capel in Western Australia) was only around $200 higher in 2006 (Australian Bureau of Statistics (ABS) 2007c). By contrast, lower income communities tend to differ from the national medium by a more significant $300 – $400.There is a distinct concentration of poorer coastal amenity communities in New South Wales, with weekly household incomes ranging between $564 per week to $635 reported in the 2006 census. Further, incomes grew at a slower rate than the national median overall during the decade 1996–2006. As many of these communities have high proportions of self-funded retirees, income growth since this time will be particularly vulnerable to global economic conditions.

Unsurprisingly, most amenity communities in our sample have higher levels of unemployment than their respective State average, however, unemployment rates in most areas decreased between 2001 and 2006 in line with national trends (Australian Bureau of Statistics (ABS) 2007c, Gurran, Squires 2008). Despite these improvements, labour force participation rates remain much lower in amenity communities, likely reflecting a lack of employment opportunity as well as older age profiles. For instance, the high growth lifestyle destination of Hervey Bay, in Queensland, had a labour force participation rate of 45 per cent in 2006, compared to 61.8 per cent for the state. Overall, 48 of the communities in the sample had a labour force participation rate lower than their respective State in 2006, and these rates actually declined over the decade in 32 amenity communities (Australian Bureau of Statistics (ABS) 2007c, Gurran, Squires 2008).

In metropolitan locations, lower incomes, declining labour force participation, and relatively high levels of unemployment usually correlate with stagnant or declining house prices and rents in sub regional housing markets. By contrast, housing price growth tends to occur when incomes and employment prospects also rise. However, in coastal amenity areas, house price inflation may occur without concomitant improvements in local economic conditions. In our sample of Australian coastal amenity communities, housing costs – both mortgage repayments and rents increased significantly between 1996–2006. Monthly mortgage repayments and weekly rent payments per household increased at a greater rate than the State average between 1996 and 2006 for the majority of communities of our sample, with changes between 15–25 per cent above rates of increase for the state overall. For instance, median home loans increased by over 88 per cent in Victoria's popular Bass Coast, compared to 64.5 per cent for the state overall, while in Capel, Western Australia, repayments increased by 88 per cent, compared to 63 per cent for the state (Australian Bureau of Statistics (ABS) 2007c, Gurran, Squires 2008). A similar story was recorded for rents, which in places such as Moyne in Victoria, have increased up to 100 per cent compared to 54 per cent for the state.

The availability of lower cost housing is declining in Australia's coastal amenity regions. For instance, caravan parks, which provide an important source of lower cost rental accommodation for retirees, have been under increasing pressure for redevelopment or for permanent tourism conversions (Squires, Gurran 2005). Between 1996 and 2006, over 3500 caravan site losses were recorded across 12 local government areas in Queensland and New South Wales (Australian Bureau of Statistics (ABS) 2007c, Gurran, Squires 2008).

Service oriented economies with limited prospects for diversity

Many amenity communities embark on strategies for growth with great optimism, assuming that new tourism or retiree developments will offset the shift in rural economies from productive industries like agriculture, fishing and forestry (Skelley 2004). Indeed, our review of industry change in the sample of amenity communities confirmed a distinct shift from these productive industries towards tourism and service industries like accommodation, retail and personal care. However, these industries tend to offer only part time, seasonal and low skilled employment opportunities and overall across the sample, employment and industry development outcomes have been disappointing for amenity growth communities. Most exhibit lower proportions of residents in higher skilled employment (categorised as 'Managers and Professionals' in the Australian census), combined with more concentrated employment in lower skilled occupations (administration, sales, labouring, machinery operators and drivers).

An example of these trends is shown in the case of Nambucca on the New South Wales north coast (Figure 11.2). Nambucca has long been a destination for retirees and downshifters, as well as a popular holiday spot for those with weekenders or second homes. While Nambucca records growing employment in construction and health care sectors, employment is declining in agriculture, despite its location amidst some of the country's most fertile farmlands.

By contrast, as shown in Figure 11.3 and Figure 11.4 below, the popular Queensland tourist destinations of the Gold Coast, and Cairns on the Great Barrier Reef record declining rates of direct employment in accommodation and hospitality as rates of employment in construction sectors increase. Employment in health care and retail sectors are increasing in these communities, reflecting the shift to permanent population settlement and perhaps a suburbanisation that may

Nambucca

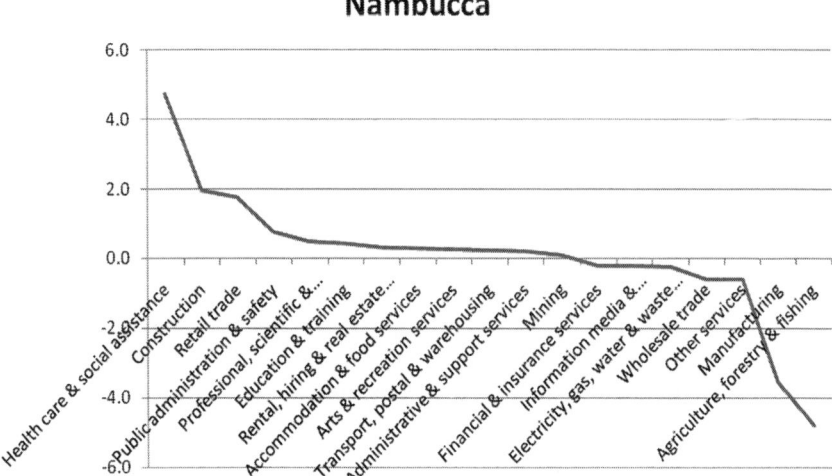

Figure 11.2   Industry of employment trends, Nambucca, New South Wales (1996–2006)

Source: Derived from Australian Bureau of Statistics (ABS) 2007c

be inconsistent with the character of a holiday destination. In this sense, these larger coastal cities, once oriented towards tourism and lifestyle are beginning to assume some of the suburban qualities (characterised by low density, functional family housing) more akin to the coastal commuter areas surrounding the major metropolitan regions.

Even without the net gains in permanent population growth discussed above, household formation rates and demand for second homes can significantly affect the demand for infrastructure and housing in amenity regions. As noted, our sample of 67 coastal communities experienced a marked shift towards smaller households of lone persons, couples without children, and single parent families, while proportions of couples with children declined at much greater rates in comparison to State and national figures (Gurran, Squires 2008). This means that coastal amenity communities require housing that is smaller and more diverse than the traditional detached home on a single block that has long epitomised the Australian housing dream. Current Australian planning policy emphasises the need for more diverse housing opportunities, for higher densities near services, and for the containment of urban areas. To examine the extent to which this policy is being implemented, we used census data to analyse broad patterns in housing development for our sample communities, between 1996–2006. The data suggests that despite the ageing populations and trend towards smaller households in these communities, for the most part housing development in coastal amenity regions has reinforced the dominant pattern of detached dwellings on a single block (Gurran, Squires 2008). Not only do most local government areas in the sample

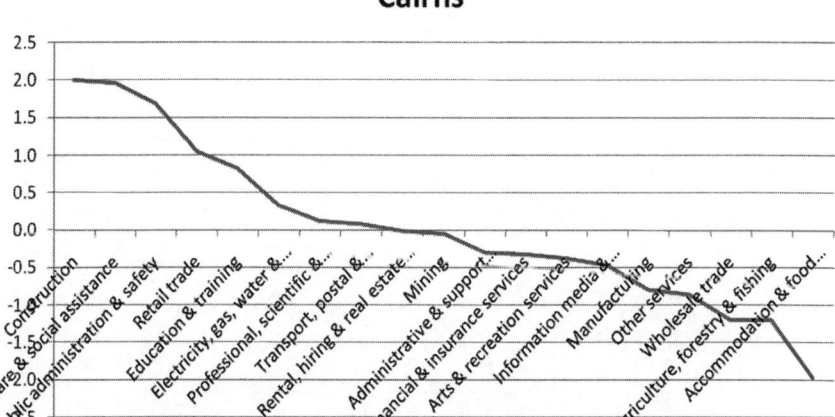

Figure 11.3   Industry of employment trends, selected Queensland sea change communities (1996–2006), Cairns

Source: Australian Bureau of Statistics (ABS) 2007c

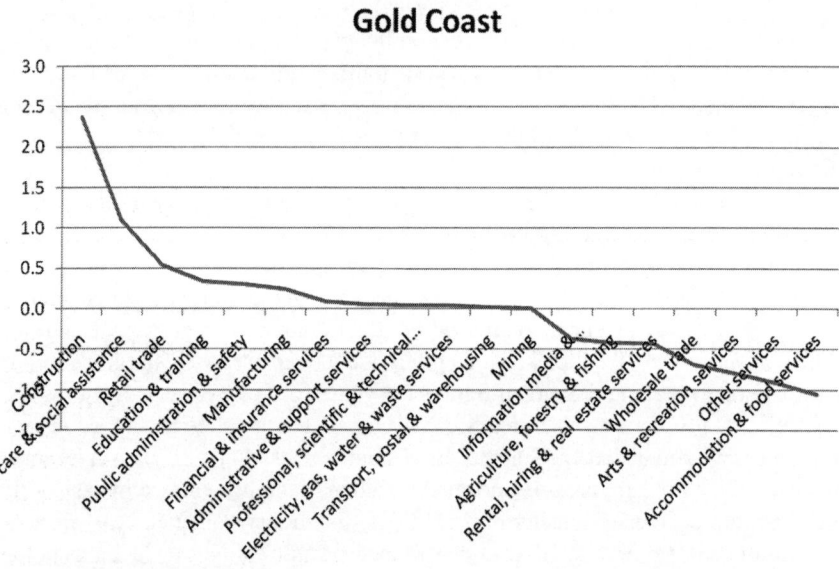

Figure 11.4   Industry of employment trends, selected Queensland sea change communities (1996–2006), Gold Coast

Source: Derived from Australian Bureau of Statistics (ABS) 2007c

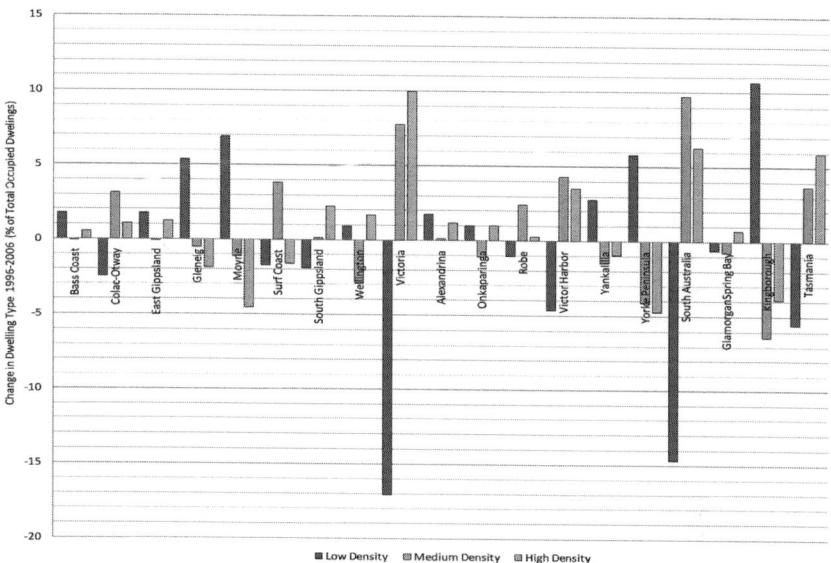

Figure 11.5   Victoria, South Australia and Tasmania, change in dwelling type (1996-2006) as a proportion of total occupied private dwellings

Source: Gurran, Squires 2008: 32 (Derived from Australian Bureau of Statistics (ABS) 2007c)

have a higher proportion of detached houses than their respective State average, but the proportional split between detached and attached (or medium density) accommodation has actually grown over the decade. Of the 67 communities, only 12 had a higher proportion of medium density dwellings (defined as semi-detached, row, terrace or townhouses) than the State average by the 2006 census, and only eight had a higher proportion of high density dwellings (apartments) (Australian Bureau of Statistics (ABS) 2007c, Gurran, Squires 2008). As expected, these communities included large coastal cities such as the Gold Coast, as well as coastal commuting areas located on the New South Wales and Queensland coast.

Figure 11.5 below summarises these trends for the states of South Australia, Victoria, and Tasmania. As shown, despite clear State shifts away from detached housing, in line with goals of environmental sustainability and the need to promote greater housing diversity, the coastal amenity communities in our sample generally intensified existing patterns of lower density suburban development. Of those that experienced declines in the proportional share of lower density housing (such as the community of Colac Otway in Victoria), these declines remained less than those of the state overall.

This basic analysis of development patterns in coastal amenity regions lends support for the argument that amenity driven growth in Australia is leading to a *suburbanisation of the coastline*. This suburbanisation is being expressed in the form of new, sprawling residential neighbourhoods stretching way beyond the original town periphery, as well as clusters of very high density, high rise apartments across the traditional town core, resulting in a significant disruption to the traditional Australian beach village typology. Distinctly suburban conurbations are stretching along the most popular coastal areas, altering the character of beach towns and representing significant social and environmental challenges – ranging from landscape degradation to social isolation and increased vulnerability to the risks associated with enhanced climate change. The small population base of coastal hamlets and lifestyle destinations means that even modest influxes of new residents can overwhelm the existing community.

Conclusions

The study of coastal amenity communities described in this chapter provides empirical evidence of several distinct characteristics of amenity driven growth and change in Australia. Firstly, amenity destinations have complex growth patterns. They tend to experience periods of very high net population growth followed by a slowing or reversal of growth rates over time. Even among those with a more stable total population, many experience influxes of new residents combined with departures, as well as seasonal fluctuation from second home owners, leading to population change and volatility. Consequently, pressure for new housing development and infrastructure may persist even in communities even when net population stabilises.

Secondly, amenity communities have older populations that are ageing more quickly than Australia overall, despite the movement of younger, working aged people to the fastest growing amenity destinations. This unbalanced demographic profile raises particular challenges for achieving social and economic diversity and meeting social programming needs. Thirdly, Australia's amenity destinations are frequently characterised by social disadvantage, with lower incomes, higher levels of unemployment, and lower labour force participation rates, than other regions (including inland centres), particularly those areas situated more than three hours from the state capital cities. Fourthly, despite the promise of an increased population base, growth has not led to a significant improvement in economic outcomes, with new employment growth in precarious or part time occupations like construction, personal care, and retail industries. These economic trends reflect a transition away from agriculture and primary production.

Finally, despite a need for smaller and more diverse forms of accommodation to reflect the ageing and small household demographic profile of coastal amenity communities, growth has largely been through single family, low density residential development and linear sprawl. These trends combine to exacerbate the vulnerability of nonmetropolitan coastal Australia to the environmental, social, and economic risks associated with climate change – which range from sea level rise, increased exposure to major storm events and flooding, to economic devastation associated with the loss of major tourist attractions such as the Great Barrier Reef (Gurran, Hamin, Norman 2008).

The socio-economic profile of Australia's coastal amenity communities also means they are currently more vulnerable to the increased risks of natural disaster associated with climate change. Lower income groups tend to occupy housing that is less well maintained and underinsured. They are typically less able to afford modifications for climate comfort or protection, and, if in rental accommodation, may be unable to carry out such changes. Residents of temporary housing like caravans and manufactured homes, which are an important source of housing for lower income retirees in coastal Australia, are particularly exposed to natural disasters such as major storms and floods (Burby, Steinberg, Basolo 2003; Cutter, Finch 2008; Levine, Esnard, Sapat 2007). Older people are often less able or willing to comply with disaster protocol, and are particularly vulnerable to chronic health risks associated with hotter temperatures, vector borne and water borne diseases. Population instability and turnover also increases community risk because newcomers lack the social ties with their new community needed to access assistance and information in times of a disaster (Levine, Esnard, Sapat 2007).

To the extent that similar processes are underway in other amenity regions around the world, the following policy considerations may resonate. Firstly, there is a need to anticipate a distorted demographic profile, with consequences for local and regional service provision over time. Secondly, there is a need to develop strong and place specific planning policies to ensure that growth in amenity regions does not replicate metropolitan forms or reinforce existing patterns of car dependency and sprawl. Thirdly, it is important to address the potential for socio-economic disadvantage to deepen in amenity regions, and for increasing polarisation between existing residents, poorer migrants, and wealthy newcomers or tourists. This means strong policies to maintain opportunities for affordable housing, irrespective of the need to manage new growth. Given the relative volatility of population patterns in amenity areas, a local economy dependent on continuing growth trends and increased housing demand is a clear vulnerability, so opportunities for economic diversification must be created and supported during times of relative prosperity.

Finally, the particular environmental and social vulnerabilities of these communities to the impacts of climate change mean that developing a suite of strategies for climate change mitigation and adaptation is a particular priority for a more low carbon and resilient coastal urban future (Norman 2010b). This will require a multidisciplinary approach better connecting climate science, urban and regional planning and socio- economic policy recognising regional difference and some of the deeper underlying causes of coastal change (Norman 2010a).

References

Australian Bureau of Statistics (ABS). 2003. *Census of Population and Housing.* Canberra.

Australian Bureau of Statistics (ABS). 2004. *Seachange – New Coastal Residents.* Canberra.

Australian Bureau of Statistics (ABS). 2007a. *Census of Population and Housing: Basic Community Profile.* Canberra.

Australian Bureau of Statistics (ABS). 2007b. *Regional Population Growth Australia and New Zealand.* Canberra.

Australian Bureau of Statistics (ABS). 2007c. *Time Series Profiles.* Canberra.

Australian Labour Party (ALP). 2006. *Meeting the Challenge of Coastal Growth: Discussion Paper.*

Beyers, W.B. and Nelson, P.B. 2000. Contemporary development forces in the nonmetropolitan west: new insights from rapidly growing communities. *Journal of Rural Studies,* 16(4), 459–74. Available at: 10.1016/S0743-0167(00)00017-6.

Burby, R.J., Steinberg, L.J. and Basolo, V. 2003. The Tenure Trap: The Vulnerability of Renters to Joint Natural and Technological Disasters. *Urban Affairs Review,* 39(1), 32–58. Available at: 10.1177/1078087403253053.

Burnley, I. 2005. Sea Change, Social Change? Population Turnaround in New South Wales. *Dialogue, Academy of the Social Sciences,* 24(2), 66–75. Available at: http://www.assa.edu.au/publications/dialogue/2005_Vol24_No2.php.

Burnley, I.H. and Murphy, P. 2004. *Sea change: Movement from metropolitan to Arcadian Australia.* Sydney: Univ. of New South Wales Press.

Casado-Diaz, M.A. 1999. Socio-demographic impacts of residential tourism: a case study of Torrevieja, Spain. *International Journal of Tourism Research,* 1(4), 223–37. Available at: http://dx.doi.org/10.1002/(SICI)1522-1970(199907/08)1:4<223::AID-JTR153>3.0.CO;2-A.

Cutter, S.L. and Finch, C. 2008. Temporal and spatial changes in social vulnerability to natural hazards. *Proceedings of the National Academy of Sciences;,* 105(7), 2301–06. Available at: 10.1073/pnas.0710375105.

Dahms, F. and McComb, J. 1999. 'Counterurbanisation', interaction and functional change in a rural amenity area — A Canadian example. *Journal of Rural Studies,* 15(2), 129–46. Available at: 10.1016/S0743-0167(98)00056-4.

Dredge, D. 2001. Leisure lifestyles and tourism: Socio-cultural, economic and spatial change in Lake Macquarie. *Tourism Geographies,* 3(3), 279–99. Available at: 10.1080/14616680110055411.

Esparza, A.X. and Carruthers, J.I. 2000. Land Use Planning and Exurbanisation in the Rural Mountain West: Evidence from Arizona. *Journal of Planning Education and Research,* 20(1), 23–36. Available at: 10.1177/073945600128992573.

Essex, S.J. and Brown, G.P. 1997. The Emergence of Post-Suburban Landscapes on the North Coast of New South Wales: A Case Study of Contested Space. *International Journal of Urban and Regional Research,* 21(2), 259–87. Available at: 10.1111/1468-2427.00072.

Green, G.P. 2001. Amenities and Community Economic Development: Strategies for Sustainability. *Journal of Regional Analysis and Policy,* 31(2), 61–75. Available at: http://www.jrap-journal.org/pastvolumes/2000/v31/31-2-5.pdf.

Greene, K. 2005. *Inquiry into infrastructure provision in coastal growth areas.* [Sydney]: Parliament of NSW.

Gurran, N. and Blakely, E. 2007. Suffer a Sea Change? Contrasting perspectives towards urban policy and migration in coastal Australia. *Australian Geographer,* 38(1), 113–31. Available at: 10.1080/00049180601175899.

Gurran, N. and Squires, C. 2008. *Meeting the Sea Change Challenge: Sea Change Communities in Coastal Australia: Update and Data Supplement 2008.* Sydney.

Gurran, N., Hamin, E. and Norman, B. 2008. *Planning for Climate Change: Leading Practice Principles and Models for Sea Change Communities in Coastal Australia.* Sydney.

Gurran, N., Squires, C. and Blakely, E.J. 2005. *Meeting the sea change challenge: Sea change communities in coastal Australia : report for the National Sea Change Taskforce, 31 March 2005.* Sydney: University of Sydney Planning Research Centre.

Gustafson, P. 2001. Retirement migration and transnational lifestyles. *Ageing & Society,* 21(04). Available at: 10.1017/S0144686X01008327.

Haas, W.H., III and Serow, W.J. 2002. The Baby Boom, Amenity Retirement Migration, and Retirement Communities: Will the Golden Age of Retirement Continue? *Research on Aging,* 24(1), 150–64. Available at: 10.1177/0164027503024001009.

Hamilton, C. 2003. *Downshifting in Australia: A sea change in the pursuit of happiness.* Deakin, A.C.T.: Australia Institute.

Hugo, G. 2005. Nomads? On the Move in Australia. *Dialogue, Academy of the Social Sciences,* 24(2), 4–24.

Jones, R.E., Fly, J.M., Talley, J. and Cordell, H.K. 2003. Green Migration into Rural America: The New Frontier of Environmentalism? *Society & Natural Resources: An International Journal,* 16(3), 221–38. Available at: http://www.informaworld.com/10.1080/08941920309159.

King R., Warnes, A.M. and Williams, A.M. 1998. International retirement migration in Europe. *Internationale Journal of Population Geography,* 4(2), 91–111. Available at: http://www.ncbi.nlm.nih.gov/pubmed/12348629.

Levine, J.N., Esnard, A.-M. and Sapat, A. 2007. Population Displacement and Housing Dilemmas Due to Catastrophic Disasters. *Journal of Planning Literature,* 22(1), 3–15.

Marcouiller, D.W., Clendenning, J.G. and Kedzior, R. 2002. Natural Amenity-Led Development and Rural Planning. *Journal of Planning Literature,* 16(4), 515–42. Available at: http://jpl.sagepub.com/content/16/4/515.abstract.

Marshall, N. 2003. *Welfare Outcomes of Migration of Low-Income Earners from Metropolitan to Non-Metropolitan Australia: Final Report.* Melbourne.

National Sea Change Taskforce Inc. *National Sea Change Taskforce.* [Online] Available at: http://www.seachangetaskforce.org.au/Home.html [accessed: 23 June 2011].

Norman, B. 2010a. *A low carbon and resilient urban future: a strategic approach to settlement planning for climate change.* Canberra.

Norman, B. 2010b. *Integrated coastal management to sustainable coastal planning:* RMIT University. Global Studies, Social Science and Planning.

Resource Assessment Commission (RAC). 1993. *Coastal Zone Inquiry: Final report.* Canberra.

Rodriguez, V., Fernandez-Mayoralas, G. and Rojo, F. 2004. International Retirement Migration: Retired Europeans Living on the Costa Del Sol, Spain. *Population Review,* 43(1), 1–36. Available at: 10.1353/prv.2004.0009.

Sant, M. and Simons, P. 1993. Counterurbanisation and coastal development in New South Wales. *Geoforum,* 24(3), 291–306. Available at: http://www.sciencedirect.com/science/article/pii/001671859390022A.

Skelley, B.D. 2004. Retiree-Attraction Policies: Challenges for Local Governance in Rural Regions. *Public Administration and Management: An Interactive Journal,* 9(3), 212–23.

Squires, C. and Gurran, N. 2005. Planning for affordable housing in coastal sea change communities. in *Building for Diversity Refereed Conference Proceedings,* edited by Australian Housing and Urban Research Institute (AHURI). National Housing Conference, Perth, 26–28 October, 381–403. Available at: http://www.nhc.edu.au/downloads/2005/Refereed/20Squires.pdf [accessed: 23 June 2011].

Stimson, R.J. and Minnery, J. 1998. Why people move to the `sun-belt': A case study of long-distance migration to the Gold Coast. *Urban Studies (Routledge),* 35(2), 123–214.

Walmsley, D.J., Epps, W.R. and Duncan, C.J. 1998. Migration to the New South Wales North Coast 1986–1991. Lifestyle motivated counterurbanisation. *Geoforum,* 29(1), 105–18. Available at: http://www.sciencedirect.com/science/article/pii/S0016718597000237.

Chapter 12

Counterurbanisation and Subjective Well-Being

Finbarr Brereton, J. Peter Clinch, Menelaos Gkartzios, Mark Scott

Introduction

Sustainable urban form and locations of settlements

Since the 1990s, spatial planning practice has increasingly focused on issues surrounding sustainable urban form and the role of planning within the context of sustainable development. For example, the European Spatial Development Perspective (ESDP) strongly advocates the 'compact city' as a method to control the physical expansion of cities, integrate land use and transport more effectively, and reduce the physical separation of daily activities (European Commission 1999). National and local policy and discussion documents within member states increasingly repeat these themes: greater densities and mixing of land uses will significantly contribute to emissions and energy consumption reductions via shorter and possibly less frequent intra urban car-based trips, and will raise the vitality and viability of urban areas. In the Republic of Ireland these sentiments have been enthusiastically embraced by planners and translated into formal guidance through the National Spatial Strategy (Department of the Environment and Local Government (DOELG) 2002), Planning Guidelines on Residential Density (Department of the Environment and Local Government (DOELG) 1999) and the Regional Planning Guidelines for the Greater Dublin Area (Dublin Regional Authority and Mid-East Regional Authority (DMERA) 2004). However, several academics argue (e.g. Jenks and Williams) that there is no proof for the postulated sustainability benefits of the compact city.

At the same time, spatial planning policy in rural localities has been increasingly concerned with growth management (Diaz, Green 2001) and restricting housing supply in rural areas on environmental and landscape grounds (Gallent, Tewdwr-Jones 2007). However, as Murdoch, Lowe (2003) highlight somewhat paradoxically, in parallel to these policy concerns for managing rural housing supply and promoting brownfield development and compact cities, has often been an increased demand for housing in rural areas from in-migration trends from counterurbanisation, people retiring to the countryside and second home ownership.

Although the rationale for promoting compact cities and preventing 'urban-generated rural growth' is well-established, in this chapter relative individual well-being and life satisfaction among rural and urban households are examined in terms of how they challenge the compact city policy agenda. Two custom-designed surveys undertaken in urban and rural areas in the Republic of Ireland in 2007 indicate that individual life satisfaction is higher in low density, dispersed settlement patterns, suggesting that individual benefits (such as privacy or space) may be valued more than a location close to employment, services and facilities. This discussion is initially located within a brief overview of the debate on counterurbanisation.

Counterurbanisation: an Irish context

The term counterurbanisation has been commonly used for more than three decades to generally describe the redistribution of population away from major cities and metropolitan areas and towards more rural areas (e.g., Dahms, McComb 1999, Escribano 2007, Fisher 2003). In the extensive literature surrounding counterurbanisation, a dichotomy is apparent between the proposed explanations of counterurbanisation, whether they are job-led or people-led, focusing on people's individual choices in seeking a more attractive rural environment to live in (see for example Grafton, Bolton 1987, Moseley 1984).

While other concepts have been used to examine dispersed, low density settlements, such as urban sprawl, rural sprawl or deconcentrated urban growth, in this chapter these spatial change processes are examined through the lens of counterurbanisation. Three forms of counterurban movements have been identified by Mitchell (2004): *ex-urbanisation* (the movement of affluent residents to the countryside surrounding urban centres); *displaced-urbanisation* (household movements to the countryside driven by economic reasons, such as employment or lower cost of living); and *anti-urbanisation* (the movement of city dwellers who wish to live in rural areas, motivated by anti-urban considerations).

In the Irish case, issues of spatial change and housing growth have been central public policy issues over the last decade as a response to rapid economic growth experienced during the 1990s, a growing population and immigration and extensive house-building activity. Dramatic changes were experienced in both urban and in selected rural localities alongside significant house-building activity. Secondary analysis of public data has showed that the emerging geographies of Ireland exhibit the following characteristics (drawing on Gkartzios, Scott 2005, Scott et al. 2005):

- High population growth (three or more times than the national average) in accessible rural areas, along road and rail transport. At the same time population decline has been recorded in less accessible rural areas (particularly in the west of the country) and in urban city wards (for example, in Dublin inner city areas);
- Remarkable housing growth during the last decade not only in urban areas, but in the hinterland of bigger cities as well. Over the 10-year period 1994–

2004, house completions increased by 190 per cent, adding more than half a million new private houses (520,317 completions) in the State. As recorded in a report by the National Economic and Social Council (NESC) (National Economic and Social Council (NESC) 2004), this increase in the level of overall construction is unprecedented and is also exceptional when compared to other European Union (EU) countries,

- Low density settlement pattern: A large part of new house-building involves single detached houses and bungalows suggesting persisting one-off housing developments (40 per cent of new houses completed in the 1994 – 2004 decade), and semi-detached houses indicative of suburban type estates development;
- Increasing house prices during the 1990s and early 2000s, particularly in Dublin city,
- High dependency on car transport and increased spatial separation of home and workplace.
- The national percentage population growth between the censuses of 1996 and 2002 was 8 per cent. The corresponding figure for County Dublin was 6.1 per cent, below the State average – however, significant population increases were experienced in counties in close proximity to County Dublin, i.e. the commuter belt[1] and counties in the west of Ireland (e.g. counties Galway 10.7 per cent and Clare 9.9 per cent). The national percentage population growth between 2002 and 2006 was 8.2 per cent. County Dublin continued to exhibit a lower percentage growth (5.7 per cent), while much greater population growth was again observed in nearby counties[2]

Figure 12.1 compares the density of new dwellings built in the period 1991–95 with that of dwellings built in the period 1996–2002. The data include all types of dwellings; bungalows, single-detached houses, semi-detached houses and apartments (the data are published aggregated by the Central Statistics Office, so it has not been possible to distinguish between different types of houses), and provide an indication of expansion and sprawl in the country. The results show a significant contrast, with the more recent period clearly showing much more widespread development spatially. Growth in the eastern region, in the South-East, around Cork, Limerick and Galway, particularly along the rail and road routes is quite evident.

---

1   Between 1996 and 2002, population increases in the counties around County Dublin were; Meath 22.1 per cent, Kildare 21.4 per cent, Westmeath 13.5 per cent, Wicklow 11.7 per cent, Wexford 11.7 per cent and Louth 10.5 per cent respectively.

2   The increase in population between 2002 and 2006 in these commuter belt counties were Meath 21.5 per cent, Laois 14.1 per cent, Kildare 13.7 per cent and Westmeath 13 per cent respectively.

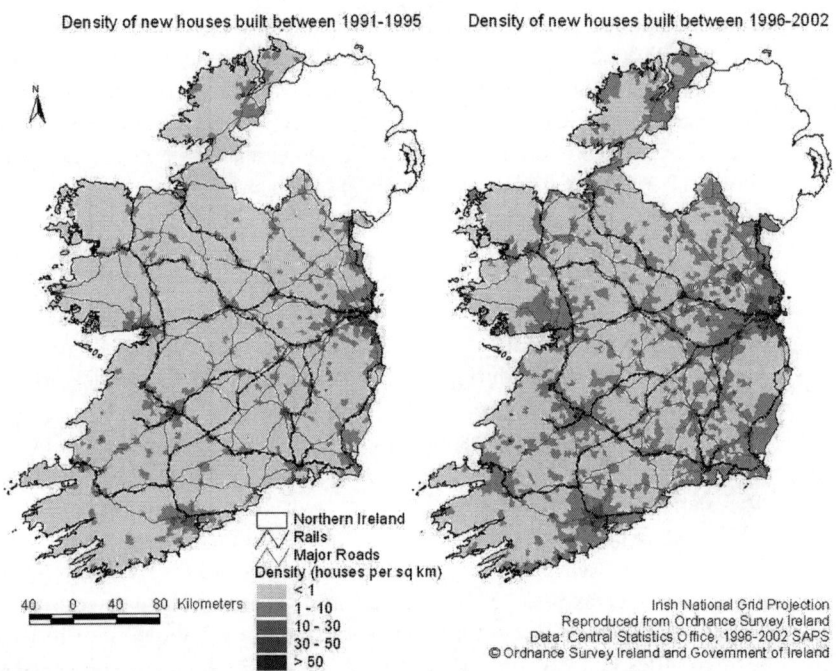

Figure 12.1   Density of new houses/apartments built between 2 different periods

Source: Data: Central Statistics Office 1996–2002 SAPS

Although the term counterurbanisation has been used to describe population flows down the urban hierarchy, more recently it has provided a framework to study wider social phenomena with a rural dimension (Champion 1989). For example, research based on rural in-migration movements has also focused on the gentrification of rural areas (e.g., Phillips 2004, Smith 2007, Smith, Holt 2005), rural regeneration and development (e.g., Stockdale 2006, Stockdale, Findlay, Short 2000), rural restructuring (e.g., Halfacree 1997, Murdoch, Lowe 2003) and residential satisfaction (e.g., Barcus 2004). Much less attention, however, has been paid to the relationship between 'place' and the factors which influence quality of life. Life satisfaction is examined with the results compared across a number of sub-populations, including: urban and rural households; long term rural residents and recent urban to rural migrants; and among households that indicated a preference to move locality in the short term.

Theoretical framework

Economists have traditionally employed the concept of 'utility' (Black 1998) to measure welfare, which in traditional economic models is assumed to be an increasing function of present and future consumption of goods, leisure and amenities. Due to the difficulty of measuring utility, income was generally used as an indicator of individual and societal welfare, using personal income at an individual level, and national income – Gross National Product (GNP) and Gross Domestic Product (GDP) – at the macro level. It has long been recognized by economists, geographers, sociologists, psychologists and others, however, that income is an inadequate measure of the performance of an economy and wider society (e.g., United Nations 1954, Erikson 1993). Such measures are unable to give value to environmental and social capital and are unable to capture the performance of a country in sustainability terms.

What are the alternatives? Psychologists have traditionally studied the determinants of subjective well-being and happiness (e.g., Diener et al. 1999, Carr 2004). Recent theoretical studies have added weight to the claim that happiness scores are useful in the analysis of welfare (e.g., Kahneman 1999, Ferrer-i-Carbonell, Frijters 2004) and that they are interpersonally comparable (e.g., Layard 2005). A new 'happiness' literature employs data from surveys as empirical approximations of individual well-being. Examples of the types of question used in the literature include 'taken all together, how would you say things are these days – would you say that you are happy, pretty happy, or not too happy?' (e.g., Oswald 1997). Moreover, evidence from neuro-science suggests that subjective well-being measures are associated with a physiological response (e.g., Layard 2005).

An obvious concern with the use of self-reported well-being is how good it is as a proxy for subjective utility and the measurement error it may introduce if respondents are unable to communicate accurately their underlying welfare level. In this regard, however, there is a broad consensus among previous (especially psychological) studies that self-reported well-being is a satisfactory empirical proxy for individual utility (e.g., Di Tella, MacCulloch 2006, Clark, Frijters, Shields 2008).

Empirical findings using these measures include a strong, negative link between life satisfaction and specific spatial and environmental attributes (e.g., van Praag, Baarsma 2005, Brereton, Clinch, Ferreira 2008). Additionally, subjective well-being scores have been used to rank quality of life across regions (Moro et al. 2008). In relation to housing and well-being, Oswald et al. (2003) in their study of older adults' housing situations in western and eastern German rural regions find that housing-related variables explain a substantial portion of variance in life satisfaction. Cattaneo et al. (2008) assess the causal impact of housing and housing improvement programs on health and welfare and find that housing improvements leave adults substantially better off, as measured by satisfaction with their housing and quality of life. In a study of quality of life in rural Ireland, individuals living in the open countryside are more satisfied with their lives than their urban counterparts (Brereton et al. 2011). This finding is attributed to a positive effect of rural amenity as represented by private goods, such as detached housing, plot size, or views. They opine that rural dwellers are not only more able to afford a property, but are also more able to afford their 'ideal home'.

Methodology

The data used in this chapter comes from two 'omnibus' style surveys addressing a number of topics related to quality of life issues in urban and rural Ireland (Clinch, Brereton, McInerney 2007a, 2007b).[3] Questionnaires were developed which included a number of topics intended to capture socio economic, socio-demographic and geographical information. The sampling procedure adopted in both cases was a proportionate random sampling procedure using probability proportionate to size (PPS). The rationale governing this choice of design was to ensure coverage of both urban and rural areas in all 'local authority' areas of Ireland.

A total of 812 interviews were obtained in the rural[4] survey and 956 in the urban survey.

Data

The satisfaction with life indicator (or proxy for individual utility) is based on the answers to the following question: 'Thinking about the good and bad things in your life, which of these answers best describes your life as a whole?' Respondents could choose a category on a scale of one to seven ('As bad as can be'; 'very bad'; 'bad'; 'alright'; 'good'; 'very good'; 'as good as can be'). The survey found a high life satisfaction in general in rural Ireland with an average of 5.7 on the seven-point scale, compared to an average of 5.4 in urban areas and the difference is significant (p=0.000).

As for the independent variables, the datasets include an employment-status variable divided into those employed (self-employed, full-time employed and part-

---

3   To test for non-response bias, in both cases four key variables from the samples (age, gender, marital status and economic activity) were compared with corresponding Irish census estimates (Central Statistics Office (CSO) 2007). With some exceptions, the characteristics of each sample are broadly similar to those of the urban and rural Irish adult populations. Some variation is to be expected due to the use of an address based sampling frame (GeoDirectory - a complete database of every building in the Republic of Ireland), where individuals in smaller households have a higher probability of being chosen. The use of an address based sampling frame was necessary due to the unavailability of the electoral register for survey purposes in 2007. However, an analysis of the sample characteristics of the survey has shown that the samples generated are generally representative of the population from which they were drawn.

4   An electoral division was deemed to be rural if its population in the 2002 Census numbered 1,500 persons or less and urban otherwise.

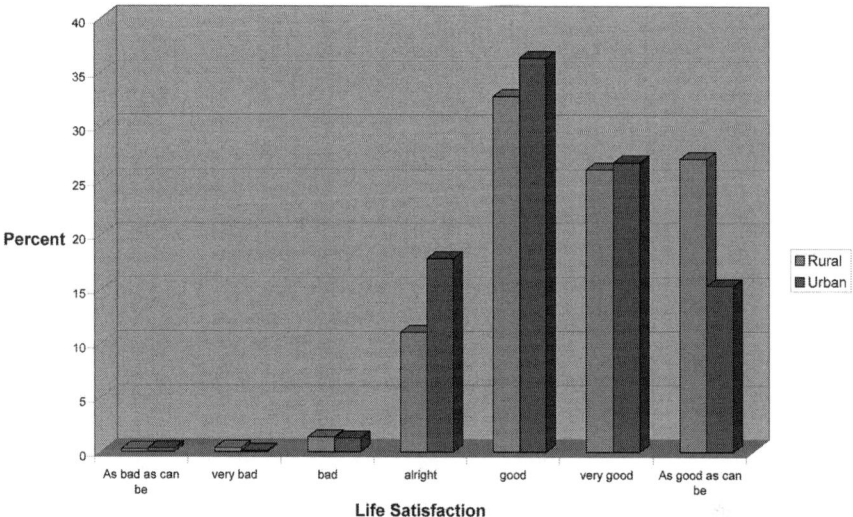

Figure 12.2 Life satisfaction in urban and rural Ireland

Source: Illustration by authors

time employed), economically inactive (student, working on home duties, disabled, retired, those not working and not seeking work) and unemployed. Additional individual characteristics contained in the datasets and typically employed in the literature are age, gender, educational attainment (primary, lower secondary, upper secondary and third level), marital status (single, married, cohabiting, widowed and separated/divorced), gross household income (Stutzer 2004)[5] and number of dependent children in the household (1, 2, 3+). As an indicator of health status, the number of times the respondent has visited the doctor in the past year (never or once, two to five times and six or more times a year) is used.

The cost of housing is an important issue in most areas in Ireland, with a 300 per cent increase in house prices between 1996 and 2006. In rural areas, 36 per cent of respondents saw the cost of housing as a major problem in their area, with 15 per cent believing this to be the most important problem in the area where they live. The corresponding figures in urban areas were 39 and 25 per cent respectively. Hence, variables capturing household tenure (owned outright, mortgaged, renting, or in public housing) were included in the regression analysis.

A composite variable corresponding to local facilities and services in the respondent's area is also included. It is a dummy that takes the value of 1 if the

---

5   Income is expressed in thousands of euro. Missing values were imputed based on the respondent's socio-demographic characteristics including age, gender, marital status, education level, area inhabited and employment status. The original income variable was divided into 14 categories, so mid-points were used.

respondent considers access to, or quality of public services to be a problem in their area. More specifically, the respondent is asked what they consider to be the 'most important' problems in their area and this variable is comprised of responses where public transport, educational facilities, shops and healthcare were seen as problematic.

The experience of 'new' rural residents (i.e., those who have recently moved from a more urban to rural area) vis-à-vis long term rural residents merits more attention. New rural groups often have higher expectations regarding local services, and these 'consumers' may be more reluctant to accept a lack of quality in service provision than long term residents, who traditionally may have relied on social networks and family for support (Moseley, Owen 2008). A variable is included in the rural regression which equals one if the respondent moved to the area less than six years ago. Also included is a variable in the urban regression which equals one if the respondent expresses likelihood to move in the near future, i.e., within five years.

The experiences of new residents in relation to volunteering also warrants further attention as gaps in local service provision in many rural areas have traditionally been addressed by the voluntary sector (Shucksmith, Shucksmith, Watt 2006), which may be under threat from a decline in support from local community volunteering. The suggestion is that as rural communities have expanded due to in migration, with many of these new rural dwellers commuting long distances to work, that the traditional sense of community has broken down. The level of social capital in each area is proxied by the respondent's participation in voluntary work. As church attendance has been perceived to have declined in rural Ireland over the past six years, variables are also included on religious beliefs and practices (attendance at religious services), to capture any influence of these variables.

Estimation strategy

Regressions of life satisfaction on socio-economic and socio-demographic variables (e.g., age, gender, employment status, educational attainment, health, marital status, and income) for urban and rural respondents are estimated and compared. These models are similar to that of, for example, Frey, Stutzer (2000). However, the regressions here also examine the influence of additional individual and location characteristics with a potential effect on subjective well-being (number of dependent children in the household, type of household tenure, civic engagement, religious beliefs and practices) not typically employed in life satisfaction regressions which may have relevance in an Irish context. Also examined is if (1) being a recent migrant to a rural area, or (2) expressing a desire to move from an urban area in the near future, has any influence on subjective well-being.

Results

Descriptive Statistics

In this section, the underlying opinions which influence the counterurbanisation decision are examined, i.e., the 'pull-factor', but also what the perceived limitations of rural living are. A section of each of the surveys was designed to capture what respondents perceived to be the main benefits and limitations of both urban and rural living (Table 12.1).

What urban dwellers perceive to be the benefits of rural living can be clustered into two general areas, environmental and quality of life issues. The specific questions asked were designed to gauge what each respondent believed to be the main benefit or limitation of rural living and one answer was recorded. The quality of life topics mentioned include the area being peaceful, a small community, less crime, no stress, easier to raise children and privacy. The environmental topics mentioned include better environment, healthy lifestyle, clean fresh air and less traffic, and these were brought up by the interviewees themselves, i.e., not prompted by the interviewer or given as part of a question. These attributes relate primarily to the 'private' benefits of rural living – more space, privacy, peacefulness – plus a perception that rural areas have a sense of community and safeness. These stated benefits are very similar to those stated by rural respondents themselves and are key to understanding counterurbanisation trends. Based on the same 2007 dataset, social features were recorded as the primary motive for previously urban dwellers moving to rural locations (Gkartzios, Scott 2008).Whereas in studies of counterurbanisation in England, environmental factors are usually most frequently cited (Halfacree 1994, Walmsley, Epps, Duncan 1998).

Table 12.1   Benefits and limitations of rural living

Main Benefits of Rural Living	Rural		Urban	
	n	Per cent	n	Per cent
Peaceful	265	32.8	294	31.1
Clean, fresh air	102	12.6	120	12.7
Space	51	6	67	7.1
Freedom	51	6	59	6.2
Friendly people	51	6	61	6.4
Healthy lifestyle	44	5.5	47	5.0
Privacy	59	7	40	4.2

Main Benefits of Rural Living	Rural		Urban	
	n	Per cent	n	Per cent
Better environment	21	2.6	23	2.4
Better class of life	40	5	21	2.2
Easier to raise children	46	5.5	36	3.8
Less traffic	15	2	29	3.1
No Stress	10	1	18	1.9
Less crime	9	1	19	2.0
Small community	14	1	18	1.9
No benefits	7	0.5	22	2.3
Main Limitations of Rural Living				
Lack of public transport	204	25.3	256	27.1
Isolation	80	10	196	20.7
Too far from facilities and services	145	18	152	16.1
No social activities	47	6	56	5.9
Lack of shops	36	4.5	57	6.0
Too far to travel	44	5.5	56	5.9
No facilities	27	3.5	35	3.7
Distance	43	5.3	30	3.2
No limitations	134	17	38	4.0

Source: Clinch et al. 2007a; 2007b

When examining what urban dwellers perceive to be the main limitations of rural living, it is interesting that these limitations are very similar to those stated by rural dwellers themselves. However, it is notable that urban respondents perceive 'isolation' to be a limitation in much greater numbers than rural dwellers (10 versus 20 per cent). The main limitations of rural living cited by urban respondents were found to centre around a lack of services and facilities and quality of life issues. A lack of public transport was the most commonly cited limitation of rural living at 27 per cent, with other issues mentioned including too far from facilities and services, lack of shops and no facilities. Quality of life limitations cited included isolation and no social activities.

Table 12.2   Limitations of urban living: urban respondents only

Main Limitations of Urban Living	Urban	
	N	Per cent
Too crowded	182	19.2
Crime	200	21.1
Traffic congestion	184	19.5
Pollution (water or air)	38	4.0
Noise pollution	77	8.1
Traffic / road works	46	4.9
House / apartment prices	71	7.5
Drugs	30	3.2
No privacy	29	3.1
None	35	3.7

Source: Clinch et al. 2007a; 2007b

Also examined is what urban dwellers perceive to be the main limitations of urban living, i.e., the 'push factors'. In almost equal numbers, urban respondents cite 'too crowded', 'crime' and 'traffic congestion' as the main limitations of urban living.

The possibility is then investigated that individuals who express a desire to move in the near future experience a lower quality of life than those who do not express this desire. It appears that this line of reasoning is borne out by the data, as those who state that they are likely to move residence in the next five years are less satisfied with life than those who do not (5.3 compared to 5.5, p<0.000).

To examine if the pull factors identified above actually do manifest themselves in higher quality of life for those respondents that move from urban to rural areas, the life satisfaction scores of recent migrants to rural areas are compared to those of long term residents. Almost 20 per cent of rural dwellers fit into the category of recent migrants, i.e., five years ago or less, and it is interesting that 50 per cent were from urban areas (small towns or larger) with the remaining from villages or the open countryside.

Overall, rural individuals are quite satisfied with their lives – very few respondents reporting in the bottom three categories of 'bad', 'very bad' or 'as bad as can be' (Figure 12.2). Since more than 95 per cent of respondents in both samples are in the top four categories, the main differences in self-reported subjective well-being between the areas are seen in the higher categories. For example, 27 per cent of rural individuals report their lives to be 'as good as can be' compared to 15 per cent in urban areas. While only 10 per cent of rural respondents report their lives as 'alright', the corresponding figure is 17 per cent in urban areas.

Life-satisfaction regressions

Table 12.3 shows the results from the estimation of ordinary least squares (OLS) life-satisfaction regressions. Such regressions minimize the sum of squared vertical distances between the observed responses in the data, and the responses predicted by a linear approximation. The reference groups for the independent variables are in parentheses.

Table 12.3 Ordinary least squares regressions/ dependent variable 'life satisfaction'

	Variable Name	Rural	Urban
Age	Age	0.0016	-0.0003
		(0.34)	(0.65)
Gender	Male	-0.1306	-0.0373
(female)		(1.23)	(0.45)
Employment status	Retired	0.2175	-0.0028
		(1.28)	(0.02)
(self-employed)	Engaged in home duties	0.2072	0.1261
		(1.25)	(0.82)
	Student	0.4901	-0.0896
		(1.62)	(0.44)
	Unemployed	-0.2405	-0.7574***
		(0.79)	(2.83)
	Not working, not seeking work	-0.1791	-0.6644**
		(0.43)	(2.14)
	Working full-time	0.0806	-0.0648
		(0.66)	(0.48)
	Working part-time	0.2326	-0.0067
		(1.26)	(0.03)

	Variable Name	Rural	Urban
	Disabled, unable to work	-0.3503	-0.5043*
		(1.13)	(1.71)
Education	Lower secondary	0.2891**	-0.1745
(primary)		(1.98)	(1.15)
	Upper secondary	0.1994	-0.0614
		(1.29)	(0.44)
	Degree	0.3109*	-0.1449
		(1.89)	(1.00)
Health	2–5 doctor visits	0.0164	-0.0631
(Visited the doctor 0 or 1 in the last year)		(0.18)	(0.81)
	6 or more visits	-0.2916*	-0.1850
		(1.92)	(1.28)
Marital Status	Married	-0.0690	0.0799
(single)		(0.49)	(0.68)
	Cohabit	0.0483	0.1430
		(0.25)	(1.00)
	Separated or divorced	-0.5715**	-0.0899
		(2.34)	(0.50)
	Widowed	-0.1850	-0.1995
		(0.87)	(0.97)
Income	Income (1,000s)	0.0075***	0.0050*
		(2.60)	(1.96)
No. of Children	1 Child	0.1611	0.0552
(no children)		(1.25)	(0.52)
	2 children	0.2336*	-0.1213
		(1.77)	(1.01)
	3 children	0.0300	-0.0891
		(0.21)	(0.70)

	Variable Name	Rural	Urban
Household tenure (own outright)	Own with a mortgage	-0.0318	-0.0725
		(0.29)	(0.78)
	Rent privately	-0.2267	-0.1472
		(1.26)	(1.20)
	Local authority	0.0340	-0.2404
		(0.16)	(1.54)
Volunteerism (more than once a month)	Volunteer monthly	0.1897	0.1765
		(0.99)	(0.71)
	Volunteer yearly	-0.2830	-0.0675
		(1.45)	(0.29)
	Don't volunteer	-0.0625	-0.2188
		(0.50)	(1.14)
Religious attendance (once a week or more)	Every couple of weeks or monthly	-0.2259*	-0.1374
		(1.87)	(1.38)
	Less than monthly or special occasions	-0.0567	-0.0816
		(0.47)	(0.83)
	Never	-0.1550	-0.2399*
		(0.70)	(1.71)
Major problems in your area (not a problem)	Access to services	0.1982**	-0.1061
		(2.00)	(1.04)
Constant		5.3159***	5.8649***
		(15.60)	(21.01)
Observations		751	859
Adjusted R-squared		0.05	0.04

Notes: Robust t statistics in parentheses * significant at 10 per cent; ** significant at 5 per cent; *** significant at 1 per cent. The 'Social Capital' question asked differed between the years

Source: Clinch et al. 2007a; 2007b

The coefficient on gender is negative, but insignificant in both areas, indicating no difference in life satisfaction between the genders in Ireland. This is in line with previous studies where gender tends to emerge as insignificant in life satisfaction regressions (e.g., Stutzer 2004, Frey, Stutzer 2000). The results show no significant relationship between life satisfaction and age.

The estimates for the employment status variables are interesting in that, in rural areas, they do not conform to priors in the literature. Firstly, the disabled, unable to work and those engaged in household activities are generally found to be less satisfied with life than the self-employed. In the rural sample they emerge insignificant. Even more interesting is that unemployment emerges negative, but insignificant in the rural regression, whereas in the urban sample and in almost all international studies, unemployment emerges significant with a large coefficient (e.g., Clark, Oswald 1994, Blanchflower, Oswald 2004b). However, these studies use nationally representative surveys while the data used here is from sub-sections of the population. An area of future research would be to determine what insulates rural dwellers from the reduction in life satisfaction that normally accompanies an unemployment spell.

In rural areas, those with lower secondary or upper secondary and third level education are more satisfied with life than those with a primary education level (see also Frey, Stutzer 2000). In some of the literature, however, university education is found to be insignificant or negatively related to life satisfaction (e.g., Veenhoven 1997). These variables emerge insignificant in the urban sample. Our objective measure of health (number of times the respondent visited their doctor in the last year) emerges significant and negative in rural areas, suggesting that those respondents visiting their doctor six or more times a year are less satisfied with their lives than those not attending or attending only once.

Among the marital status variables, being separated or divorced emerges significant in rural areas and such respondents are less likely to be satisfied with their lives than single respondents by half a life satisfaction category. Being married emerges insignificant in both regressions, but this result is in contrast to those in previous studies such as Clark, Oswald (1994) and Blanchflower, Oswald (2004a) which generally find married individuals to be happier than all other marital status categories. This contrasting result is not all that surprising in an Irish context however. Ireland is a predominately Roman Catholic country with a very low divorce rate compared to most developed nations and there is still a stigma associated with divorce amongst the older generation. Evidence suggests that living in a nation with a low rate of divorce is associated with lower levels of reported happiness among the married (Stack, Eshleman 1998). In terms of family composition, in rural areas we find that having two children emerges significant and positive, which conforms with Pittman, Lloyd (1988) who find that the number of children is positively related to life satisfaction. This variable emerges insignificant in urban areas.

Income is significantly related to life satisfaction in both samples, but its coefficient is low, i.e., an increase in income of €1,000 raises well-being by 0.0075, other things being equal. To give an indication of the small size of the effect, an increase of €100,000 would raise well-being by less than one category.

Of the variables not typically included in regressions of this nature, the negative and significant coefficients on the attending religious services variables suggests that increased attendance at religious services increases well-being and this is the case in both urban and rural areas. Examining our proxies for social capital, i.e., the level of volunteerism that the respondent is engaged in, these emerge insignificant in both samples. This is surprising, as studies of respondents in the United States find that regular club attendance, volunteering, entertaining or church attendance is the happiness equivalent of getting a college degree or more than doubling one's income (Putnam 2000). Household tenure emerges insignificant in the regression in both areas. This is also surprising given the concern over the cost of housing expressed by both urban and rural dwellers.

In additional regressions (not shown, available on request), variables were included that capture if the respondent is a recent migrant in the rural case, and if the respondent considers themselves likely to move in the near future in the urban sample. Both of these variables emerge insignificant in their respective regressions. This is interesting in the case of the rural regression as it indicates that there is no significant difference between the well-being of long term residents and recent migrants.

Conclusions

Since the 1990s, spatial planning practice has increasingly focused on issues surrounding sustainable urban form and the role of planning within the context of sustainable development. At the same time, spatial planning policy in rural localities has been increasingly concerned with growth management and restricting housing supply in rural areas on environmental and landscape grounds. However, in parallel to these policy concerns for managing rural housing supply and promoting brownfield development and compact cities, there has often been an increased demand for housing in rural areas from in-migration trends from counterurbanisation, people retiring to the countryside and second home ownership.

In this chapter, the underlying reasons behind the counterurbanisation decision have been examined. Life satisfaction considerations were analyzed and the results were compared across a number of sub-populations, including: urban and rural households, long term rural residents and recent urban to rural migrants, and among urban households that indicated a preference to move locality in the short term. The results show that in general, life satisfaction is high in both areas, but individuals living in rural areas are more satisfied with their lives than their town dwelling counterparts and we attribute this result to a positive effect of a tranquil life outweighing a lack of facilities and services. This may reinforce the argument that the availability of green space and more natural environments, may have important restorative effects on individual well-being, and space is valued above services in residential satisfaction (Verheij, Maas, Groenewegen 2008). What individuals perceive to be the main benefits and limitations of rural life is very similar for both urban and rural dwellers with environmental and quality of life issues seen as the main benefits of rural life, while lack of facilities and services are seen as the limitations. Quality of life issues cited include both positive (e.g., friendly people) and negative (e.g., isolation) traits. However, the positive effects of rural life appear to outweigh the negative effects.

Additionally, socio-economic and socio-demographic variables are found to be important determinants of life-satisfaction in Ireland, with the results generally in line with expectations. The exceptions may be due to the concentration in the international literature on nationally representative samples, while this study deals with sub-samples. For example, unemployment, found in the literature to be the primary economic source of unhappiness (Oswald 1997) emerges insignificant in our rural regression. This is a result that merits further research. In keeping with priors, we find that the separated and divorced are less satisfied with their lives than single respondents, a result that may be linked to stigma still attached to separation and divorce in rural areas (divorce was only introduced in Ireland in 1996) and also the importance of personal relationships to individual well-being. Education emerges as a significant determinant of life satisfaction, with the more highly educated happier. A positive, but weak relationship is found between income and life satisfaction, a result generally found for developed countries.

While spatial planning orthodoxy increasingly emphasizes concentrating residential development into existing urban centres and brownfield sites, the findings suggest that individual life satisfaction is higher in low density, dispersed settlement patterns, suggesting that individual benefits (such as privacy and space) are valued more than a location close to services and facilities. However, further global economic impacts may increasingly challenge this perspective, such as rising fuel costs adding to the expense and availability of transport, issues of transport lie at the heart of problems of inclusion in service provision in rural areas (Shucksmith, Shucksmith, Watt 2006). Similarly, with Ireland having been the first country within the European Union to enter a recession, pressure on public finances is inevitable, suggesting that 'uneconomical' rural services are at risk. In this way, the economic costs of rural living may increasingly be transferred to rural dwellers, who at present experience primarily private benefits. These pose real problems to the ability of vulnerable groups to fully participate in society and to access services, and may reinforce rural gentrification processes leading to the rural as an increasingly middle class space.

References

Barcus, H. 2004. Urban-Rural Migration in the USA: An Analysis of Residential Satisfaction. *Regional Studies,* 38(6), 643–57. Available at: http://www.informaworld.com/10.1080/003434042000240950 [accessed: 15 June 2011].

Black, C.R.D. 1998. Utility. in *The new palgrave: A dictionary of economics,* edited by J. Eatwell. London: Macmillan, 776–78.

Blanchflower, D. and Oswald, A.J. 2004a. Money, sex and happiness. An empirical study. *The Scandinavian journal of economics,* 106(3), 393–415.

Blanchflower, D. and Oswald, A.J. 2004b. Well-being over time in Britain and the USA. *Journal of public economics,* 88(7/8), 1359–86.

Brereton, F., Clinch, J.P. and Ferreira, S. 2008. Happiness, geography and the environment. *Ecological Economics,* 65(2), 386–96. Available at: http://www.sciencedirect.com/science/article/pii/S0921800907003977.

Brereton, F. Bullock, C. Clinch, J.P. and Scott, M. 2011. Rural change and individual well-being: the case of Ireland and rural quality of life. *European Urban and Regional Studies,* 18 (2), 203–27

Carr, A. 2004. *Positive psychology: The science of happiness and human strengths.* Hove: Brunner-Routledge.

Cattaneo, M., Galiani, S., Gertler, P., Martinez, S. and Titiunik, R. *Housing, Health and Happiness.* [Online] Available at: http://siepr.stanford.edu/publicationsprofile/1763 [accessed: 15 June 2011].

Central Statistics Office (CSO). 2007. *Census 2006: Principal Demographic Results.* Dublin: Stationery Office.

Champion, A.G. 1989. *Counterurbanisation : the changing pace and nature of population deconcentration: The changing pace and nature of population deconcentration.* London: Arnold.

Clark, A., Frijters, P. and Shields, M. 2008. Relative income, happiness, and utility. An explanation for the Easterlin paradox and other puzzles. *Journal of Economic Literature,* 46(1), 95–144. Available at: http://eprints.qut.edu.au/30738/.

Clark, A.E. and Oswald, A.J. 1994. Unhappiness and unemployment. *The economic journal,* (424), 648–59.

Clinch, J.P., Brereton, F., & McInerney, D. (2007a), Quality of life in Urban Ireland: Methodology [mimeo]. Dublin: UCD School of Geography, Planning and Environmental Policy.

Clinch, J.P., Brereton, F., & McInerney, D. (2007b), Quality of life in Rural Ireland: Methodology [mimeo]. Dublin: UCD School of Geography, Planning and Environmental Policy.

Dahms, F. and McComb, J. 1999. 'Counterurbanisation', interaction and functional change in a rural amenity area — A Canadian example. *Journal of Rural Studies,* 15(2), 129–46. Available at: 10.1016/S0743-0167(98)00056-4.

Department of the Environment and Local Government (DOELG). 1999. *Residential density: Consultation draft of guidelines for planning authorities.* Dublin.

Department of the Environment and Local Government (DOELG). 2002. *The national spatial strategy 2002–2020: People, places and potential.* Dublin.

Di Tella, R. and MacCulloch, R. 2006. Some uses of happiness data in economics. *The journal of economic perspectives,* 20(1), 25–46.

Diaz, D. and Green, G.P. 2001. Growth Management and Agriculture: An Examination of Local Efforts to Manage Growth and Preserve Farmland in Wisconsin Cities, Villages, and Towns. *Rural Sociology,* 66(3), 317–41. Available at: 10.1111/j.1549-0831.2001.tb00070.x.

Diener, E., Suh, E.M., Lucas, R.E. and Smith, H.L. 1999. Subjective Well-Being: Three Decades of Progress. *Psychological Bulletin,* 125(2), 276–302. Available at: http://www.sciencedirect.com/science/article/pii/S0033290902001521.

Dublin Regional Authority and Mid-East Regional Authority (DMERA). 2004. *Regional planning guidelines: Greater Dublin area 2004–2016.* Dublin.

Erikson, R. 1993. Descriptions of inequality. The Swedish approach to welfare research. in *The Quality of life,* edited by M.C. Nussbaum and A. Sen. Oxford England, New York: Clarendon Press; Oxford University Press.

Escribano, M.J.R. 2007. Migration to Rural Navarre: Questioning the Experience of Counterurbanisation. *Tijdschrift voor Economische en Sociale Geografie,* 98(1), 32–41. Available at: 10.1111/j.1467-9663.2007.00374.x.

European Commission. 1999. *ESDP: European spatial development perspective: Towards balanced and sustainable development of the territory of the European Union; agreed at the informal Council of Ministers responsible for Spatial Planning in Potsdam May 1999.* Luxembourg.

Ferrer-i-Carbonell, A. and Frijters, P. 2004. How Important is Methodology for the estimates of the determinants of Happiness?. *The Economic Journal,* 114(497), 641–59. Available at: 10.1111/j.1468-0297.2004.00235.x.

Fisher, T. 2003. Differentiation of Growth Processes in the Peri-urban Region: An Australian Case Study. *Urban Studies,* 40(3), 551–65. Available at: 10.1080/0042098032000053914.

Frey, B.S. and Stutzer, A. 2000. Happiness, Economy and Institutions. *The Economic Journal,* 110(466), 918–38. Available at: 10.1111/1468-0297.00570.

Gallent, N. and Tewdwr-Jones, M. 2007. *Decent homes for all: Planning's evolving role in housing provision.* London: Routledge.

Gkartzios, M. and Scott, M. 2005. Urban-generated rural housing and evidence of counterurbanisation in the Dublin city-region. in *Renewing urban communities: Environment, citizenship, and sustainability in Ireland,* edited by N. Moore and M. Scott. Aldershot, Hampshire, England ;, Burlington, VT: Ashgate, 132–56.

Gkartzios, M. and Scott, M. 2008. *Rural idyll versus rural living: Insights from 3 Irish rural case studies.* European Network for Housing Research Conference, 6–9 July 2008 in Dublin.

Grafton, D. and Bolton, N. 1987. Counter-urbanisation and the rural periphery: some evidence from North Devon. in *Managing the city: The aims and impacts of urban policy*, edited by B.T. Robson. London: Croom Helm, 191–210.

Halfacree, K.H. 1994. The importance of 'the rural' in the constitution of counterurbanisation: Evidence from England in the 1980s. *Sociologia Ruralis,* 34(2–3), 164–89. Available at: 10.1111/j.1467-9523.1994.tb00807.x.

Halfacree, K.H. 1997. Contrasting roles for the post-productivist countryside. A postmodern perspective on counterurbanisation. in *Contested countryside cultures: Otherness, marginalisation, and rurality*, edited by P. Cloke. London: Routledge, 70–93.

Kahneman, D. 1999. Objective Happiness. in *Well-being: The foundations of hedonic psychology*, edited by D. Kahneman. New York: Russell Sage Foundation.

Layard, P.R.G. 2005. *Happiness: Lessons from a new science.* New York: Penguin Press.

Mitchell, C.J.A. 2004. Making sense of counterurbanisation. *Journal of Rural Studies,* 20(1), 15–34. Available at: http://www.sciencedirect.com/science/article/pii/S0743016703000317.

Moro, M., Brereton, F., Ferreira, S. and Clinch, J.P. 2008. Ranking quality of life using subjective well-being data. *Ecological Economics,* 65(3), 448–60. Available at: 10.1016/j.ecolecon.2008.01.003.

Moseley, M.J. 1984. The revival of rural areas in advanced economies: a review of some causes and consequences. *Geoforum,* 15(3), 447–56. Available at: http://www.sciencedirect.com/science/article/pii/0016718584900502.

Moseley, M.J. and Owen, S. 2008. The future of services in rural England: The drivers of change and a scenario for 2015. *Progress in Planning,* 69(3), 93–130. Available at: 10.1016/j.progress.2007.12.002.

Murdoch, J. and Lowe, P. 2003. The preservationist paradox: modernism, environmentalism and the politics of spatial division. *Transactions of the Institute of British Geographers,* 28(3), 318–32. Available at: 10.1111/1475-5661.00095.

National Economic and Social Council (NESC). *Housing in Ireland: Performance and policy.* [Online] Available at: http://www.nesc.ie/docs/housing/NESCHousingReport.pdf.

Oswald, A.J. 1997. Happiness and Economic Performance. *The Economic Journal,* 107(445), 1815–31. Available at: 10.1111/1468-0297.00260.

Oswald, F., Wahl, H.-W., Mollenkopf, H. and Schilling, O. 2003. Housing and Life Satisfaction of Older Adults in Two Rural Regions in Germany. *Research on Aging,* 25(2), 122–43. Available at: 10.1177/0164027502250016.

Phillips, M. 2004. Other geographies of gentrification. *Progress in Human Geography,* 28(1), 5–30. Available at: 10.1191/0309132504ph458oa.

Pittman, J.F. and Lloyd, S.A. 1988. Quality of family life, social support and stress. *Journal of Marriage and Family,* 50(1), 53–67. Available at: http://www.jstor.org/stable/352427.

Putnam, R.D. (ed.). 2000. *Bowling alone: The collapse and revival of American community.* New York, NY: Simon & Schuster.

Scott, M., Gkartzios, M., Redmond, D., Williams, B. and Clinch, J.P. 2005. *Emerging settlement trends and implementing the National Spatial Strategy.* Dublin.

Shucksmith, M., Shucksmith, J. and Watt, J. 2006. Rurality and Social Inclusion: A Case of Preschool Education. *Social Policy and Administration,* 40(6), 678–91. Available at: 10.1111/j.1467-9515.2006.00526.x.

Smith, D.P. 2007. The changing faces of rural populations: '"(re) Fixing" the gaze' or 'eyes wide shut'? *Journal of Rural Studies,* 23(3), 275–82. Available at: 10.1016/j.jrurstud.2007.03.001.

Smith, D.P. and Holt, L. 2005. 'Lesbian migrants in the gentrified valley' and 'other' geographies of rural gentrification. *Journal of Rural Studies,* 21(3), 313–22. Available at: 10.1016/j.jrurstud.2005.04.002.

Stack, S. and Eshleman, J.R. 1998. Marital Status and Happiness: A 17 Nation Study. *Journal of Marriage and Family,* 60(2), 527–36. Available at: http://www.jstor.org/stable/353867.

Stockdale, A. 2006. Migration: Pre-requisite for rural economic regeneration? *Journal of Rural Studies,* 22(3), 354–66. Available at: 10.1016/j.jrurstud.2005.11.001.

Stockdale, A., Findlay, A. and Short, D. 2000. The repopulation of rural Scotland: opportunity and threat. *Journal of Rural Studies,* 16(2), 243–57. Available at: http://www.sciencedirect.com/science/article/pii/S0743016799000455.

Stutzer, A. 2004. The role of income aspirations in individual happiness. *Journal of Economic Behavior & Organization,* 54(1), 89–109. Available at: 10.1016/j.jebo.2003.04.003.

United Nations. 1954. *Report on international definition and measurement of standards and levels of living.* New York.

van Praag, B.M.S. and Baarsma, B.E. 2005. Using Happiness Surveys to Value Intangibles: The Case of Airport Noise*. *The Economic Journal,* 115(500), 224–46. Available at: 10.1111/j.1468-0297.2004.00967.x.

Veenhoven, R. 1997. Advances in the understanding of happiness. *Revue Québécoise de Psychologie,* 18(2), 29–74.

Verheij, R., Maas, J. and Groenewegen, P. 2008. Urban--Rural Health Differences and the Availability of Green Space. *European Urban and Regional Studies,* 15(4), 307–16. Available at: 10.1177/0969776408095107.

Walmsley, D.J., Epps, W.R. and Duncan, C.J. 1998. Migration to the New South Wales North Coast 1986–91. Lifestyle motivated counterurbanisation. *Geoforum,* 29(1), 105–18. Available at: http://www.sciencedirect.com/science/article/pii/S0016718597000237.

Chapter 13

Socio-Environmental Impacts of New Housing Development at Infill and Greenfield Sites – Methical Design for a Multicriteria Assessment

Sophie Schetke, Theo Kötter, Dagmar Haase

Overview

Despite decreasing population in an increasing number of German urban agglomerations, urban expansion and land development pressure is still the main driver behind massive land consumption. This negatively affects natural resources and fosters the loss of ecosystem services in the surrounding suburban areas. Since the high annual land consumption rates have not yet abated, the German Federal government established a quantitative benchmark which aims to reduce land consumption from 113 hectares (280 acres) per day in 2008 to 30 hectares (75 acres) per day in 2020 (http://www.nachhaltigkeitsrat.de). In order to realize this significant step, stakeholders need to focus on more compact settlement development and to use infill strategies. Options include both brownfield development and densification strategies. Despite obvious positive effects of reduced land consumption and protection of natural resources in suburban areas, the specific socio-environmental impacts of infill development remain unclear, especially with regard to residents´ quality of life (QoL) and the provision of urban ecosystem services (UES) including the provision of local climate regulation, recreation or aesthetic features. This study introduces an innovative methical design for a multicriteria assessment (MCA) of the socio-environmental impacts of new infill development compared to suburban – especially greenfield – development. The multicriteria assessment focuses on the provisioning benefits of urban green space for urban residents. So doing, it bridges the gap between the two concepts of quality of life and urban ecosystems services. The study presents an integrative multicriteria assessment scheme which can be applied by both urban planners and scientists. We show that infill development does not equal a decrease in the environmental conditions in cities.

Introduction

Currently, we see a paradoxical disparity of urban land development in most of the German urban agglomerations. Simultaneously we are witnessing ongoing suburbanisation, considerable proportions of inner-urban housing stock which are old and no longer marketable, and an increasing amount of industrial and residential brownfields (see for example, Schetke, Haase 2008, Schetke 2010). As urban policy makers aim to attract more residents in order to offset the decreasing population numbers, cities are under ongoing development pressure (Couch, Karecha 2006). In the light of political targets such as the 30 hectare (75 acre) per day benchmark to promote compact and resource preserving settlement growth, infill strategies are needed. These strategies not only address ways to sustain future settlement growth, they also respond to new lifestyle considerations and living preferences (Haase et al. 2008). Considering the German Ruhr-Area, where the case study city Essen is located, infill development has become necessary due to limitations of spatial expansion into the outskirts. Neighbouring growing cities tend to merge which leads to an urban mélange of blurred transition spaces between inner and suburban areas (Schetke 2010).

According to the literature, a densification of existing settlement structures is typically followed by the decreasing potential of urban ecosystem services and negative impacts on resident's quality of life (Schetke 2010, Douglas 1983 in Priego, Breuste, Rojas 2008, de Ridder, Adamec, Banuelos . 2004, Tyrvainen, Mäkinen, Schipperijn 2007). According to Schetke 2010: 9 'the acceptance of infill development is critically discussed among planners and scientists, as in most cases, local residents strongly disapprove of [...] higher densities. This highlights the gap in values between local residents´ preferences and urban policies'.

Following studies on the social and environmental effects of demolition in housing estates we know that a simple quantitative omission of built-up space does not necessarily lead to improved ecological functions and an enhanced provision of a suitable quality of life (Schetke, Haase 2008). Again, Schetke states:

> 'We have to carefully focus on prerequisites, preconditions and socio-environmental circumstances accompanying each change – both reduction and expansion – of the urban fabric' (Schetke 2010: 11).

In doing so, this study introduces a quantitative approach to the impact assessment of different forms of settlement growth which integrates both the concepts of quality of life and urban ecosystem services. In the following, we address three major questions:

- Which socio-environmental preconditions exist in inner-urban and suburban areas determining their quality as housing areas in terms of quality of life and urban ecosystem services?
- What socio-environmental impacts occur as a consequence of either

infill (re-densification, revitalisation of former industrial brownfields) or greenfield development?
• Does infilling of the inner-urban fabric lead to negative socio-environmental impacts in terms of quality of life and urban ecosystem services and how can we evaluate this?

The multicriteria assessment approach

As a major part of the introduced multicriteria assessment approach we developed a scenario-based socio-environmental impact assessment procedure of housing estates according to Schetke, Haase, Breuste 2010 (see also Schetke 2010) integrating the concepts of quality of life and associated urban ecosystem services (specified according Bolund, Hunhammar 1999, Costanza et al. 1997, de Groot, Wilson, Boumans 2002). This study focuses on the quantitative analysis of the functionality of urban green spaces under conditions of settlement growth and housing development. As discussed in Schetke 2010 and Schetke, Haase, Breuste 2010, during the development special emphasis was put on the question of green spaces and structures which might be modified by processes of suburbanisation and infill development. As the emerging new land uses, urban patterns and green structures are diverse,

> 'a made-to-measure and integrated methodology for on-site analysis and small-scale observation' (Schetke, Haase, Breuste 2010: 144) is presented here.

This multicriteria assessment procedure has been developed as a Visual Basic Decision Support System (VB-DSS) addressing the needs of both planners and scientists (Schetke 2010).

> 'The concept of 'quality of life' represents more than the private 'living standards' and refers to all the elements of the conditions in which people live, that is, all their needs and requirements' (Fadda, Jiron 1999: 262).

Furthermore, there is no doubt that this concept is difficult to grasp, to measure but also to define (Fadda, Jiron 1999). Accordingly, we have developed the assessment procedure under the framework of sustainable urban development. According to the literature (Bolund, Hunhammar 1999, de Groot, Wilson, Boumans 2002, Santos, Martins 2007, Schetke 2010, Schetke, Haase, Breuste 2010, Tyrvainen, Mäkinen, Schipperijn 2007), urban green spaces and green land uses are considered as one essential contributor to urban residents' quality of life and as linking elements in bridging the gap between the concepts of quality of life and urban ecosystem services (Schetke, Haase, Breuste 2010, Schetke 2010, Millennium Ecosystem Assessment (MEA) 2005).

The Case Study: Essen

The City of Essen, located in the German Ruhr-Area, serves as the case study for this research. The city has around 580,000 inhabitants and

> 'is characterized by spatially limited urban expansion and challenging infill development with brownfield (re-)development of former industrial sites and re-densification' (Schetke 2010: 77).

It is a densely built-up urban area with an industrial past. Despite considerable existing housing potential in inner-urban areas, the existing demand for specific segments of the housing market, including single-family homes and high-quality housing, cannot be met. Thus, housing in new areas is being planned for and developed. In most cases, a lack of marketability of the existing inner-urban housing estates is seen as a crucial factor for these paradoxical trends.

The analysis includes 31 potential housing sites spread over the municipal area of Essen (Schetke 2010). Their formal planning status and time horizon for coming onto the market vary due to various adjustments based on either preparatory planning or binding land use planning. Of the 31 sites, 19 are infill development and therefore located in inner-urban neighbourhoods. The remaining 12 sites are located in more remote locations of the city and represent greenfield development. The potential future housing sites were displayed in the draft (2008) of the regional land use plan for the City of Essen. The regional land use plan is the instrument of preparatory land use planning and no legal claims can be asserted. The compilation of all analyzed sites does not entirely meet the compilation of housing sites displayed in the final version of the regional land use plan (2010). Also the status of infill and greenfield development refers to the initial reference year of 2008.

Methodology

Multicriteria Assessment

A multicriteria assessment

> 'allows the integration of manifold aspects of a problem and considers conflicts of interest of different stakeholders [...] within a planning process' (Schetke, Haase 2008: 489 referring to Nijkamp, Torrieri, Vreeker 2002; Nijkamp, Vreeker 2000).

In their article titled 'A decision support system for regional sustainable development,' Nijkamp and Ouwersloot (1997) propose the application of critical threshold values (CTV), which refer to a sustainable state of a system or an urban region (Figure 13.1).

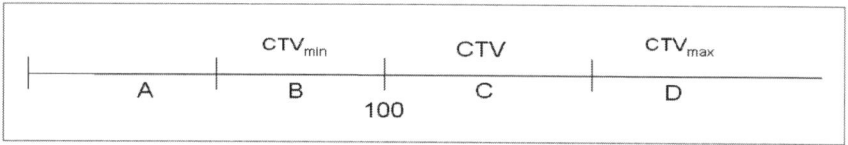

Figure 13.1   CTV-scheme of the assessment

Source: Schetke, Haase 2008 modified according to Nijkamp, Torrieri, Vreeker 2002

For all indicators of the assessment minimum and maximum threshold values (CTVMin and CTVMax) can be provided and were calculated according to local conditions. Both threshold values of each indicator refer to the respective weighted mean values of the whole city area and to the wider living surroundings of each potential housing site (buffer distance = 1,000 metres).

The indicator set

The indicator set represents a nested framework starting from the dimension of sustainability (Schetke, Haase 2008: 490; eq.1):

$$D_S = \sum_{1,2,...} w * C_S \qquad (1)$$

where DS is the respective dimension of sustainability, w the weighting and CS the respective criterion. Each criterion consists itself of a set of quantifiable sustainability indicators (eq.2):

$$C_S = \sum_{1,2,...} w * I_S \qquad (2)$$

where w is the weighting and IS represents the indicator.

Data compilation and processing

As the analysis of the impacts on quality of life and urban ecosystem services has an anthropocentric focus, special emphasis is put on the analysis of closer living surroundings, as this area has immediate influence on the residents living conditions and quality of life (Schetke 2010). German planning literature (von Fritsch, Fritzsche, Naumann 2004: 22) defines a radius of 500 metres (one third of a mile) which represents about a 5 to 10 minute walking distance. Therefore a

500 metre buffer where a walking distance coefficient of 1.2 is included and was applied around all analysed potential housing sites. Since some of the respective sites are in close distance to each other the 31 original sites were aggregated to 14 buffer sites in total.

The availability of data on urban development and land use in Essen is fairly good. Table 13.1 presents the categories used for the integrative multicriteria assessment on quality of life and urban ecosystem services. Compiling the database, analogous and digital data are primarily used in order to get an initial picture of the overall data quality. This covers the district, block and building scale. Besides existing municipal land use data, modified cadastral data are used. To get closer insights into the performance of urban ecosystem services of specific land use classes an attribution of cadastral data has been applied based on the approach of Singer 1995, who defined regulative functions or biotope quality related to urban land use types using a simple scale ranging from 0 (= very low performance) to 4 (= very high performance) Schetke 2010. The attribution of cadastral land use data with respect to explicitly hydrological indicators is based on the Berlin Environmental Atlas (Senatsverwaltung für Stadtentwicklung 2005, Schetke 2010).

Additionally, to provide detailed data on green space distribution, accessibility and property rights, a geographic information systems (GIS) based green space mapping for the whole municipal area of Essen has been used with municipal land use data at the block level and cadastral land use data (Schetke 2010). Despite the expenditure of time and money, efforts to create such a detailed data base on the urban open space and its differentiation between private and public access to greenery have been very worthwhile not only for assessing the quantitative supply of green space, but also its accessibility and availability for residents.

Table 13.1 Categories of QoL/UES-assessment (modified according to Schetke 2010, Schetke et al. 2010)

Concept of quality of life determinants deriving from urban green infrastructure*	Associated Urban Ecosystem Services (UES) directly affecting residents**	Social function, amenities, values, ecosystem function***	Data set
Recreation	Air filtering/climate regulation recreation noise reduction	Contact with nature & provision of favorable living conditions, providing opportunities for recreational activities, regulation at local level, feeling of comfort, temperature regulation	Cadastral Data
	Habitat/ biotope provision, conservation refugia	Species richness, habitat for resident an transient population, feeling of naturalness; heterogeneous/ unaffected green spaces	Cadastral Data
	Recreation	Contact with nature & provision of favorable living conditions, providing opportunities for recreational activities	Cadastral Data
Regulation and environmental health	Water and climate regulation	Soil formation processes, regulation of hydrological flows, feeling of naturalness, climate regulation	Cadastral Data
	Refugia	Habitat function (of soil)	Cadastral Data
	Reduction of pollutants	Gas regulation, regulation at local level, provision with healthy living conditions, air filtering	Cadastral Data

Concept of quality of life determinants deriving from urban green infrastructure*	Associated Urban Ecosystem Services (UES) directly affecting residents**	Social function, amenities, values, ecosystem function***	Data set
Social cohesion/ community and local identity	Recreational & cultural values, spiritual and historic information	Consolidation of a community, privacy, identity, psychological benefits, contact with nature	Green mapping using Cadastral Data & land use classifications on block level
	Recreational & cultural values, spiritual and historic information	Information function, provision of meeting facilities, design of the public domain, Interaction of different social groups, strengthening of the social network, attractiveness of a place	See above
	Recreational & cultural values, spiritual and historic information	Information function, fulfilment of privacy needs	See above

Notes: *e.g., Burgess, Harrison, Limb 1988, MEA 2005, Priego, Breuste, Rojas 2008, Schetke, Haase 2008, Schetke, Haase, Breuste 2010 **Bolund, Hunhammar 1999, Costanza et al. 1997, Chan et al. 2006, de Groot, Wilson, Boumans 2002, Schetke, Haase, Breuste 2010 ***Definition see Costanza et al. 1997, Chan et al. 2006, de Groot, Wilson, Boumans 2002, MEA 2005, Norberg 1999, Singer 1995, Schetke, Haase, Breuste 2010

Scenarios of urban growth

For the impact assessment according to quality of life and urban ecosystem services, planning scenarios for three housing structure types according to cadastral land use classes have been implemented. We assume a full realisation of the new housing development to be able to quantify socio-environmental impacts due varying urban structure types. We also know that a single site will probably not consist of one single structure type but will be more heterogeneous. Taking into account that the majority of the sites are not subject to binding land use planning, a homogeneous scenario application seems appropriate (Schetke 2010).

Those sites planned as single-family homes are allotted to three scenarios based on structure types (1) detached houses, (2) semi-detached houses, and (3) row-houses. They represent not only different densities within the urban fabric, but also imply more diversity among residents, as well as various types of green spaces. For those sites dedicated to multi-storey housing, future housing structures have been categorised as (1) group houses and (2) block structures. The modification of green spaces and their provision due to settlement growth was calculated according to local standards of green quality and quantity of cadastral land use classes. The number of new residents was calculated using the variables structure-type, associated gross building land, housing density and occupancy rate. A closer insight into the complete underlying methodology can be derived from Schetke (2010).

Decision Support System (DSS)

The assessment was integrated into the prototype of a visual basic graphical user interface (VB GUI) being executed within MS Excel® (Schetke 2010). The method realises the impact assessment of the mentioned scenarios (Figure 13.2) and the indicator weighting.

Results

Impacts of settlement growth

In order to gain a closer insight into the socio-environmental impacts of settlement growth, the following initial research questions were investigated: Which socio-environmental preconditions exist for housing areas in inner-urban and suburban districts in terms of quality of life and urban ecosystem services? Should industrial cities like Essen be perceived of as 'environmental aggressors' (Priego, Breuste, Rojas 2008)? The following paragraphs give a short insight into selected preliminary results and directly compare the status quo analysis distinguishing between sites of infill and greenfield development. Note that the impacts due to settlement growth and indicator values at individual sites always refer to not

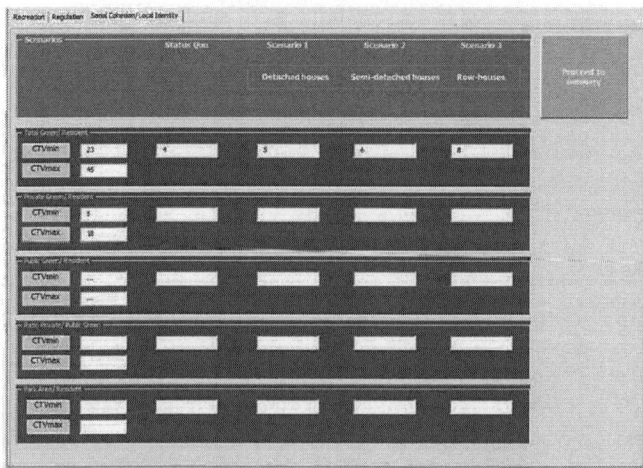

Input of scenario-dependent indicator-values for an integrated assessment of Quality of Life and Urban Ecosystem Services

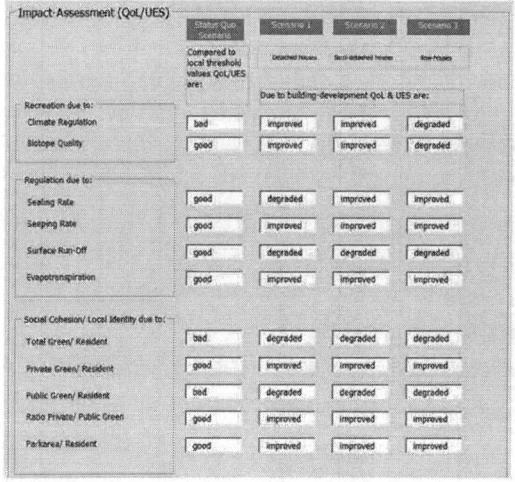

Summary of scenario-outputs according to varying structure types: detached, semi-detached or row-houses

Figure 13.2 **VB-DSS of the integrated Quality of Life/UES-assessment (modif. acc. to Schetke 2010)**

only the new building land itself but also to its closer surroundings (radius = 500 metres) as outlined in subsection *The indicator set*. All calculated values which are presented in the following sections are based on a study by Schetke 2010.

Status-Quo Analysis

The status-quo analysis shows an overall worse performance for infill sites in terms of urban ecosystem services and a comparatively good performance for greenfield sites. In order to get a closer insight into status quo conditions of different sites and the associated impacts due to settlement growth, it is useful to consider single indicator performances, as well as different measures of development. These are brownfield revitalisation, re-densification and new development.

The mean value of the regulative function indicator (Figure 13.3) within the city of Essen is at a medium level (value: 2.14). (This estimation is based on the classification of Singer 1995, which enables an attribution of cadastral land use classes according to urban ecosystem services). Compared to that, park areas are defined with a value of 4, implying a very high regulative function. Due to the high density of the built-up central and northern parts of the City of Essen and a more agrarian character in its southern parts, the average urban values of biotope quality and diversity are also comparatively low, at 1.65. The optimum value of 4.0 applies to land use types such as forests or wetlands.

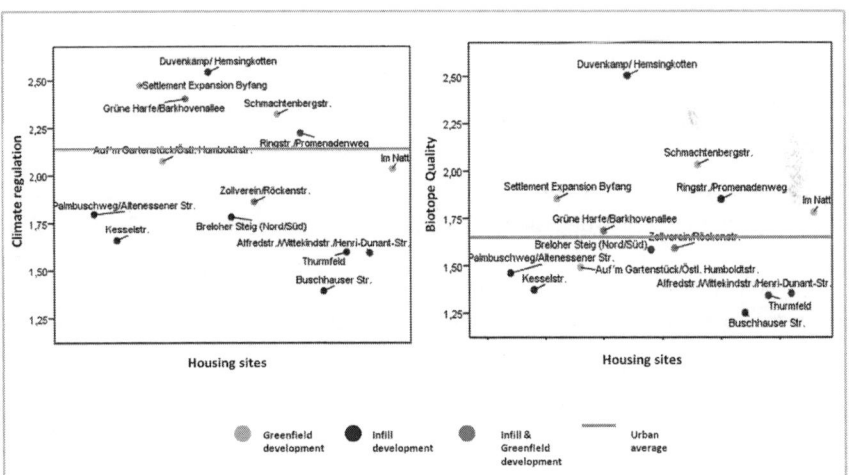

Figure 13.3   UES-indicator samples 'climate regulation' and 'biotope quality' (author´s own illustration)

The indicator values of the infill sites mostly fall below these benchmarks indicated by the urban average whilst greenfield sites show a better performance, but do not exceed them significantly (see light blue bars in Figure 13.3). The same counts for the results of the indicator surface sealing rate (urban mean value: 34 per cent) which show a quite clear distinction between sites of infill development (above mean value) – and greenfield sites (below mean value).

Also, associated hydrological indicators show a similar distinction between infill and greenfield development sites. Here, the indicator 'water surface run-off' is positively lower at greenfield sites than at infill development sites (with values below the urban mean value of 19 per cent of total precipitation). Results of the indicator evapotranspiration of greenfield sites are positively above urban mean value of 55 per cent of total precipitation and show a better performance than those of inner urban sites. Also the values of the indicator seeping rate remain above urban mean value of 26 per cent at greenfield sites.

Regarding the overall green provision and its differentiation into private and public green we find an above threshold provision with total green which is estimated at 6 square metres per resident (von Fritsch, Fritzsche, Naumann 2004) at sites of infill and greenfield development. Even the urban mean value itself is very high with more than 200 square meters (2,100 square feet) per capita due to agrarian and rural lands south of Essen. Despite the fact that the overall provision of private green space around inner urban sites remains below the urban mean value of around 74 square metres (800 square feet) per resident (including private gardens and courtyards), it significantly exceeds threshold values from the planning and scientific literature. The same is true for the overall provision of public green around most inner urban sites. The provision of private parks as a major contributor to interaction and local identity is far above planning threshold values of 6–7 square metres per capita (Richter 1981) at most sites (inner urban and suburban). Suburban provision of public parks shows overall lower values than inner-urban sites (Schetke 2010).

Scenario Analysis

As the preceding status-quo analysis of the indicators of quality of life and urban ecosystem services shows a clear distinction between sites of infill and greenfield development, we want to answer two remaining research questions: What socio-environmental impacts occur as a result of either infill (such as, densification or revitalisation of former industrial brownfields) or greenfield development? Does infill of the inner-urban fabric lead to negative or positive socio-environmental impacts in terms of quality of life and urban ecosystem services, and how can we evaluate this?

The overall impact assessment of settlement growth throughout all scenarios based on the urban structure types of detached, semi-detached and row-houses is very heterogeneous and dependent on the means of settlement growth (Schetke 2010). While greenfield sites and their closer living surroundings show decreasing values of the indicators climate regulation (**Figure 13.4**) and sealing rate (**Figure 13.5**) throughout all building scenarios, sites of infill development show a very heterogeneous picture in terms of infill measures and aspirational structure types.

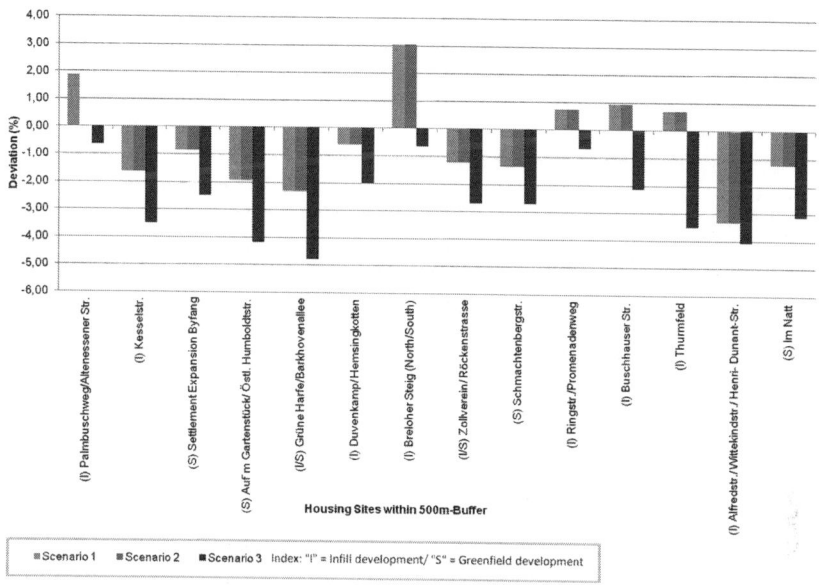

Figure 13.4   **Deviation of UES-indicator 'climate regulation' from status quo (modif. acc. to Schetke 2010)**

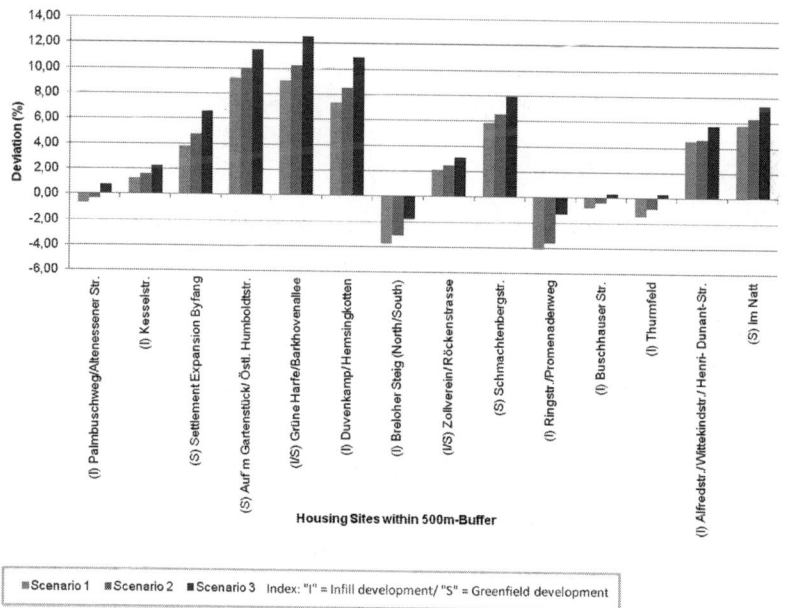

Figure 13.5   **Deviation of UES-indicator 'sealing rate' from status quo (modif. acc. to Schetke 2010)**

Here, brownfield revitalisation sites are benefiting from additional housing, while densification sites show a similar picture to greenfield sites.

Indicators of hydrological regulation show analogous results regarding a clear decrease in surface runoff, for example. Also the indicator evapotranspiration showed increasing values at brownfield revitalisation sites. Improvements to the respective seeping-rates are unclear. Compared to the overall impression of positive socio-environmental impacts at infill-sites for detached and semi-detached housing, we observe a clear transition to more negative impacts for the scenario with row-houses, which is the densest scenario in the single-family homes sector. These negative results are witnessed at both infill and greenfield sites.

The results of overall green space provision throughout the housing scenarios show a very heterogeneous picture. It is clear that a distinction between private and public green provision is necessary in order to get a closer insight into the detailed impact assessment on quality of life and associated urban ecosystem services (Schetke 2010, Schetke, Haase, Breuste 2010). While the total and overall public green space provision per resident decreases throughout all scenarios, the provision of private green spaces and therefore the provision of private recreation areas increases at infill-sites. Here, better accessibility for more residents results from brownfield revitalisation and the transformation of former industrial sites to private gardens shows major positive effects in terms of pure green space provision, but also social identity and cohesion. Negative impacts on the provision of private green were identified at greenfield-sites. Regarding the provision of public parks, an overall decrease of the total park area per resident has to be recognised due to additional residents being attracted by new housing areas at all sites. Moreover, no additional parks have been included within the scenario as is predicted. However, the overall situation even in inner-urban areas remains at an acceptable level (Schetke 2010).

Conclusions

Contributions from research on the shrinking city have highlighted the heterogeneous and site specific effects of demolition and dilapidation on socio-environmental conditions and green spaces (Haase 2008, Schetke, Haase 2008). In this chapter, it was demonstrated that similar findings can be made in terms of settlement growth. We have shown that a compact infill development does not necessarily mean a threat to quality of life and associated urban ecosystem services but, conversely, can provide ecologically attractive development paths, as well as positive influences on environmental health, living conditions and therefore residents' quality of life (Schetke 2010). While the indicator values of revitalised brownfield sites have shown positive impacts on both quality of life and urban ecosystem services, densification sites and also suburban housing sites provide similar unfavourable indicator performances (Schetke 2010). The hypothesis of a tensed green space provision by default even in a densely built-up city like Essen could be refuted for both infill and greenfield development sites. A differentiated mapping of green space makes it clear that additional urban fabric can diminish the overall amount of green space, but cannot be generalized for all types of urban green space.

We presented an integrative multicriteria assessment scheme, which has application potential for both urban planners and scientists, and also serves as a bridge between the two concepts of quality of life and urban ecosystem services by providing quantitative indicators to integratively analyse both. Moreover, the Visual Basic based multicriteria assessment has enabled a site-specific assessment of the status quo conditions of quality of life and urban ecosystem services in inner and suburban areas, as well as a scenario-driven impact analysis of different options of land development and settlement growth. Finally, it remains to be said that – as with all tools which strive to aid the decision making process in urban planning – the interpretation of results in the light of the local context and spatial development objectives is of vital importance.

References

Bolund, P. and Hunhammar, S. 1999. Ecosystem services in urban areas. *Ecological Economics,* 29(2), 293–301. Available at: 10.1016/S0921-8009(99)00013-0.

Burgess, J., Harrison, C. and Limb, M. 1988. People, Parks and the Urban Green: A Study of Popular Meanings and Values for Open Spaces in the City. *Urban Studies,* 25(6), 455–73. Available at: 10.1080/00420988820080631.

Chan, K.M.A., Shaw, M.R., Cameron, D.R., Underwood, E.C. and Daily, G.C. 2006. Conservation Planning for Ecosystem Services. *PLoS Biology,* 4(11), e379. Available at: 10.1371/journal.pbio.0040379.

Costanza, R., d'Arge, R., Groot, R. de, Farber, S., Grasso, M., Hannon, B., Limburg, K., Naeem, S., O'Neill, R.V., Paruelo, J., Raskin, R.G., Sutton, P. and van den Belt, M. 1997. The value of the world's ecosystem services and natural capital. *Nature,* 387(6630), 253–60. Available at: 10.1038/387253a0.

Couch, C. and Karecha, J. 2006. Controlling urban sprawl: Some experiences from Liverpool. *Cities,* 23(5), 353–63. Available at: 10.1016/j.cities.2006.05.003.

de Ridder, K., Adamec, V. and Banuelos A. 2004. An integrated methodology to assess the benefits of urban green space. *Science of the Total Environment,* 334–335, 489–97. Available at: 10.1016/j.scitotenv.2004.04.054.

Fadda, G. and Jiron, P. 1999. Quality of life and gender: a methodology for urban research. *Environment and Urbanisation,* 11(2), 261–70. Available at: 10.1177/095624789901100220.

Fritsch, A. von, Fritzsche, R. and Naumann, M. 2004. *Indikatoren für eine nachhaltige Umweltentwicklung in Leipzig.*

Groot, R.S. de, Wilson, M.A. and Boumans, R.M.J. 2002. A typology for the classification, description and valuation of ecosystem functions, goods and services. *Ecological Economics,* 41(3), 393–408. Available at: 10.1016/S0921-8009(02)00089-7.

Haase, D. 2008. Urban Ecology of Shrinking Cities: An Unrecognized Opportunity? *Nature and Culture,* 3(1), 1–8. Available at: 10.3167/nc.2008.030101.

Haase, D., Haase, A., Kabisch, S. and Bischoff, P. 2008. Guidelines for the 'Perfect Inner City'. Discussing the Appropriateness of Monitoring Approaches for Reurbanisation. *European Planning Studies,* 16(8), 1075–100. Available at: 10.1080/09654310802315765.

Millennium Ecosystem Assessment (MEA). 2005. *Ecosystems and human well-being: Synthesis : a report of the Millenium Ecosystems Assessment.* Washington, DC: Island Press.

Nijkamp, P. and Vreeker, R. 2000. Sustainability assessment of development scenarios: methodology and application to Thailand. *Ecological Economics,* 33(1), 7–27. Available at: 10.1016/S0921-8009(99)00135-4.

Nachhaltigkeitsrat 2008. Das Ziel-30-ha: Nachhaltigkeit auf dem Prüfstand. Presentation of Dr. Günther Bachmann, Rat für Nachhaltige Entwicklung, Geschäftsstelle. Available at: http://www.nachhaltigkeitsrat.de/fileadmin/user_upload/dokumente/beitraege/2008/Bachmann_Refina_Hof_26-11-2008.pdf

Nijkamp, P., Torrieri, F. and Vreeker, R. 2002. A Decision Support System for Assessing Alternative Projects for the Design of a New Road Network. Methodology and Application. *Int. J. management and decision making,* 3(2), 114–38. Available at:DOI: 10.1504/IJMDM.2002.002468.

Norberg, J. 1999. Linking Nature's services to ecosystems: some general ecological concepts. *Ecological Economics,* 29(2), 183–202. Available at: 10.1016/S0921-8009(99)00011-7.

Priego, C., Breuste, J.-H. and Rojas, J. 2008. Perception and Value of Nature in Urban Landscapes: a Comparative Analysis of Cities in Germany, Chile and Spain. *Landscape Online. Available at:* 10.3097/LO.200807 [accessed: 19 July 2011].

Richter, G. 1981. *Handbuch Stadtgrün: Landschaftsarchitektur im städtischen Freiraum.* München: BLV-Verl.-Ges.

Santos, L.D. and Martins, I. 2007. Monitoring Urban Quality of Life: The Porto Experience. *Social Indicators Research,* 80(2), 411–25. Available at: 10.1007/s11205-006-0002-2.

Schetke, S. 2010. *Socio-environmental impacts of settlement growth under conditions of fostered infill development: a methodological framework for a multicriteria assessment.* Bonn. urn:nbn:de:hbz:5N-22543

Schetke, S. and Haase, D. 2008. Multi-criteria assessment of socio-environmental aspects in shrinking cities. Experiences from eastern Germany. *Environmental Impact Assessment Review,* 28(7), 483–503. Available at: 10.1016/j.eiar.2007.09.004.

Schetke, S., Haase, D. and Breuste, J. 2010. Green space functionality under conditions of uneven urban land use development. *Journal of Land Use Science,* 5(2), 143–58. Available at: 10.1080/1747423X.2010.481081.

Senatsverwaltung für Stadtentwicklung. *Digitaler Umweltatlas Berlin: 02.13 Oberflächenabfluss, Versickerung, Gesamtabfluss und Verdunstung aus Niederschlägen.* [Online] Available at: http://www.stadtentwicklung.berlin.de/ umwelt/umweltatlas/da213_04.htm [accessed: 20 July 2011].

Singer, C. 1995. *Stadtökologisch wertvolle Freiflächen in Nordrhein-Westfalen.* 1st Edition. Dortmund: ILS.

Tyrvainen, L., Mäkinen, K. and Schipperijn, J. 2007. Tools for mapping social values of urban woodlands and other green areas. *Landscape and Urban Planning,* 79(1), 5–19. Available at: 10.1016/j.landurbplan.2006.03.003.

Chapter 14

Redeveloping the Redundant Defence Estate in Regions of Growth and Decline – Challenges for Spatial Planning

Robin Ganser

Introduction

Challenges and opportunities of restructuring the defence estate

The end of the cold war, along with new asymmetrical threats by groups organised outside formal political systems, are decisive factors in the development and disposal of the defence estate. The process of restructuring opens up a window of opportunity for the transition of redundant military estate – sites and buildings – to civil uses and is defined as a specific form of 'conversion' (Grundmann 1998 49; Wieschollek 3). The terms 'defence estate conversion'; 'base conversion' and 'site conversion' are used synonymously hereafter. All of them describe the process of planning and implementing the reuse of former military sites and buildings – including infrastructure – which are usually in national ownership or have been handed back from foreign forces.

The conversion of redundant sites can be a successful strategy for avoiding population loss and economic decline that frequently occurs following the closure of military facilities. Conversions generally involve complex statutory and informal planning procedures, social, environmental, economic and political considerations. So far few studies have looked explicitly at the planning challenges associated with military conversion in England.

More recent work related to the study of conversion projects has been limited to a cursory international comparative analysis and an equally brief discussion of planning issues – mainly focusing on urban design and participation (Bagaeen 2006a, Bagaeen 2006b). There is also no conclusive discussion of the different impacts of conversion sites in dissimilar spatial contexts – namely growing and shrinking regions. In both cases the statutory planning system can play a decisive role for the successful redevelopment of redundant defence estate as a contribution to sustainable development of growing and shrinking regions. At the same time problems and hindrances in the planning process can delay or even prevent conversion.

This chapter explores planning problems and potential solutions with a view to help planning practice and to inform the further development of the planning system. In doing so the spatial context in terms of growth and slow growth or shrinkage is given particular consideration. In England there are significant differences in different parts of the country. For example, the South East is characterised by development pressure and the North West is dominated by large swathes of brownfield land and much slower take up of developable sites.

In England the paradigm for restructuring the defence estate is based on the comprehensive 1998 'Strategic Defence Review', which postulates a focus of military activities on fewer, larger sites – so called 'Core Sites'. The entire defence estate was analysed, in doing so the operative requirements and status quo of use were the main criteria to identify 'Core Sites' on the one hand and to identify redundant military land on the other. However, site characteristics and quality of sites respectively were also considered (Benson 2005 48). The Treasury stipulation, namely to adhere to the 'Best Value Principle' in terms of maximising the potential revenue from the sale of redundant sites, is also significant here. Finally, the aforementioned strategic and programmatic approaches are closely linked to the 'Lyons Report', which postulates considerable public sector relocations in general, and of military positions specifically, away from the South East of England.

The recent 'Defence Estate Development Plan 2008' has defined three 'timeframes' for restructuring of the estate up to 2030. It also foresees spreading Ministry of Defence facilities and operations across the regions as evenly as possible, whereby the focus of potential future disposal of sites clearly is on the South East region (Defence Estate (DE) 2008).

In summary this implies that the disposal of military sites, which have to be dealt with in the scope of spatial plans and strategies, will continue in the foreseeable future. It also implies that areas of development pressure, such as London and the South East, may benefit from the release of sites. At the same time areas which are historically weaker in terms of economic development and linked population growth or development pressure, such as the North West of England, may not be hit quite as hard from the negative aspects of conversion, for instance the loss of jobs and dereliction. This strategic approach can therefore facilitate planning in the context of conversion in growing and shrinking regions.

Conversion challenges – the academic discussion

The literature on brownfield redevelopment – including conversion sites – is largely conclusive about its wider role in regeneration and sustainability agendas, recognising that both 'sustainable development' and 'brownfield regeneration' agendas have dominated the urban redevelopment debate in recent years in Europe, which is of particular importance in shrinking regions. The contributions to regeneration were mainly in the form of residential and employment hard-end reuse. This, however, only works well in regions with high development pressure. Brownfield developments are also considered a key way to improve the sustainability of urban form in England (Dair, Williams 2006). Further to this, 'soft-end' uses on brownfields can contribute to leisure and open space provision. This is particularly important in areas with a lack of such amenities.

Environmental improvements to the sites themselves and wider economic and social regeneration are also listed as key benefits; often reinforced by international experience (Dixon 2006). Brownfield regeneration is often expected to happen in an 'ecological' way, balancing both the positive and negative effects within often competing dimensions of sustainability (Gareth et al. 2007). Some redundant defence estate is of high ecological value. The preservation of such sites – and if possible linking them into a network of habitats – contributes to sustainable spatial development. Additionally, conversion sites may be suitable for ecological upgrading in the scope of environmental compensation measures which cannot be accommodated on the site of the development which is accountable for certain environmental impacts.

The existing research on brownfield redevelopment examines a range of issues, including general constraints and barriers (McCarthy 2002; Adams, Watkins 2002; Adams 2004); and the more technical aspects, including contamination challenges (Eisen 1999; Syms 2004; Nathanail, Bardos 2004). A number of researchers have analysed local experiences of defence land and property disposal, many of which are based on US examples, and largely focused on the economic impacts of redevelopment (Woodward 1998; Hill 2000; Gallo, Sullivan 2002; Bludau 2002; Benneworth, Bradley 2004). Several studies examined the contested process of military site reuse across rural England identifying some good practice but also – among other things – policy tensions between environmental protection and conversion (Woodward 1998; Gallent, Howe, Bell 2000; Northumberland Information Network 2006).

Policy context – emphasis on sustainable brownfield redevelopment

In England conversion sites are in most cases covered by the definition of *previously developed land* and *brownfield land* (Department of Communities and Local Government (CLG) 2006 26). Prioritising the reuse of appropriate conversion and other brownfield sites in order to further urban regeneration and to reduce greenfield development is a long established objective of English planning policy (Ganser 2005). This is manifested in the national target to deliver 60 per cent of all new housing on previously developed land and through conversions of existing building stock (Department of Communities and Local Government (CLG) 2006 Section 41). This target is a material consideration in local land use planning procedures and for the determination of planning applications.

Two central methodological approaches have been established for the implementation of this target and for the general prioritisation of the reuse of previously developed land. The first is the central idea of the 'sequential approach,' which is that appropriate brownfield sites should be allocated in regional and local planning documents with priority before 'greenfields' are allocated (Department of the Environment Transport and the Regions (DETR) 2000). Secondly, a sequential element is built into the implementation of planning documents which calls for the phased release of allocated housing sites – again with a view to further the effective use of land by prioritising the redevelopment of appropriate brownfield sites. In this context it is important to emphasize the adjective 'appropriate'; it was not intended to promote a blanket approach to allocating and developing previously developed land before other sites are considered (Ganser 2005). In fact, only brownfield sites which are suitable with regards to the site characteristics should be given priority when allocating sites in statutory planning documents or when releasing sites for development (Department of Communities and Local Government (CLG) 2006 Section 41).

First and foremost this relates to location, accessibility and quality of the land, as well as existing buildings and infrastructure. In this context it is particularly important not to shy away from sites which are hard to develop due to their physical characteristics, but which provide an important opportunity for future urban or rural development (Ganser 2005). With regard to military site conversions, the central task of the planning system is to determine the suitability of redeveloping such sites and giving them priority in the scope of statutory planning processes. This priority is partially compromised through the government's postulate (PPS3) to provide a continuous five-year supply of deliverable housing sites (Department of Communities and Local Government (CLG) 2006 Section 60), which potentially has to rely on a larger proportion of greenfield sites characterised by more predictable and quicker planning processes.

The effects and consequences of such planning policies vary in different spatial contexts of growth and shrinkage. In regions characterised by growth and consequent development pressure, the prioritisation of brownfield land, with longer lead times due to more complex planning processes, can lead to an overall shortage of sites. As a consequence, more greenfield sites allocated as reserve sites for later phases of the defined planning horizon will have to be brought forward if the shortage of available land for development is to be overcome. Such actions may then lead to a shortage of sites in later phases of plan implementation.

In regions characterised by shrinkage it is conceivable that a general prioritisation of brownfield development can be problematic, particularly where selective short term greenfield development is necessary to support declining areas (Ganser 2005 112). In this context holding back or preventing essential infrastructure development or realisation of alternative building types and qualities on greenfields may lead to further decline and therefore exacerbate the dereliction and brownfield problem in the long term, resulting in a negative spiral which it is difficult and costly to escape.

Further to this it may not be possible to find appropriate interim or long term hard-end uses for conversion sites in a shrinkage scenario. This leads to the question of how these sites should be treated, including (1) interim uses, (2) so-called soft-end reuse, or (3) 'resting' the site, but keeping it open for long term reuse or renaturalisation of sites where this is ecologically practical. In both cases – growth or shrinkage – the success of (hard-end) site conversion will also depend on whether the location of the military site and the long term spatial development priorities of the relevant local authorities are compatible.

Planning practice – redevelopment of conversion sites through statutory planning procedures

Coordination problems and complex planning processes

The conversion process is closely linked to the statutory spatial planning process. During the 1990s considerable coordination and communication problems occurred, particularly between responsible Ministry of Defence directorates and statutory planning agencies. A cursory analysis of regional and local planning shows that throughout the 1990s a lack of coordination between Ministry of Defence internal processes and statutory planning processes led to a situation in which even some large strategic conversion sites were not allocated in statutory planning documents. This was because the release of those sites had been unclear for too long or this information was fed into the planning process too late (see Fig. 14.1 below). This led to significant hindrances and delays in the conversion process.

Although these hindrances have largely been overcome as a consequence of restructuring, the complexity of the process due to the large number of stakeholders involved, as well as their intricate relationships, still pose considerable challenges. In this context the military estate strategy, as well as the site release programme, needs to be coordinated with strategies and planning policies at the national, regional and local level.

A central objective is to identify potential conversion sites as early as possible and to ensure that these are either directly allocated in the Development Plan for reuse or are earmarked for future redevelopment in the scope of plan reviews (Ministry of Defence (MoD) 2007 3 et seq.). Due to the complexity of this process there is still the danger that information is passed on to the planning agencies at a late stage of the statutory process which makes it more difficult to accommodate conversion sites than greenfield sites or other brownfields. The following diagram gives an overview of the conversion process, on the one hand, and relevant statutory planning tiers, documents and procedures, on the other hand.

In this context it is important to note that the most recent push towards less regional and more local guidance will further complicate this situation in the short term (The Localism Bill Department of Communities and Local Government (CLG) 2011). In the longer term more direct contact between military and local authorities may be helpful in cases where conversion sites can be well integrated into the existing settlement structures and where strategic coordination is of less importance.

However, in spatially more complex situations, such as shrinkage or growth scenarios with competing (neighbouring) local authority interests, weak or limited regional guidance can lead to further problems for site conversions. Also, in situations where a large pool of conversion sites needs to be coordinated across a region, it will be more difficult to achieve this through locally organised authority

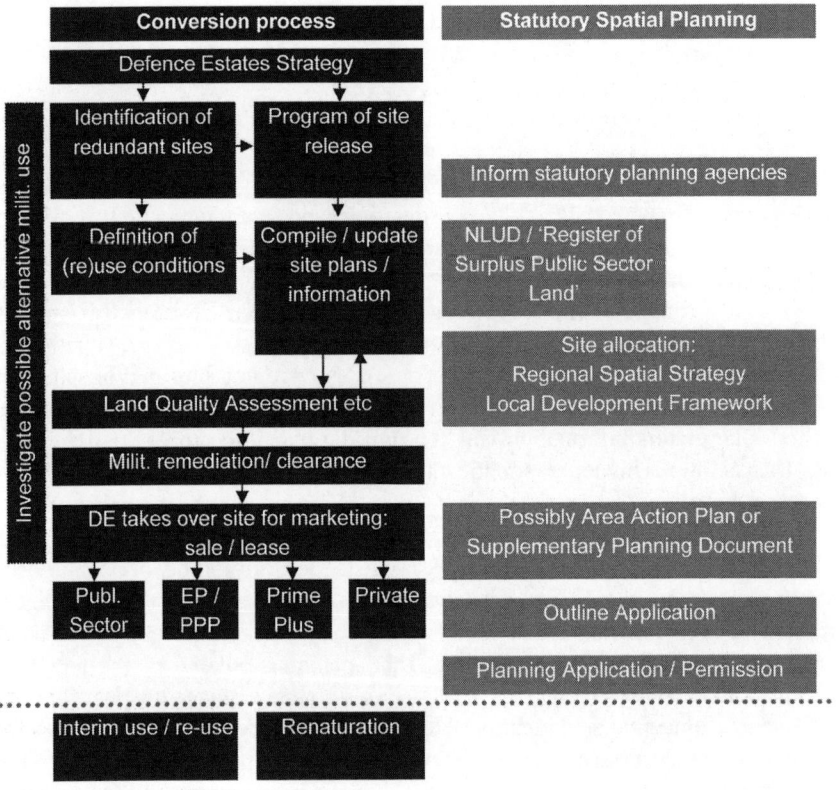

Figure 14.1   Key elements of the conversion and statutory planning process

Source: author's own illustration

cooperation rather than by means of a regional planning body with strategic responsibilities and objectives.

A key factor adding uncertainty to the statutory planning process is the power of the Ministry of Defence to identify alternative military uses for conversion sites even after they have been declared redundant. In fact, this is legally possible right until the penultimate phase of the conversion process before a sale of a conversion site has been finalised. The identification of an alternative military use thereby terminates the conversion process. This in turn can lead to a shortfall in land supply which has to be addressed by allocating alternative sites in the local planning documents.

This problem is more pressing in areas of fast growth than in regions which are characterised by slow growth or shrinkage. This kind of uncertainty may cause local authorities to be more and more reluctant to include conversion sites in their development plans. They may choose to treat conversion sites merely as reserve sites.

Different Conversion Models and Partnership Working

Different approaches or 'models' for the conversion of redundant defence estate are currently pursued in practice. These can be characterised and categorised as follows

- The 'classic' form of conversion is characterised by incremental development whereby the site is usually not part of a wider planning strategy – or is accommodated in a planning strategy only retrospectively. Instead the short- to medium-term reuse of the site is pursued by means of interim land uses while the search for long-term development options continues.
- The 'strategic approach' to conversion entails the inclusion of redundant sites in an overarching spatial strategy and planning concepts such as 'Growth Areas' or 'Eco Towns'.
- The 'Prime Plus Contracting' approach includes a combination of site conversions and development of core sites. In doing so it relies on innovative and complex Public Private Partnership working.

All of these models are characterised by specific benefits and challenges. What they all have in common is that various forms of partnerships are at the heart of each model.

The interdependency of public and private partners can be described as follows developers depend directly on the decisions made by local authorities for investment opportunities, while the latter require such investment to fulfill their broader place-shaping objectives (Raco 2003). This interdependency is certainly played out in relation to redeveloping conversion sites where the Ministry of Defence is the developer or cooperates with a private sector partner. While the Ministry of Defence has typically sought planning permission prior to disposal, more recently it has introduced a different approach in 'packaging up' sites and partnership with the private sector (Defence Estates (DE), South East England Regional Assembly (SEERA) 2006).

Although there is a general body of literature and research dealing with partnerships, which primarily identify several models for describing them, there is no research yet into the structure or operations of such partnerships in the specific context of conversion processes. These are characterised by particularly high complexity due to the fact that commonly national as well as regional and local public and private stakeholders are involved.

A prominent example of the difficulties arising in this context is the conversion of the former Royal Air Force Upper Heyford, Oxfordshire, which follows the 'classic' conversion model. The planning process was characterised by conflicting interests between different stakeholders, mainly with regards to the proposed size and impacts of the development in this rural location. This can largely be blamed on the lack of specific policies and allocations in the local development plan due to the poor coordination of the planning and conversion process (Ganser 2008).

This in turn was at least partially due to a lack of communication between the Ministry of Defence and the local authority. In addition to the process related problems the following substantive issues certainly added to the planning problems a rural location; historic as well as nature conservation challenges on site and contamination issues.

Recent public private partnership approaches appear to be more successful. A good example is the planned Eco-town pilot at Northstowe comprising the former Royal Air Force Oakington Barracks and adjacent sites (South Cambridgeshire District Council 2007). English Partnerships (now part of Homes and Communities Agency) and Gallagher Longstanton Ltd. have formed a public private partnership with equal financial and land stakes in the development proposal (personal communication of the author with Department of Communities and Local Government, English Partnerships 2008). Strong public sector involvement and the setting up of the infrastructure delivery vehicle 'Cambridgeshire Horizons' certainly facilitated communication and alignment of the interests of the different stakeholders. This resulted in a swift planning process with less than two years between English Partnership's acquisition of the site and handing in a joint planning application within the framework of the Core Strategy and the Northstowe Area Action Plan (AAP), both coordinated with the conversion process and adopted 2007 (South Cambridgeshire District Council 2007). A major remaining challenge for this partnership approach is the complex coordination of planning teams and relevant stakeholders.

This is also true for the project 'Ministry of Defence Estate London' (MoDEL) following the 'Prime Plus Contracting' conversion model which involves a private consortium of prime plus contractors which are responsible for both the development of a core site and conversion of redundant sites (www. defencemanagement.com 2011). As this model relies on pooling several sites in different local authorities the complexity of conversion and planning processes is increased. In case of MoDEL the local authorities and Prime Plus Contractors cooperated closely in drafting new local planning documents such as area action plans and supplementary planning documents for the sites in question. This helped to align the public and private interests in the context of identifying the preferred planning alternatives for the conversion sites (Ganser 2008).

The public private partnership approaches outlined above, all have in common that they are set in a spatial context which is characterised by growth and relatively high development pressure. It appears questionable whether such a partnership would work in regions characterised by shrinkage where as a consequence the site conversion would have to be phased over a longer planning horizon, which in turn means that only long term profits appear realistic, and where the success of hard-end development is a lot less certain. In this context the public partner may have to take the lead and/or carry a larger burden in terms of overall development cost or underwriting the risk involved.

Environmental requirements adding to complexity

As part of the statutory planning process it is obligatory to notify the environmental agencies in case designated areas may be affected by the conversion of sites. Such designations and their associated requirements had major implications for the reuse of conversion sites, principally due to the incompatible frameworks – in terms of procedures, standards and regulations. Examples are the 'Deepcut' project and two North Hampshire projects located close to the Thames Basin Special Protection Area and other Natura 2000 sites.

The profile of such designations was raised when the European Court of Justice ruled that the United Kingdom government had failed to correctly transpose the Habitats Directive into national law. This directive applies the precautionary principle to protected areas so plans and projects can only be permitted having ascertained that there will be no adverse effect on these areas (Scott Wilson et al. 2006). Natural England acted as the key consultee for implementing the 'Habitat Regulations' at the local level (Department of Communities and Local Government (CLG) 2006). The case was argued that any housing development near to special protection areas (SPAs) should be planned and designed to incorporate areas of natural green space for recreation uses to prevent conflict, for example, by diverting human movement away from certain areas (English Nature 2006). The planning process is still wrestling with this requirement, but the underlying ambiguity about how projects in these localities can be achieved without impacting special protection area habitats continues to stifle development.

Considering all of the above, it is to be expected that a larger number and area of designations necessarily lead to an increased probability of planning conflicts and greater complexity of the planning process. These problems have not yet been resolved nor have they been analysed comprehensively.

In spite of these challenges, there are promising signs for the future. The informing of environmental consultees takes place early in the planning process. Therefore potential problems can be identified and discussed before detailed planning decisions have been taken which may make it more difficult to avoid, minimise and/or compensate negative environmental impacts. The investigation of these mitigation measures is a statutory requirement as part of the Strategic Environmental Assessment (SEA) and Environmental Impact Assessment (EIA) procedures. Because there already is a lot of practical experience in mainstream planning, there is scope for the quality of assessments to increase and the synchronisation with the conversion and planning process to improve (Levett-Therivel Sustainability Consultants 26.05.2009).

The environmental considerations may be less problematic in regions which are dominated by shrinkage or slow growth as conversion sites will usually feature a mix of hard and soft-end land uses. In fact, the real or perceived problem of slow growth or shrinkage can be turned into an advantage, offering more ecological value and also more attractive living and working environs. Where it is important to maximise the efficiency of redevelopment in terms of high densities in a growth scenario, there is less scope for buffer areas or larger proportions of soft-end uses.

Strategic planning tiers set to change – again

Regional development agencies (RDAs) often had an indirect role in regenerating brownfield sites by means of supporting major projects and infrastructure provision in the past (Ganser 2005). Regional development agencies, were set to be of growing importance in the conversion process as they were to replace regional planning bodies and take the lead in developing and reviewing the Regional (Spatial) Strategy jointly with local authority leaders' boards. The Localism bill now calls for an even more radical change with less regional and more local responsibilities in plan making (Department of Communities and Local Government (CLG) 2011).

Due to the complexity of the planning processes it is to be expected that this change in responsibilities will lead to procedural issues and delays, at least during a transitional phase. In this context a smooth transition will be partially determined by how successful the knowledge base and experience which exists in regional planning bodies can be preserved and transferred. This in turn may to a large extent be determined by the existing organisational structures.

Another important challenge for strategic plan making across different local authority borders is the release of large conversion sites. Such sites, potentially covering several hundreds of hectares, can lead to a massive oversupply of developable land and can result in a detrimental effect on the real estate market. In order to avoid such problems the site conversion needs to be integrated sensibly into the overall regional real estate portfolio of developable and deliverable land.

One way of approaching the dichotomy of reusing conversion sites and at the same time avoiding stifling the land market in the region, is to carefully define clusters of specific uses for the conversion sites which complement existing site allocations. To give an example only industrial uses in the context of renewable energy could be permitted on the large conversion site, other 'ordinary' industrial uses would have to locate on existing allocations for industrial land. Additionally strategic phasing of site release can further facilitate this process. In areas of slow growth or shrinkage the analysis of the 'aptitude' of conversion sites is absolutely crucial. This means that only a careful analysis of all relevant site characteristics, such as location, size, existing buildings and infrastructure, can help us to understand which kind of reuse – if any – will be desirable and acceptable in planning terms as well as financially viable. Once the 'aptitude' of a site is clear (e.g., use for renewable energy and related industries), innovative concepts in informal as well as statutory planning documents can help to achieve the reuse.

To summarise the above, regional guidance in the context of site conversion is therefore of particular importance in order to (1) avoid negative competition, (2) enable the pooling of conversion sites (packaging hard to develop, as well as most desirable sites), and (3) allow clustering of special land uses and (4) permit phasing into the overall regional site portfolio. As already set out above both spatial contexts – shrinkage and growth – will be affected in different ways by these changes to the strategic tiers in the planning system.

Alignment of interests

Another key issue influencing the planning and conversion process is the complex relationship of relevant stakeholders and their individual interests. In this context Defence Estates is keen to 'ensure that Ministry of Defence's requirements are fed into development plans as part of ongoing work with Government Offices (currently being restructured) and Planning Authorities' (Defence Estates (DE), South East England Regional Assembly (SEERA) 2006 6). This requires more than merely stating the aspiration to redevelop a site when making representations on an emerging regional strategy (possibly obsolete in future) or core strategy at the local level. In fact any inclusion of a conversion site as a strategic site in the core strategy needs to follow the preparation of a robust evidence base and information on its deliverability (Department of Communities and Local Government (CLG) 2008).

With regard to the preferred reuse option of conversion sites the individual interests of the Ministry of Defence and local authorities (LAs) recently showed a congruence of planning objectives when the local authority favoured residential reuse of conversion sites. In the case of local authorities this interest was influenced by the statutory duty to provide an adequate supply of land for (affordable) housing in order to meet their regionally prescribed housing targets. In parallel to this it is Ministry of Defence policy that 'best value' is achieved in the disposal of surplus sites within Treasury Guidelines (Government Accounting 2000 Rules).

In cases where the local authority prescribes a preferred reuse option in their planning documents which in their view best caters for future urban development, but is not in line with achieving the highest possible profit for Ministry of Defence land sales, conflicts with regards to the preferred planning alternative arise. In the wake of discussions over abolishing regional spatial strategies, local authorities have started recently to reduce their housing targets considerably (Marrs 3, June 2011). Additionally a conflict over the reuse of conversion sites is conceivable when different reuse options are set out in local and strategic planning documents or when one of the documents does not foresee the allocation of the conversion site. In both cases the local authority's position to pursue its preferred reuse option is relatively weak, due to the far reaching control and default powers of the Secretary of State at the national level.

Local planning tiers facing dichotomy of certainty versus flexibility

Local authorities can further the conversion process considerably by prioritising such sites and providing guidance and certainty for redevelopment through the statutory planning process in the plan led system. This can be achieved by allocating conversion sites in the core strategy and site allocations document of the local development framework.

Even if a conversion site is allocated in an area wide planning document – this still allows considerable agency discretion in the scope of development control which makes the redevelopment a rather speculative undertaking. The amount of certainty can be increased by *area action plans* or site specific *supplementary planning documents* as both provide more detail with regards to spatial development options and therefore reduce the amount of discretion in decision making. On the other hand, more detailed planning documents are inevitably less flexible and are therefore less able to accommodate future alterations which may be necessitated by a change in the local spatial context.

But even the preparation of area action plans and/or supplementary planning documents does not come without its difficulties as not all local authorities have the necessary expertise or resources to develop meaningful detailed planning documents, which particularly require urban design and spatial analysis skills as well as financial resources. In theory these potential problems could be overcome by drawing on external funding and expertise. However, this in turn may not be possible due to material or political considerations.

In summary it is therefore clear that in addition to the quest for reduced process duration, local authorities face one of the greatest dichotomies in spatial planning in the context of site conversions the provision of certainty versus long term flexibility.

In both spatial scenarios – shrinkage and growth – these issues arise with slightly different connotations. In growth regions flexibility is particularly important when requirements and development interests change rapidly. Certainty is mainly of importance when comparing conversion sites to competing greenfield sites. It is crucial to reduce the risk of developing military brownfields in terms of availability and other site constraints in order to attract development to these sites, as opposed to more straightforward development options on greenfield land.

In a shrinkage scenario flexibility is required mainly to allow changes over the necessarily longer period of development, usually spanning several development phases, and potentially decades rather than years. Certainty by means of reliable and sufficiently detailed planning documents is also required based on the same arguments which have been set out for the growth scenario above.

Development control challenges – appeals and planning obligations

It is evident from planning practice that a lack of a clear policy framework usually leads to a prolonged planning application process. Classic examples are the conversion of the Queen Elizabeth II Barracks and also the redevelopment of the former Royal Air Force Upper Heyford, Oxfordshire. In both cases appeals against the failure to issue a decision within the statutory period, against refusal to grant outline planning permission, or to grant planning permission had to be investigated by a planning inspector and both cases were subsequently recovered for determination by the Secretary of State (Inspector's report on RAF Upper

Heyford dated 25.02.08). The appeal and call-in procedure adds considerably to the overall duration of the planning and application process. In addition to this, the negotiation of planning obligations – which set out what developers are expected to contribute financially or in kind to make the development acceptable in planning terms – can be time consuming.

These constraints and additional costs have been identified (Callcutt 2007 45). Developable brownfield sites must not be rendered unviable as a result of unrealistic demands made by regulators, which in this case include local authorities who set the local framework for developer contributions through *development plan policies* and *supplementary planning documents*. A core problem in this context still is the lack of a standardized approach to setting and collecting developer contributions. In the absence of standard charges the contributions from each conversion project have to be individually assessed, calculated and negotiated.

In this context it is obvious that the system of developer contributions, or a new community infrastructure levy, as far more difficult to operate (if at all) in regions characterised by shrinkage and resulting lack of development interest. Only where private sector developers can hope to achieve sufficient (short term) profits, in addition to offsetting development costs and contributions towards infrastructure, will they be able and willing to undertake such development and sign up to (and honour) linked obligations.

Monitoring and databases

The monitoring of redundant defence estate available for redevelopment is an essential basis for all of the conversion and statutory planning processes mentioned above. The Register of Surplus Public Sector Land, for example, helps to identify sites for allocation in statutory planning documents (Homes and Communities Agency (HCA) 2011). The National Land Use Database – Previously Developed Land (NLUD-PDL), which is based on annual local authority returns, identifies all available previously developed land within the local authority area. Unfortunately the two databases are not (yet) linked up which complicates the strategic assessment of the availability of conversion sites and previously developed land in general for redevelopment. Unfortunately, the National Land Use Database is riddled with several problems, some of which relate to the methods of data collection and the structure of the database (Department of Communities and Local Government (CLG) 2008).

These monitoring instruments are of equal importance no matter what the spatial development challenge may be growth or shrinkage. With regard to the former, it is essential to ensure the most effective and efficient use of land (where possible prioritising the reuse of previously developed land), in order to prevent further loss of greenfield land in already densely populated areas with high development pressure. Considering the latter, it appears crucial to highlight development opportunities and to actively seek to promote development on appropriate sites, while avoiding 'perforated' settlement structures characterised by a patchwork of vital settlement areas and derelict sites. It is therefore of crucial importance to improve the existing monitoring instruments – thereby remedying the problems highlighted above.

Addressing the challenges

It is clear from the analysis of planning practice that, on the one hand, several planning instruments are suited to facilitate the conversion of former military sites, but that they are not always employed. This is often to avoid the potentially considerable duration of the statutory planning process. This indicates that there is no need for yet more new planning instruments, rather the improved implementation of existing tools is required.

In this context master planning offers a possibility to provide more certainty by setting out the local authorities' ideas for the future of a conversion site while at the same time allowing flexibility as a statutory planning process is not required. However, there will most likely still be the need for a robust supporting policy background to set parameters in order to bind in private partners and to avoid inconsistent development control decisions.

It also appears that more practice experience and skills are needed to successfully implement the planning instruments. These requirements will have to be met through continued professional development and in the scope of higher education. Additionally the sharing of experiences between local authorities as well as the identification and dissemination of best practice including the evaluation of pilot schemes should be encouraged.

As described above, improved organisational structures and clear communication pathways have already resolved some coordination problems. The current overhaul of the planning system should therefore strive to carefully avoid the old problems and ensure a smooth transition.

With regards to environmental requirements, it would be important to exploit strategic environmental assessments at the regional level which could help to identify specific environmental challenges for conversion sites early in the planning process. It is unclear as to how this may be implemented when regional spatial strategies cease to exist.

Nonetheless, a pooling approach should be explored whereby alternative soft-end uses are explored for conversion sites which potentially face difficult mitigation measures due to their proximity to designated areas or in areas of shrinkage. Additionally these sites could provide for compensation measures required for conversion to hard-end land uses on other sites in the pool. In this context, it is conceivable to adapt the German practice of establishing 'eco-accounts' which local authorities use to record ecological upgrading of sites which can subsequently be used to off-set certain past, present and future impacts on the environment (Bunzel 1999 69).

A classic bone of contention – and an important time constraint to address – is the negotiation of planning obligations. Already local authorities are encouraged to employ formulae and standard charges where appropriate, as part of their framework for negotiating and securing obligations (Department of Communities and Local Government (CLG) 2005). This approach can help speed up negotiations, and also further predictability, by indicating the likely size and type of contributions in advance.

In case of large scale developments it is also conceivable that the approach pioneered by Milton Keynes is employed. This includes an infrastructure tariff as part of an overarching legal agreement which sets out the facilities required and how they will be provided in a framework agreement (Milton Keynes Partnership (MKP) 2007).

Only sites which the planning authorities are aware of can be considered in the statutory planning process. In this context continuous monitoring and comprehensive databases play an important role. A major improvement would certainly be the merger of National Land Use Database – Previously Developed Land (NLUD-PDL) and the Register of Surplus Public Sector Land, as well as further developing this into a geographic information systems-based solution providing a one-stop shop for local authorities and developers (Department of Communities and Local Government, English Partnerships 2008). In order to overcome the challenge of flawed or ambiguous site data, influenced by the interpretation of the collecting authority, it would be helpful to categorise redundant defence estate with particular consideration of reuse options and viability as early as possible in the planning process.

An adaptation of the so called 'ABC Model' (Ferber 2006) could prove beneficial as it categorises brownfields and conversion sites according to the potential drivers of the redevelopment whereby, depending on the cost of regeneration and the value of the land, sites can be classified as

- A Sites – which represent development projects that are driven by private funding
- B Sites – which are characterised by marginal profitability. These projects tend to be funded through public-private co-operation or partnerships
- C Sites – which represent mainly projects driven by public funding or specific legislative instruments.

This model should be adapted in order to consider spatial structures, e.g., in terms of centrality, and demand of development land to make it a meaningful tool for the selection of conversion sites in areas of growth and of shrinkage (Beutler 2008). This could assist institutions responsible for regional development and investment, and review strategies for dealing with different types of conversion sites and other brownfields. If applied to the whole of the defence estate, this tool could also inform the defence estate strategy, alongside purely military decisions.

Conclusions

It is clear from the above discussion that the challenge posed by military site conversions is of importance both in areas of growth and decline. In England the spatial planning challenge is eased slightly due to the strategic decision to focus site conversions in the South East. This regional focus means that the measures suggested above can facilitate conversion efforts such as (1) the pooling of sites, with a view to balance risks and opportunities within the conversion portfolio, (2) local authority cooperation and exchange of best practice experiences, which can build on existing organisational and communication structures within the region, and (3) directing the still relatively high development pressure towards conversion sites by means of formal planning documents, thereby helping to overcome the disadvantage when compared to greenfield sites.

In spite of the improved communication and organisational structures of the Ministry of Defence which makes clear reference to the spatial planning system and sets out clear lines of communication it is still difficult to synchronise conversion and statutory planning processes. This may be exacerbated by yet another radical change to the planning system – eradicating regional spatial strategies.

Recent planning reforms (including 2004, 2008, and 2010/11) have already facilitated the synchronisation of processes by means of the flexible local development framework 'folder approach', but the planning system still needs time to settle in – as practice struggles with the implementation of these instruments. It is therefore safe to argue that yet more change of structures and instruments will be detrimental. We do not need different or more planning instruments to further conversion but more experience and best practice dissemination to make the current system work more effectively.

Further to this there appears to be particular value in an international comparative analysis as similar challenges are being addressed in Germany and France. Particularly Germany has a wealth of experience to offer and the restructuring of military sites is not regionally focused but a ubiquitous challenge, calling for even more innovative planning concepts.

With regard to reuse options it appears that soft-end uses will be of increasing importance in the future – particularly as interim uses, while sites wait to be redeveloped or as permanent uses in regions characterised by shrinkage or slow growth. In this context the experiences gained with the land (restoration) trust's program of reclaiming brownfields for soft-end reuse should be utilised for conversion sites (The Land Trust). After all, the objective would be similar namely to reclaim previously used land either for nature or for the public (e.g., providing green infrastructure) and increasing quality of the living and working environment. Particularly the two final suggestions will require further and more detailed research in order to allow adaptations with a view to provide tailored solutions which can facilitate site conversions in areas of growth as well as in shrinking regions.

References

Government Accounting 2000 Rules Chapter 24 Disposals of Assets. Local Democracy Economic Development and Construction Bill [HL Session 2008–09] Section 69.

Adams, D. 2004. The changing regulatory environment for speculative housebuilding and the construction of core competencies for brownfield development. *Environment and Planning A,* 36(4), 601–24. Available at 10.1068/a3557.

Adams, D. and Watkins, C. 2002. *Greenfields, brownfields and housing development.* Oxford Blackwell Science.

Bagaeen, S.G. 2006a. Brownfield sites as building blocks for sustainable urban environments a view on international experience in redeveloping former military sites. *Urban Design International,* 11(2), 117–28. Available at 10.1057/palgrave.udi.9000168.

Bagaeen, S.G. 2006b. Redeveloping former military sites Competitiveness, urban sustainability and public participation. *Cities,* 23(5), 339–52. Available at 10.1016/j.cities.2006.05.002.

Benneworth, P. and Bradley, D. 2004. *The Potential Closure of RAF Boulmer A First Review of the Local Impacts.* Newcastle.

Benson, W.L.P. 2005. *Determining significant effects within environmental management a case study of the UK Ministry of Defence.* Oxford.

Beutler, K. 2008. Konversionsflächentypisierung. in *Konversionsflächenmanagement zur nachhaltigen Wiedernutzung freigegebener militärischer Liegenschaften REFINA-KoM,* edited by C. Jacoby and K. Beutler. Neubiberg, 265–77.

Bludau, O.W. 2002. Base reuse in an environmentally sensitive locality. *Economic Development Journal,* 1(1), 29. Available at http//search.ebscohost.com/login. aspx?direct=true&db=a9h&AN=7548943&site=ehost-live.

Bunzel, A. 1999. *Bauleitplanung und Flächenmanagement bei Eingriffen in Natur und Landschaft.* Berlin Dt. Inst. für Urbanistik.

Callcutt, J. 2007. *The Callcutt Review of housebuilding delivery.* London Communities and Local Government Publications.

Dair, C.M. and Williams, K. 2006. Sustainable land reuse the influence of different stakeholders in achieving sustainable brownfield developments in England. *Environment and Planning A,* 38(7), 1345–66. Available at 10.1068/a37370.

Defence Estate (DE). 2008. *The Defence Estate Development Plan 2008 Appendix 1 to Annex B.* London.

Defence Estates (DE) and South East England Regional Assembly (SEERA). *Joint Studies on the Development Potential of the Ministry of Defence Estate in the South East Region.* [Online] Available at http//www.eipsoutheast.co.uk/downloads/documents/20061030114220.pdf [accessed 20 July 2011].

Department of Communities and Local Government (CLG). 2005. *Circular 5/2005 Planning Obligations (published 18 July 2005).*

Department of Communities and Local Government (CLG). 2006. *Consultation on Planning Policy Statement 3 Housing (PPS3) a summary of responses and key issues.* London.

Department of Communities and Local Government (CLG). 2008. *Planning Policy Statement 12 Local Spatial Planning.* London The Stationary Office (TSO).

Department of Communities and Local Government (CLG). *The Localism Bill Local government.* [Online] Available at http//www.communities.gov.uk/localgovernment/decentralisation/localismbill/ [accessed 21 July 2011].

Department of Communities and Local Government and English Partnerships. 2008. *National Land Use Database (NLUD) NLUD scoping study final report. (Project Report).* London.

Department of the Environment Transport and the Regions (DETR). 2000. *Planning to Deliver The Managed Release of Housing Sites.* London The Stationary Office (TSO).

Dixon, T. 2006. Integrating Sustainability into Brownfield Regeneration Rhetoric or Reality? – An Analysis of the UK Development Industry. *Journal of Property Research,* 23(3), 237–67. Available at 10.1080/09599910600933889.

Eisen, J.B. 1999. Brownfields policies for sustainable cities. *Duke Environmental Law and Policy Forum,* 9(2), 187–229. Available at http//www.law.duke.edu/shell/cite.pl?9+Duke+Envtl.+L.+&+Pol%27y+F.+187 [accessed 20 July 2011].

English Nature. 2006. *Thames Basin Heaths Special Protection Area Mitigation Standards for Residential Development (Final Report October 2006).* Newbury.

Ferber, U. (ed.). 2006. *Sustainable Brownfield Regeneration CABERNET network report.* Nottingham Univ. of Nottingham.

Gallent, N., Howe, J. and Bell, P. 2000. New uses for England's old airfields. *Area,* 32(4), 383–94. Available at 10.1111/j.1475-4762.2000.tb00154.x.

Gallo, A. and Sullivan, M. 2002. Oakland Army Base. *Economic Development Journal,* 1(3), 43. Available at http//search.ebscohost.com/login.aspx?direct=true&db=a9h&AN=7553900&site=ehost-live [accessed 21 July 2011].

Ganser, R. 2005. *Quantifizierte Ziele flächensparsamer Siedlungsentwicklung im englischen Planungssystem Ein Modell für Raumordnung und Bauleitplanung in Deutschland?* Kaiserslautern Techn. Univ. Lehrstuhl Stadtplanung.

Ganser, R. 2008. Militärflächenkonversion in England – Vergleichende Studie der Vorgehensweisen und Erfahrungen. in *Konversionsflächenmanagement zur nachhaltigen Wiedernutzung freigegebener militärischer Liegenschaften REFINA-KoM,* edited by C. Jacoby and K. Beutler. Neubiberg, 119–54.

Gareth, J., Thornton, C., Nathanail, P., Franz, M. and Pahlen, G. 2007. The development of a brownfield-specific sustainability and indicator framework for regenerating sites proposing a new definition of 'sustainable brownfield regeneration'. *Land Contamination & Reclamation,* 15(1), 41–54. Available at 10.2462/09670513.836.

Grundmann, M. 1998. Truppenabbau, Konversion und die Möglichkeiten einer eigenständigen Regionalentwicklung in Deutschland. in *Konversion – Chance für eine eigenständige Regionalentwicklung?*, edited by J.-J. Carmona-Schneider. Bonn Kuron, 49–63.

Hill, C. 2000. Measuring Success in the Redevelopment of Former Military Bases Evidence from a Case Study of the Truman Annex in Key West, Florida. *Economic Development Quarterly,* 14(3), 267–77. Available at 10.1177/089124240001400306.

Homes and Communities Agency (HCA). *Register of Surplus Public Sector Land.* [Online] Available at http//www.homesandcommunities.co.uk/ourwork/register-surplus-public-sector-land [accessed 26 July 2011].

Inspector's report on RAF Upper Heyford dated 25.02.08. *Secretary of State decision letter regarding QE II barracks, dated 24.07.08.*

Levett-Therivel Sustainability Consultants. *Recommended strategic environmental assessment / sustainability appraisal 2006.* [Online] Available at http//www.levett-therivel.co.uk/index_files/SEArec06.htm [accessed 21 July 2011].

Marrs, C. 3 June 2011. Councils warned about delays to development plans. *Planning,* 3 June. Available at http//www.planningresource.co.uk/Economic_Development/article/1072866/councils-warned-delays-development-plans/ [accessed 21 July 2011].

McCarthy, L. 2002. The brownfield dual land use policy challenge reducing barriers to private redevelopment while connecting reuse to broader community goals. *Land Use Policy,* 19(4), 287–96. Available at 10.1016/S0264-8377(02)00023-6.

Milton Keynes Partnership (MKP). 2007. *Framework Section 106 Agreement.*

Ministry of Defence (MoD). 2007. *Defence Lands Handbook.* London.

Nathanail, C.P. and Bardos, R.P. 2004. *Reclamation of contaminated land.* Chichester Wiley.

Northumberland Information Network. 2006. *Military Base Closures in Rural Areas Best Practice & Cautionary Tales, Prepared for the Raf Boulmer 2012 Group, Final Report.* Morpheth, Northumberland.

Raco, M. 2003. Assessing the discourses and practices of urban regeneration in a growing region. *Geoforum,* 34(1), 37–55. Available at 10.1016/S0016-7185(02)00040-4.

Scott Wilson, Levett-Therivel Sustainability Consultants, Treweek Environmental Consultants and Land Use Consultants. 2006. *Appropriate Assessment of Plans.*

South Cambridgeshire District Council. 2007. *Northstowe Area Action Plan adopted July 2007.*

Syms, P.M. 2004. *Previously developed land Industrial activities and contamination.* 2nd Edition. Oxford Blackwell Publishing Ltd.

The Land Trust. *Managing land for you.* [Online] Available at www.thelandtrust.org.uk [accessed 21 July 2011].

Wieschollek, S. *Konversion ein totgeborenes Kind in Wünsdorf-Waldstadt? Probleme der Umnutzung des ehemaligen Hauptquartiers der Westgruppe der Truppen zur zivilen Kleinstadt.* Bonn Bonn International Center for Conversion BICC.

Woodward, R. 1998. *Rural development and the restructuring of the defence estate A preliminary investigation (Research Report).* Newcastle University of Newcastle upon Tyne.

www.defencemanagement.com. *A MoDEL construction project – defence estates – Defence Management Journal Issue 36.* [Online] Available at http//www.defencemanagement.com/article.asp?id=249&content_name=defence%20estates&article=7489 [accessed 09 August 2011].

Chapter 15

The Regeneration of a Naval City: Portsmouth

Fabiano Lemes de Oliveira, Lorraine Farrelly

Introduction

One of the key themes in contemporary urban design debates is the redevelopment of brownfield sites. It not only refers to the restructuring of specific sites and districts of post-industrial cities, but also to the redefinition of the urban form and its functions in naval urban contexts. Despite being different phenomena, these processes of spatial change fit within major global economic, financial and technological structural shifts. While specialised sites were necessary for the capitalist industrial model of development with regard to production, distribution and transportation (Castells 2003: 23); the development of the global economy and ways of communication, particularly since the last quarter of the twentieth century, led them to obsoleteness, frequent dissolution and abandonment mostly in the United States and western European countries. This has often been accompanied by a loss of population and other marks of decline. Not only former industrial plants and dockyards have been affected by these processes, but also significant historic sites associated with military use have been closed after having gone through periods of rationalization. In brief, the decay of these sites in many cities around the world coupled with the economic pressure for their redevelopment offered the opportunity for re-shaping extensive urban territories.

Among many interesting examples, the redevelopment of Gunwharf Quays in Portsmouth, South East coast of England, is one of the latest most interesting transformations in the country and will be the object of analysis in this chapter. Portsmouth has a population of around 199,200 people today, living in an area of 40 square kilometres (15.5 square miles). Since the beginning of the new millennium, the city's population has been growing slowly and the forecast is that it will reach 207,170 by 2026. The South East is facing unprecedented levels of urbanisation and population growth, exceeding a total of 9.5 million people by 2026. Although its gross value added (GVA) per head is high, the region faces the widest range of social deprivation and economic disparities of the country (South East, 2009). In this context, Portsmouth has been redefining itself in the last decades, aiming at becoming a globally competitive knowledge economy in the near future. Building upon its maritime heritage and privileged location, the city is today developing ways to suppor economic growth, innovation and enterprise and the competitiveness of the city to attract investment and visitors. Gunwharf Quays is part of this process. Not only is it of interest to explore its role in the context of contemporary Portsmouth, but also to include it into the wider debate on urban regeneration of Brownfield sites.

Towards urban regeneration

The changes in the world urban economy across the twentieth century were accompanied by new ways of looking at the urban space. While large-scale plans were the basis upon which laid the development of town planning as a specific discipline until the crisis of the modern movement after World War II, urban design emerged as a new field of study aimed at tackling the transformation of the post-war city. The totalitarian ideas and historical process that finally led to the war put at stake the very same belief in the progress as the path to social equity and instigated the reaction to top-down decisions and plans(Benjamin, Tiedemann 1999; Giedion 1969). One of the foremost criticisms to the paradigmatic modernist master plans and their generic buildings were posed particularly by human geography and urban sociology, opening the path to the conception of the city as a fragmented place, to the understanding of the importance of history, tradition and diversity in social, local and community needs (e.g., Rowe, Koetter 1978, Jacobs 1961, Harvey 1989, Lang 2005). Therefore, the understanding of the city as a complex phenomenon and the necessity to face immediate local problems led – in the post-war period – to the emergence of a variety of trends in urban design (Cuthbert 2007), some based upon the physical nature of the cities (Cullen 1961, Rowe, Koetter 1978, Lynch 1960), while others focused upon social involvement (Jacobs 1961), social theory and the role of economic processes in the construction of the urban space (Castells 2003).

In terms of policy in the United Kingdom in the period, five distinct phases have been identified: (1) reconstruction, (2) revitalisation, (3) renewal, (4) redevelopment and (5) regeneration (Roberts 2000:14). By the mid-1970s, typical inner-city areas had lost between 16 and 20 per cent of their populations, due to loss in manufacturing jobs and rationalization processes (Hall, Tewdwr-Jones 2011: 137). To change the existing city became a fundamental issue to trigger economic growth and avoid widespread deprivation. It is remarkable how, in the laissez-faire attitude of the 1980s, the role of private sector started to be decisive to the development of cities, with a clear raising of the importance of services and shift towards the production of spaces of consumption. Instead of the focus on community life of the previous decades – ultimately on the public realm of the welfare state – urban design interventions started to follow a new agenda.

Needless to say, industrial and maritime heritage became key business opportunities for private developers. The public sector has become more and more interested in attracting investment and renewing entire parts of cities, particularly in Britain. In this context, urban regeneration has been one of the most common strategies to give new uses to decayed sites, while promoting profitable investments particularly to the private sector (e.g., Tallon 2010, Lang

2005, Cuthbert 2007). Under the conservative government of Margaret Thatcher, Canary Wharf in London was a prominent example of urban redevelopment of an obsolete site, ruled mainly by private investors. Several other examples followed the case of East London, frequently revising the aspects of the project that led to the failure of the redevelopment in its first phase. The reconversion of brownfield sites has become essential to the growth of cities in the global economy and to the change in their images, as can be seen in contemporary complex strategies, such as in Barcelona's 22@ project (Rota 2005).

The relationships between private investors' interventions and public control have been a way to combine public interests with economic viability of developments. Urban regeneration, therefore, theoretically, needs to combine collective needs with private interests. New paradigms have consolidated their importance in every typology of urban design in the last decades and are almost consensual, such as the need for diversity in use, sustainability, accessibility and the importance of connections with public transport. However, some are controversial and reflect how much society is dependent on the market and on consumerist behaviours, in such a way that it has been seen as almost unconceivable that new urban regeneration projects escape from the need to create large areas for retail and from increasing property speculation. Public life has been linked so tightly to consumption that this new scenario of economic crisis might also establish new perspectives towards the production of urban space.

In the following sections, the history behind the creation of Gunwharf Quays is discussed, along with the questions of (1) how it can be analysed within the premises discussed above, and (2) how it avoided further decline to become a thriving development. Within this framework, key arguments, such as how this project attempted to respond to the context of the site, city and region as part of its strategy to enhance local cultural and socio-economic aspects, are of special interest. Moreover, it is fundamental to look at the discourses on sustainability that informed this development.

From HMS Vernon to Gunwharf Quays

In the past few decades, regions and cities across Europe have had to redefine their identities by reinventing major areas within them to attract investment and be competitive internationally. This was also the case of Portsmouth, one of the major ports on the south coast of United Kingdom. Originally a Roman port, where goods entered the island of Great Britain, Portsmouth has grown due to its location on a natural harbour, and is still one of the important strategic ports of the United Kingdom and home for Naval ship building. Its population peak occured in the 1930s, when the city population reached 26,000. Between 1931 and 1981 there was a decline in population in each consecutive census. The 1980s and 1990s saw some fluctuations in the population of the city, which reached 188,000 by the end of the millennium. (Portsmouth City Council 2011a; Portsmouth City Council 2011b).

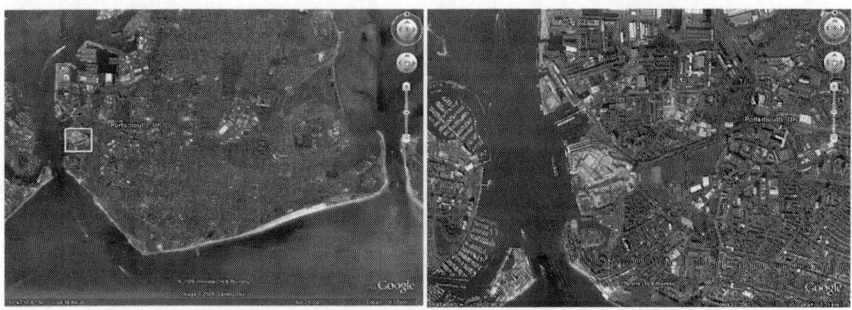

Figure 15.1   Portsmouth and the location of Gunwharf Quays

Source: Google Earth. Highlights by Fabiano Lemes

Over the last few decades, the country's navy has redefined itself, focusing on more sophisticated ships and weaponry and thus needing less manpower and physical space. In 1981, the Ministry of Defence undertook a review of the defence provision in the United Kingdom, and published a document entitled 'The Way Forward', which considered the future of the navy. It recommended the closure of naval sites within Portsmouth and adjacent Gosport. As a consequence, whole urban areas which once serviced the navy needed to be redefined and the identity of the naval city and its future depended upon this redefinition. It was, on the other hand, an opportunity to enhance Portsmouth's competitiveness to attract investment and thrive economically, as well as to promote a more integrated urban fabric and new facilities to its citizens. Evidently, the navy played a major role in the economy of the city, as an employer and consumer, and any regeneration project resulting from its rationalisation needed to minimise demographic and economic shrinkage, to stimulate the economy in the area and to create a new momentum for employment.

For such an undertaking, a bid was put forward by the local business consortium to the Millennium Commission, a major government funding body that supports regeneration projects, entitled 'The Renaissance of Portsmouth Harbour'. The proposal included the following key aims:

- To transform Portsmouth harbour into an international heritage arena and in doing so, create a world-class attraction, which should act as a catalyst for the economic regeneration of both Portsmouth & Gosport.
- To create new, highly accessible amenities (e.g., public open space/ performance areas), in addition to construct five kilometers of new promenade to form a trail around the harbour mouth to open up land closed off for centuries.
- To link new and enhanced attractions on both sides of the harbour to reflect the area's maritime history.
- To develop new facilities, including the landmark harbour observation

tower, which would create future development opportunities.

- To mark the renaissance of the harbour from one dominated by the defence industries to one where leisure, commerce and defence are all important elements (Portsmouth City Council 2006)

Within this proposal, Gunwharf was identified as a key development site. There were additional development sites in Priddy's Hard and the Royal Clarence Yard, which have developed subsequently.

Gunwharf Quays, formerly known as HMS Vernon, was used as a naval ordnance yard from the late seventeenth century onwards and expanded to its current size in the 1870s. In the 1980s, it was clearly a brownfield, disused naval storage area, on the sea edge, inaccessible to the public. With the Ministry of Defense (MoD) review, the site was put on the open market and bought by the Berkeley group in 1996, which started to envision a redevelopment plan.

Dealing with the dilemmas of permanence and change, the master plan incorporated existing historic structures that had been part of the original storage area of Gunwharf, as the planning brief required its restoration as well as the boundary walls from the 1870s. Older buildings on the site that needed to be retained included the Vulcan Building, the Infirmary building and the Board of Ordnance offices.

The development of the site was included in the local plan as a mixed-use residential, retail and office area. Further requirements listed in the brief, included a millennium promenade, a millennium boulevard, a city quay and a 170m tower, which had a separate brief. The tower was the key element of the scheme to celebrate the new millennium. Some architects signalled their interest in designing it such as Foster and Santiago Calatrava (Portsmouth Society April 1997), but HGP Greentree Allchurch Evans's spinnaker plan was ultimately selected after public consultation.

An outline planning application was submitted in 1997, which included details of the proposed layout, location and design of the main buildings. There were objections to the vast amount of retail area proposed, concerns over potential traffic jams and lack of affordable houses (Portsmouth Society September 1997). However, there was extensive consultation in Portsmouth and Gosport, as well as extensive studies and investigations into the impact of the retail area proposal locally and regionally to determine its viability. Soon afterwards, the construction started.

The final proposal

The initial idea indicated what the future development of the area would be like, and few major changes to the concept and general arrangements were made. The choice of a mixed-use development is a common option in urban renewal projects, as discussed previously, and was a key argument to achieve diversity in use and economic sustainability. The 'mixed-use' included housing, restaurants, the Aspex gallery and leisure facilities such as cinemas, health clubs and bowling. Moreover, its location – alongside Portsmouth Harbour – provides waterside views, a canal

Figure 15.2 View of the canal

Source: photo by Fabiano Lemes

and a marina facility, which offers berthing facilities for boats, also allowing tall ships and pleasure boats to moor alongside.

The canal runs east-west and is a fundamental element in the layout of the site. Originally the plan for the canal also had a northern wing which led to a proposed hotel and an open-air amphitheatre, which were not actually built. Instead, the canal ends at its eastern side at a circular open space destined for festivals and to house public art. The canal's presence in the design reinforces the waterside nature of the project, and provides a link to the site's historical background. However, its most important function is to delineate two different zones within the project: the residential units, on its southern side, and the main shopping/leisure areas on the northern.

As a result, there is a definite sense of calm within the residential areas, which also benefits environmentally as most of the units have south orientation. There is a wide range of building types which accommodate many housing configurations, from single-bedroom or studio units to townhouses for families. The homes are located around a variety of different spaces, from formal courtyard gardens to smaller streets and squares. The residential areas are grouped into two, with a series of streets and squares (some pedestrianised) to the southeast of the site incorporating the historic structures, including the Vulcan building.

The retail/recreation area, on the other hand, anchors the project and is a dynamic and multifunctional space. This sector is usually heavily used, especially during the day. The proximity to the sea and the interstitial public space are also

Figure 15.3   Central Piazza in Gunwharf Quays

Source: photos by Fabiano Lemes

Figure 15.4   View of the retail area

Source: photos by Fabiano Lemes

key elements of its success, linking it to the Millennium promenade. This retail area is connected to the canal by many links. Other public spaces leak into the commercial areas, and there is a clear gradation of scale from the canal side, to the central square and finally to the pedestrianised streets.

The scheme mixes the restoration of historic buildings with a range of contemporary architecture and the layout and massing of the development is variable. Alongside the three-storey blocks of the historic naval structures, the housing is limited to three stories to respond to this existing context. The scale increases towards the water's edge and canal side to six stories. There are larger-scale structures across the site near the newly constructed retail areas, including social housing and a new hotel. This massing is dominated by two elements: the Spinnaker tower (not 'Millennium Tower' as originally defined), approximately 170 metres tall opened to the public in 2005, and Number 1 Gunwharf, a 29-storey apartment block. Both of these structures offer incredible views across Portsmouth Harbour. They are monumentally located on opposite sides of the site and are clear reference points that act visually, to cite Lynch 1960, as important elements of legibility. Sculptures and art pieces were incorporated into key open spaces, mainly reinforcing the naval character of the site.

It was imperative that this proposal responded carefully to several needs, including establishing strong links with the city. These links assumed several dimensions, with special regard to creating visual links and to enhance the physical connections to the territory; but also filled a gap in the urban fabric sensibly enough to attend to social wishes and expectations. The respect for history – observable in many of the buildings and in the urban design proposal– is a feature of Gunwharf Quays, which is intended to gain the local population's approval and to boost their sense of belonging. It is important to explore this last argument, particularly how the insertion of the project into the territory has been planned at different scales.

In a large-scale context, it is part of the Millennium Promenade, a route along Portsmouth's water edge, from Clarence pier to the historic dockyards. It is three kilometres long, crossing through the territory and connecting the most significant of Portsmouth's historic monuments and sites, including the historic battlement in Old Portsmouth. The route also opens up the waterfront land that had been previously closed to the public.

Following the Millennium Walkway and to enhance the pedestrian's experience within the site, the canal-side edge and the main shopping area in Gunwharf Quays were completely pedestrianised with ground level walkways along the marina and walkways at upper levels connecting bars and restaurants.

Good links to public transport have become fundamental to the success of any urban design/regeneration project. Firstly, it allows great numbers of people to use the site, encouraging diversity of social groups; and secondly, as challenges automobile dependence, it contributes environmentally to a more sustainable city. Gunwharf Quays benefits from very good transport links to train and bus stations all within walking distance. The site is adjacent to a major transport interchange in Portsmouth, the Hard – the main bus terminal for the city and a major railway

Figure 15.5   Southwestern part of the Milennium Promenade in Gunwharf Quays

Source: photo by Fabiano Lemes

station. There are ferry services to the Isle of Wight – a 15-minute journey – and Gosport – approximately five minutes.

The site has two road access points: one for visitors of the waterfront area and another for the housing part of the development. This allows access to an underground parking area and to a private road with allocated parking for residents. The residential part of the site is laid out with clear pedestrian areas and clearly defined roadways.

The various elements of the scheme use a range of materials, which aim to relate to the materials and shapes of the previous buildings, to respond to technological needs and to produce a contemporary architectural expression. An example of the first is the use of local bricks both by the existing Vulcan buildings on the site, which used to be naval storehouses, and by the surrounding new buildings of apartments and townhouses. The newer houses and apartment blocks use rendered panels, while the newest building, Number 1 Gunwharf, is a concrete framed structure with a proprietary glazed system.

Conclusion

Gunwharf Quays has been transformed with the creation of housing, shopping, offices, leisure equipment and public space. Today it is, however, more than a successful mixed-use scheme. It is a collection of experiences moulded through a large process of collective work by public and private sectors, which has had a significant impact upon Portsmouth's social, cultural, economic and physical contexts. It is important to highlight that the site was developed through a range of projects executed by various architectural practices over a whole decade.

The main Gunwharf retail and leisure area went into business in 2001. It opened up an area that had been in naval ownership for over 300 years, providing public access to the sea front. The area is used for local events and has been developing its own character with street markets, festivals and performances scheduled all year round. It plays its part in the creative economy of Portsmouth (Florida 2002). The success of the Gunwharf Quays development lies in the integration of a range of living, working and leisure facilities on a unique site. The previously walled quays have been opened up to the city, creating new routes along the water edge and through its main pedestrianised shopping areas. It is fair to say that a new neighbourhood has been created from nothing, providing self-contained living in a range of property types, from one-bedroom apartments to townhouses. The various aspects of the scheme complement one another to create a particular urban experience that has proved popular and successful both as a place to live and as a destination for a day out.

This proposal is connected to the idea that the Harbour could become a World Heritage Site in the future. A heritage bid was compiled and submitted to the World Heritage Committee in 2006 for consideration as the world's first 'cultural seascape'. With the prospect of moderated population growth and the city's ambition to enhance its global competitiveness and economic growth, as part of the South Hampshire sub-region, Portsmouth is currently investing in partnerships with private sector for further regeneration projects (Portsmouth City Council 2011c). Gunwharf Quays is part of a story that connects the site to its past and future success, working within the local, regional and international context to redefine the future of the city.

References

Benjamin, W. and Tiedemann, R. 1999. *The arcades project.* Cambridge, Mass: Belknap Press.

Castells, M. 2003. The Process of Urban Social Change. in *Designing cities: Critical readings in urban design*, edited by A.R. Cuthbert. Malden, Mass: Blackwell Pub, 23–27.

Cullen, G. 1961. *The concise townscape.* New York: Van Nostrand.

Cuthbert, A.R. 2007. Urban design: requiem for an era – review and critique of the last 50 years. *Urban Design International,* 12(4), 177–223. Available at: 10.1057/palgrave.udi.9000200.

Florida, R. 2002. *The rise of the Creative Class: And how it's Transforming Work, Leisure, Community and Everyday Life.* 1st Edition. New York (NY): Basic Books.

Giedion, S. 1969. *Mechanization takes command: A contribution to anonymous history.* New York: Norton.

Hall, P.G. and Tewdwr-Jones, M. 2011. *Urban and regional planning.* 5th Edition. London: Routledge.

Harvey, D. 1989. *The condition of postmodernity: An enquiry into the origins of cultural change.* 1st Edition. Oxford: Blackwell.

Jacobs, J. 1961. *The death and life of great American cities.* 3rd Edition. New York: Random House.

Lang, J. 2005. *Urban design: A typology of procedures and products ; illustrated with over 50 case studies.* Amsterdam: Elsevier.

Lynch, K. 1960. *The image of the city.* Cambridge [Mass.]: Technology Press.

Portsmouth City Council. 2006. *The Rennaisance of Portsmouth Harbour and Gunwharf Quays: Information Sheets.*

Portsmouth City Council. *Forecasts for Portsmouth Wards, 2010–2013.* [Online] Available at: http://www.portsmouth.gov.uk/yourcouncil/1516.html [accessed: 22 June 2011].

Portsmouth City Council. *Portsmouth population totals from 1971.* [Online] Available at: http://www.portsmouth.gov.uk/yourcouncil/3817.html [accessed: 22 June 2011].

Portsmouth City Council. 2011c. *Shaping the future of Portsmouth Portsmouth.*

Portsmouth Society. April 1997. Gunwharf – the story so far. *Portsmouth Society News: The Newsletter of the Portsmouth Society,* April 1997.

Portsmouth Society. September 1997. Gunwharf – Outline Permission Granted. *Portsmouth Society News: The Newsletter of the Portsmouth Society,* September 1997.

Roberts, P. 2000. *Urban regeneration: A handbook.* London: SAGE.

Rota, M.B. 2005. 22@Barcelona: a New District for the Creative Economy. in *Making spaces for the creative economy,* edited by W. Ng and J. Ryser. Madrid.

Rowe, C. and Koetter, F. 1978. *Collage city.* Cambridge, Mass: MIT Press.

Tallon, A. 2010. *Urban regeneration in the UK.* London: Routledge.

Conclusions Spatial Planning for the Dichotomy of Growth and Shrinkage

Evolution of planning paradigms and planning systems

Settlement growth and shrinkage are not new phenomena (see Ward, Chapter 1) but have had different environmental, economic, and social impacts which have been, and continue to be, addressed by urban and regional planning or integrated spatial planning. An initial impulse may therefore be to turn to the wisdom of the past to find lessons which can be learned to resolve our current planning problems. While it is certainly not necessary, or even helpful, to 'reinvent the wheel' when developing planning policy documents, great care has to be exercised regarding the identification of the appropriate planning solution. A key issue in this context is a tendency of the planning response to focus on long term growth. This is not surprising, as modern urban and regional planning has been formed with a view to respond to the growth problems of the industrial revolution (Hall 1992: 12). Additionally the political interpretation (or wishful thinking) and reality of spatial development appear to diverge frequently. Clearly, it is more politically palatable, for example, to open up new schools and kindergartens – rather than to be responsible for scaling back infrastructure. Therefore, in situations of parallel growth and decline, more emphasis will (quite naturally) be placed on planning solutions to address problems linked to the former.

Depending on the planning system, as well as the political and legal context, there usually is a certain time lag before (innovative) planning solutions are implemented. Hall aptly assigns the main responsibility for this phenomenon to 'the inertia of people's minds, and still more to the inertia of social and political processes' (1992:12).

We therefore have to be particularly careful not to implement planning policy aimed at growth management, or increased growth stimulation, in situations where management of shrinkage is required and vice versa. A particularly harmful situation would be where growth stimuli lead to unhealthy competition between local authorities, thereby wasting public financial resources and exacerbating the problems linked to slow growth or shrinkage in the long term.

In Chapter 1, Ward identifies different 'eras' of spatial planning responses: from major and strategic interventions to the acceptance of general spatial development trends with more local planning measures. He also develops the hypothesis that spatial planning philosophy may be linked to economic and political development. Considering the historic waves of changes which planning systems around the world have been subjected to, Ward suggests that real fundamental changes to planning systems, based on more control of global economic development, may occur as a consequence of and as a response to global environmental crisis. If we take this train of thought a step further we may expect to see an 'ecologicalisation' of spatial planning due to the source of, and reason for, this further development of the planning systems.

The core question is how we can ensure that future spatial planning 'leitmotifs' or paradigms lead us in the right direction. In a situation of urban shrinkage, there may possibly be more time to develop plans and policies, but resource and revenue needs may prove to be the major challenge. In such a context the only possible answer might be the use of public subsidies linked to planning frameworks to guide spatial development. This may significantly limit opportunities to truly affect change.

The paradox appears to be that it is not any easier to implement spatial planning frameworks in a rapid growth scenario, since spatial planning would be under pressure and would probably be pushed into a reactive role. It is difficult, or in most cases virtually impossible, to direct spatial development against market forces.

Further to this point of future development Hall (Chapter 2) suggests that the occurrence of new mega-city regions – a new element in the history of global spatial development – simultaneously offers challenges and opportunities for economic development. In this context he mentions the possibility for each place to discover its economic niche based on human capital which, he argues, is absolutely critical in the new knowledge economy. If this is the case, a critical factor in competition will undoubtedly be a healthy and attractive living and working environment, in order to attract the 'high potential' workforce of the future which can bring forward the necessary innovations and therefore economic advantages (see also: Roth et al. Chapter 4). This may add to the trend of downright 'ecologicalisation' in certain areas of spatial planning or may ensure that long term environmental and economic material issues will be treated with more equal weighting in planning decision making. A challenge in this context will certainly remain in environmental fields which are not directly linked to the working and living environment. Here, it would require a very strong environmental and planning framework to coordinate the forces of global competition.

At the same time it appears that the physical demarcation between built up areas and landscape becomes more fluid as the relation between growing and shrinking parts of a city region (Laursen, Chapter 5). This poses new challenges for spatial planning which will have to deal more and more with an increasingly complex urban and landscape patchwork.

It also appears safe to assume that a major challenge – at least for urban planning in shrinking cities and regions – will take the form of resource constraints (Jessen, Chapter 3) with regards to human capital but also funding. This will no doubt impact on environmental considerations and could hold back the 'ecologicalisation' envisaged above.

The above may indicate that a planning paradigm which leans more towards state intervention is probably the more natural fit in situations characterised by shrinkage, and a 'go with the flow' liberal approach is probably easier to implement in the context of growth. Either way it appears to be necessary to closely monitor and control the implementation of planning policy. Only then will it be possible to ensure timeliness and aptness of planning responses. It would obviously be quite advantageous to address problems of growth and shrinkage before they manifest themselves. There appears to be some hope that broad indicators of spatial development can help identify cities or regions that are more likely to face huge transformations than others (see Jessen, Chapter 3). However, further research is still needed to devise the appropriate planning measures which soften or avoid spatial development problems at their roots, that is, before they are fully manifested.

Strategic planning

There is general consensus among practitioners and academicians, that rapid urban growth and related major development projects require strategic planning tiers and documents to achieve coordination across local authority and regional boundaries. Lessons from the past –such as the development of the London Docklands throughout the 1980s, which tried to achieve major urban expansion and regeneration without strategic planning and infrastructure coordination – demonstrate forcefully that market forces alone coupled with streamlined project by project ad hoc planning decisions, are inadequate.

This understanding ensured that planning systems around the globe have been, or are currently being, equipped with formalised strategic (i.e., regional) planning with a clear statutory purpose. However, recently in England, a complete political and paradigmatic change can be observed at the heart of which is the abolishment of regional planning documents and planning tiers.

In Germany, where regional planning is traditionally strong due to the federal political structure which is mirrored in the planning system, there is a move towards more bottom-up participation in regional coordination efforts. This is mainly based on the belief (or hope) that local authorities will see a win-win situation through strategic coordination at the regional level and as a result facilitate implementation of strategic regional objectives at the local level.

In the United States there continues to be an evolution of the regional planning process to become even more comprehensive and multidimensional – expanding the relationship established between land use, economic, and transport planning to also incorporate environmental protection and restoration, systems approaches and design, social equity, and human health. The organizing principle of environmental sustainability provides an overarching framework for bringing these various issues together. This appears to be of crucial importance for both growing and shrinking city regions to develop more integrated approaches to strategic planning. For growing regions there is the inherent danger that due to high development pressures and speed of development, environmental degradation can occur. For shrinking regions, due to a lack of financial resources, environmental issues may not be given the weight they deserve when compared with other material issues which are part of planning decision making.

A challenge and an opportunity for spatial planning at the same time appears to be the fact that cities choose similar strategies or planning approaches to solve their problems (see Roth et al. Chapter 4). With regards to global competition this contradicts the postulated uniqueness of cities and may therefore be seen as problematic. At the same time this situation opens up opportunities for international benchmarking and cooperation with a view to further improve spatial planning instruments and processes. This may also help to overcome or reduce the resource constraints mentioned above.

The key question for strategic planning in the context of parallel patterns of growth and decline is whether more or less planning direction is required in these differing spatial development contexts. Strauß (Chapter 5) argues that in a spatial context of shrinkage (in Germany), strategic planning direction and focus on urban and villages cores is necessary. In this context, it is postulated that urban qualitative improvements should be at the heart of such a planning agenda. This could then lead to more flexible future urban structures which adapt more easily to changing spatial demands, for example, reverting urbanised lands to non-urban uses.

Following this train of thought a clear challenge for spatial planning will arise with regards to achieving political consensus and implementation. This appears to be very different to a growth scenario, where development pressures, but also benefits linked to new development, can be spread around and city centres as well as suburban and rural areas can all have a piece of this cake. Simultaneously it is fairly common to distribute public funding, for example for regeneration, according to the scatter gun principle. In a shrinkage scenario this is no longer possible and tough decisions with regards to planning future development and funding focus will have to be made. On a positive note Strauß argues that learning from planning for shrinkage may lead to more flexible urban structures which would more easily allow the reversal of spatial development. This of course would be beneficial for the environment and an assessment similar to the life cycle assessment of buildings could be devised for urban and rural developments: from developing land for hard-end uses right through to turning them into soft-end uses or complete rehabilitation.

Again, looking at the German planning system, Kuebler et al. (Chapter 7) postulate new forms of cooperation between local authorities to meet the challenges of parallel growth and decline. In Germany's political and legal system these must mainly remain informal due to constitutional reasons, with the advantage that within informal patterns of cooperation it is easier to follow individual and joint objectives. However, it appears that in some situations –for example, when competition between neighbouring local authorities cannot be overcome – a clear statutory requirement for strategic planning, alongside informal cooperation, is needed to achieve meaningful spatial coordination. Strengthening cooperation across boundaries between different administrative authorities would optimize land use policy and generally make a valuable contribution to a more sustainable use of land and related service provision.

Kuebler et al. (Chapter 7) discuss, amongst other things, a cap on land allocations for greenfield development with a view to saving habitats and preserving land for agriculture. With regards to the environmental challenge of safeguarding greenfields, it was already mentioned above that shrinkage tendencies do not automatically lead to a situation of less greenfield development. It is therefore a pertinent topic for spatial planning to address. In the context of their case study they suggest, due to the relatively weak nature of German strategic planning documents, an independent 'cooperation agency,' the core remit of which would be the provision of information for local authorities in the hope that more of them would recognise a win-win situation in cooperation with neighbouring authorities. This could bring about financial savings and environmental benefits through better coordinated development across local authority boundaries. This is a good example for the spatial planning challenge to find an appropriate combination of statutory and informal planning instruments – including organisational or procedural approaches – with a view to setting up a planning framework that can actually deliver. This implies that there cannot be a simple 'one size fits all' solution. In fact, it will be important to assess exactly what characteristics the formal planning procedures and instruments possess with regards to participation but also regarding their binding character for lower tier planning authorities.

Depending on the (national) planning culture there will be parallel approaches in different countries or regions. This raises interesting ethical planning issues with regards to fairness and democratic legitimacy. After all, approaches range from strictly binding planning documents and planning processes with a fairly rigid framework of stakeholder participation to weak planning documents and very open planning procedures.

Further to the point of planning challenges, and more specifically challenges across different planning tiers, Fina et al. (Chapter 8) point out that clearly visible conflicting interests at the local level are much more difficult to detect at the regional or national levels as they can balance each other out. With regards to shrinking regions they argue that the unhealthy competition amongst local authorities still prevails. In particular, the resulting oversupply of cheap land for buildings and speculative residential development leads to negative environmental impacts which could be avoided if local authorities cooperated more closely, as suggested above.

An objective analysis of this situation leads to the conclusions that there is the inherent danger that spatial planning will be blamed – at least partially – for such negative impacts although it is not necessarily the planning system but the political power structures or wider societal policy including fiscal policy which appears to be the root cause for conflicting interests and unhealthy competition in developing land for housing and industry.

A different set of challenges appears to arise in coastal amenity communities which follow a very distinctive, yet volatile and fairly fast paced, pattern of growth and stagnation which is characterised by long term as well as seasonal demographic growth and shrinkage Gurran et al. (Chapter 11). Here fundamental challenges for spatial planning and the environment are identified as low density greenfield development and car dependent settlement structures with negative effects similar to metropolitan sprawl. Additionally the vulnerability of coastal locations to the effects of climate change is highlighted. The authors therefore call for a multidisciplinary approach including climate science and urban and regional planning.

Considering the above it appears that an integrated spatial planning approach which goes beyond the realm of land use planning would be beneficial in this context. Dealing with climate change issues as well as with negative impacts of sprawl also imply that it would be valuable to implement this at the strategic as well as at the local planning level.

Sustainable residential development and quality of life

Housing is probably the field of spatial development in which problems associated with high growth or shrinkage are most obvious. At one end of the scale, there is physical dereliction and declining property values, in which a downward spiral occurs. Income from rents decreases and there is a subsequent lack of investment in the maintenance of real estate. At the other end of the scale, demand for housing and affordability issues in high growth areas are typically observed.

Malottki, et al. (Chapter 8) argue that the demolition of 'problematic' housing stock which is no longer marketable, particularly in areas of housing market failure due to demographical shrinkage, can free up land for other uses or housing types which are still in demand (see also Kaido, Chapter 9). This in turn may help to avoid additional greenfield development and therefore has a beneficial effect on the environment. At the same time two great challenges for spatial planning in this context are identified – these are: avoiding the unhealthy competition between local authorities mentioned above and convincing all concerned owners of 'problematic' housing stock that demolition is a viable tool for reviving a housing market area, as it will only work in a fair way when all concerned stakeholders contribute in the form of demolitions and/or redevelopments. Malottki et al. argue that detailed market surveys are a key to success in this context.

Building on these conclusions it appears safe to assume that a mix of 'strong' statutory planning instruments and 'soft' communicative informal instruments will be necessary to accomplish the twin objectives of reducing environmental impacts (i.e., additional greenfield development) and increased vacancy rates, by means of demolition and redevelopment. It may not be necessary to employ the statutory instruments, including compulsory purchase, if the relevant stakeholders buy into schemes to overcome market failure on the basis of informal planning instruments and surveys which clearly show the win-win-situation for all concerned parties. This in turn requires sufficient resources for spatial planning so it can take on the pivotal role of coordinator and communicator. This takes us back once again to the challenge of resource provision, already mentioned above.

Interestingly the impacts of growth and of shrinkage on quality of life can be fairly similar. In both scenarios the soft-end use of sites and high quality urban design are equally important. Brereton underlines this postulate and argues that green infrastructure is important for quality of life based on results of comparative analysis of quality of life in urban and rural areas (Chapter 12). Additionally, socio-economic and socio-demographic variables are found to be important determinants of life satisfaction. An assessment tool linking concepts of quality of life and urban ecosystem services could therefore be an important planning and decision-making tool, which could be used for the prioritisation of projects. This analysis suggests that spatial planning should find ways to emphasize the 'positives' in shrinkage, as well as in growth areas. In this context shrinkage can feasibly lead to a better quality of life, for instance, in circumstances in which more space becomes available per capita and housing becomes more affordable even in urban areas. In this context it appears that the sustainability of a city and city region strongly affects the sustainability of suburban housing estates within it (see Kaido, Chapter 9).

Malottki et al. (Chapter 9) argue that the housing market and spatial planning are closely linked. Consequences produce infrastructural, social, economic and ecological effects.

Effective and efficient use of land by means of reuse of sites

A specific form of shrinkage and spatial restructuring is linked to the closure of military bases as it results in both the removal of personnel and loss of civil sector jobs (double blow) in the same area (see Farrelly and Lemes, Chapter 15). Swift regeneration in this context appears to be of particular importance in order to avoid a downward spiral and instead reap a so-called 'peace dividend' by converting the former military sites for civil reuse.

This is not easily accomplished and poses an even greater challenge than 'normal' brownfield reuse, due to the specific configuration of actors and planning processes involved (see Ganser, Chapter 14; Farrelly and Lemes, Chapter 15). With regards to material success factors of site conversions, Farrelly and Lemes argue that the integration of a range of living, working and leisure facilities on a unique site is of core importance.

In line with this argument, the aptness (or appropriateness) of a site – depending on parameters such as size, location, and possible functions for the city region as a whole as well as for the immediate neighbourhoods is crucial for the successful conversion of sites (see Ganser, Chapter 14).

The desirability of 'hard-end' reuse – including new buildings and physical infrastructure –is more difficult, if not impossible, to pursue in areas characterised by shrinkage. Therefore more 'soft-end' reuse – in quantitative as well as in qualitative terms – is a more reasonable option. Also in the context of regeneration and conversion, the importance of addressing planning issues at a strategic level has to be underlined. An important example is the need for regional coordination to allow the pooling of sites – particularly in slow growth or shrinkage areas (see Ganser, Chapter 14).

Ganser (Chapter 14) concludes that conversion sites are of importance in a spatial context of growth as well as in declining regions but he also points out different focal points of these problem areas. Two central challenges with regards to spatial planning and the environment include, on the one hand overcoming brownfield development disadvantages when compared with the development of greenfield sites, and on the other hand soft-end reuse of conversion sites.

With regards to the former, Lemes and Farrelly's case study based analysis of brownfield redevelopment highlights the benefit of a location which is integrated in the urban fabric and of a mixed use approach, which can both provide much more character than a greenfield site (Chapter 15). However, before these benefits can come to fruition it is necessary to streamline the conversion planning process and to remove the planning obstacles highlighted by Ganser, otherwise development on 'easy' greenfield sites will come first.

It appears safe to assume that all of the above can lead to great opportunities for an improved environment in growing and shrinking regions. The former mainly profit from the windfall of developable land and possible additional scarce open space and green infrastructure which would not be possible otherwise, and the latter benefit from the clearance of derelict sites and the creation of quality green space, helping to make the shrinking part of a city or a region a better place to live, thereby preventing additional segregation and out migration.

Finally it appears important to consider the debate on different spatial contexts, trends of shrinkage and growth, in the light of what this means for quality of life and individual life satisfaction. Brereton et al. (Chapter 12) find that individual life satisfaction in rural areas with low density dispersed settlement patterns is generally higher than in urban centres. They also conclude that currently privacy, space, cheaper land and similar elements are valued higher than access to infrastructure and services. The authors do attach a word of warning that the cost of transport and service provision in rural areas may change this picture in the future. In fact, across Europe and also on other continents service provision, particularly in sparsely populated and shrinking rural areas, is a major planning concern. Considering the high satisfaction rates noted above, several challenges for spatial planning become apparent. The pull factors to rural areas further classic suburbanisation with all its recognized environmental problems. Additionally long term service provision is more expensive (per individual) in low density settlement structures. These problems will be exacerbated in the case of shrinkage in the long term future. The key objective for spatial planning must therefore be to strike the right balance between concentrating settlement development in urban areas and diversified well-connected rural locations in order to provide living environments with a high (perceived) quality of life. Again this will require a strategic planning tier which coordinates development in entire city regions and rural areas.

Spatial planning for growth and decline

In the context of rapid growth, more resources – including human resources – have to be made available if spatial planning is to have a pro-active role which includes emphasis on safeguarding the environment and social well-being while at the same time coordinating necessary infrastructure for economic prosperity. In a scenario of shrinkage or slow growth we are not simply looking at the reversal of growth, as most settlement structures and infrastructure were not planned to be rolled back at a later date, and particularly in the case of physical infrastructure a minimum as well as a maximum capacity limit is usually a fairly fixed parameter. This in turn backs up the argument that a different kind of spatial planning is needed in shrinking cities and regions. Of course, parallel patterns of shrinkage and growth mean that the challenges discussed above will often have to be addressed in parallel. This again may lead to a situation of competition, where it will be of importance to find the right balance in addressing these spatial planning challenges.

Considering all of the above it becomes clear that within the environmental sustainability principle, very specific challenges but also opportunities are associated with the parallel trends of growth and decline. The parallelism of these spatial developments makes it particularly hard to address these challenges effectively through statutory planning instruments and informal planning tools. It appears that an appropriate mix of both is of the essence – and this applies to all tiers of planning from strategic to local levels.

References

Hall, P.G. 1992. *Urban and regional planning.* 3rd Edition. London: Routledge.

Index